THE YOUNGEST YUGOSLAVS

THE YOUNGEST YUGOSLAVS

An Oral History of Post-Socialist Memory

Jovana Babović

INDIANA UNIVERSITY PRESS

This book is a publication of

Indiana University Press
Herman B Wells Library
1320 East 10th Street
Bloomington, Indiana 47405 USA

iupress.org

© 2025 by Jovana Babović
All rights reserved

No part of this book may be reproduced or utilized in any form or by any means, electronic or mechanical, including photocopying and recording, or by any information storage and retrieval system, without permission in writing from the publisher.

First Printing 2025

Cataloging information is available from the Library of Congress.

ISBN 978-0-253-07394-5 (hdbk.)
ISBN 978-0-253-07395-2 (pbk.)
ISBN 978-0-253-07397-6 (ebook)
ISBN 978-0-253-07396-9 (web PDF)

To baba Olivera,
who gave me resilience

To Eric,
who gives me strength

CONTENTS

Acknowledgments ix

Introduction 1
Glossary of Key Concepts 23
1. Interview with Luka Lisjak Gabrijelčič 42
2. Interview with Krisztina Rácz 69
3. Interview with Artan Sadiku 87
4. Interview with Iva Radivojević 110
5. Interview with Gordan Pejić 128
6. Interview with Elena Stavrevska 153
7. Interview with Bojan Števin 179
8. Interview with Melinda Vuković 199

Suggested Discussion Questions 219
Bibliography 221
Index 235

ACKNOWLEDGMENTS

When the COVID-19 pandemic derailed the archival project I was working on, I developed *The Youngest Yugoslavs* to stay intellectually engaged. Conducting the interviews turned out to be a lifeline for me in more ways than one. Every interviewee certainly gave me new insights into the past. They also inadvertently offered me a social outlet when I had little access to other people. In our conversations about their childhoods, themes of community and belonging in late socialist Yugoslavia came up again and again. It did not take me long to realize that remembering their shared experiences of growing up in a country that no longer exists created a new form of community and belonging for many members of the youngest Yugoslav generation. While no individual had a universally positive perspective on Yugoslavia, interviewees actively engaged with its history and one another. In doing so, those I spoke to facilitated the creation of a sort of Yugoslav diaspora between the pages of this book. They invited me into that world when I was most starved for community during the pandemic, and now *The Youngest Yugoslavs* extends the invitation to you, the reader.

First and foremost, I would like to thank all the interviewees who shared their time and memories with me. I am grateful to them for trusting me with their stories and allowing me to use them to tell a bigger one about the legacies of Yugoslav socialism and multinationalism. I would also like to thank everyone who put me in touch with potential interlocutors in their circle of family, friends, colleagues, and acquaintances.

I would like to thank Bethany Mowry and Sophia Hebert at Indiana University Press for shepherding *The Youngest Yugoslavs* from initial vision to final iteration. I am fortunate to have worked with an editorial team that saw my dream of this book and helped me realize it. I am grateful to the two anonymous readers who offered valuable advice and thoughtful suggestions for sharpening the text.

I am incredibly fortunate to work at SUNY Geneseo, an institution that gives me space to follow my curiosities in research and teaching. I would like to thank the members of the Department of History, especially Cathy Adams, Sadegh Ansari, Justin Behrend, Ryan Jones, Jordan Kleiman, Kathy Mapes, and Michael Oberg, for their encouragement. I would also like to thank administrators Bev Rex-Burley and Angie Briggs. Beyond the department, I am indebted to the diligent work of the staff at Geneseo's Milne Library.

I was fortunate to receive a number of grants funded by the Geneseo Foundation to support the development, research, and writing of this project. I am grateful to the director of the Office of Sponsored Research, Anne Baldwin, for facilitating much of this funding. Geneseo's Department of History provided additional support for research and conference travel. I could not have been able to complete this project without extraordinarily valuable course releases and financial support from Geneseo.

I would like to thank Geneseo students who worked as my research assistants over the course of three years. Adam Comstock, Emma Furnari, Jack George, Heather Matela, Liam Murphy, Terra Peter, and Lizzy Wisniewski contributed to the transcription, annotation, and indexing of this project. Their engagement with history never ceases to impress me.

As I worked on this project, I benefited greatly from the insights of several scholarly communities. I'd like to thank the Balkan Reading Group, particularly James Robertson, Maddie Fichter, Jovana Knežević, and Filip Erdeljac. I would also like to thank the Upstate REEES Workshop, especially Heather DeHaan, Katherine Zubovich, Shoshana Keller, and David Kaminsky. I found it valuable to present early versions of this project at conferences of the Association for Slavic, East European, and Eurasian Studies and the Oral History Association.

I would like to thank my family for their support. I am grateful to my parents, Dušica Babović-Vuksanović and Srdjan Babović, my siblings, Nikola Babović and Mihajlo Babović, and my sisters-in-law, Kimberly Bentjen-Babović and Alyssa Babović. My paternal grandmother, Olivera Babović, passed away long before I even conceived of this project but I could imagine dialoguing with her about my work, as we always did while she was alive.

I am so deeply grateful to my beautiful circle of chosen family. I would like to thank Adrienne Aldredge, Sasha Allgayer, Leigh Cressman, Shannon Curley, River Drosera, Silvia Duque, Éléonore Forêt, Gene Gallagher, Jeff Hayton, Adrienne Harris, Raluca Iancu, Steven Jug, Emi Kanemoto, Mace McDonald,

Brenna McCaffrey, Bill Mercer, Preston Mohr, Sally Morris, Peter Nicholson, Brian Preston, Bruno Renero-Hannan, and Elier Suárez for sharing my enthusiasm about this project. The people I have loved over the years brought immeasurable joy into my life while I worked. I wrote this book in Rochester, NY, in a little paradise I share with my intellectual companion Eric Garcia McKinley and our two beasts.

Thank you all so much. My heart is so full.

THE YOUNGEST
YUGOSLAVS

Introduction

The Youngest Yugoslavs: An Oral History of Post-Socialist Memory is a collection of interviews with the last generation of Yugoslavs to live in the unified state as children. The volume showcases how these individuals remember childhood during the final decades of socialism and how they conceptualize the impact of Yugoslav multinationalism on their lives. The collection gives readers the opportunity to explore why the idea of Yugoslavia continues to resonate prominently among members of the state's youngest cohort. It contributes to our understanding of the afterlife of unified Yugoslavia's brief though exceedingly dynamic twentieth century.

The Youngest Yugoslavs brings together the voices of former Yugoslav citizens born between 1971 and 1991 as a generational group. Scholars argue that age cohorts cut across social categories such as gender, class, and race; they form when people share similar life experiences and are aware of sharing them.[1] Anthropologist Monika Palmberger suggests that generational positioning impacts how individuals narrate their lives, think about the past, and imagine the future.[2] Several distinctive experiences unite the generational group born in the last twenty years of Yugoslavia's existence. One definitive experience is having grown up at the height of socialist Yugoslavia. Many interviewees recalled having access to a rich mainstream culture, a society that recognized ethnic, religious, and national differences, and an inherited sense of belonging. Another shared generational experience is the violent dissolution of Yugoslavia. This period impacted individuals differently depending on their background and where they lived, but the Yugoslav wars of the 1990s shaped the childhood

---

1. Spaskovska, *The Last Yugoslav Generation*, 9.
2. Palmberger, *How Generations Remember*, 3.

or adolescence of everyone of this generation. A third distinctive experience is loss of homeland by the time of early adulthood. Whether they continued to reside in the region or moved far from it, the members of the youngest Yugoslav generation have now lived more than half their lives in a world in which their birth country no longer exists. Many interviewees reflected on their experiences as generationally shared. Some referred to their cohort as a "transition generation" or "bridge generation," and all deeply considered how the former state shaped their childhood, how its demise impacted their life trajectory, and how its social ideals continue to resonate in their adult life.

Scholars have primarily studied older Yugoslav generations, those born after World War I in the Kingdom of Yugoslavia and those born after World War II in the Socialist Federal Republic of Yugoslavia. In her recent study of generational memory, Palmberger found that the cohort born during the interwar years was least impacted by the Yugoslav wars and thus often expressed nostalgia for the physical, social, and economic security that characterized their adult lives in Yugoslavia.[3] Comparatively, those born shortly after World War II—the generation of the parents of interviewees included here—lived through the dissolution of the state in midlife. Scholars have devoted attention to this generation's struggles to adapt to the market economy and new national identities of the post-Yugoslav world.[4] Historian Ljubica Spaskovska explains that members of this generation were ambivalent about the past because they had faced great obstacles in rebuilding their lives and felt insecure about the future.[5]

Only a few studies consider the experiences of the youngest Yugoslav generation. These studies primarily focus on individuals who remained in the region and thus articulated their relationship to the past through the prism of successor states. Palmberger conducted her fieldwork in Bosnia and found that members of this age cohort pitted positive childhood memories in Yugoslavia against dissatisfaction with social, educational, and economic opportunities in present-day Bosnia.[6] In her study of youth in Serbia, anthropologist Jessica Greenberg similarly writes that "people too young to have experienced 'the good life' in socialist Yugoslavia nonetheless compared their fortunes to those of their parents and older siblings."[7] While much of this youngest generation's

---

3. Palmberger, *How Generations Remember*, 132.
4. Burić, "Dwelling on the Ruins of Socialist Yugoslavia"; Kojanic, "Nostalgia as a Practice of the Self in Post-Socialist Serbia"; Kolstø, "Identifying with the Old or the New State"; Petrović, "'When We Were Europe.'"
5. Spaskovska, *The Last Yugoslav Generation*, 10.
6. Palmberger, *How Generations Remember*, 205.
7. Greenberg, "On the Road to Normal," 92–93.

memory might be based on imagined ideals of the Yugoslav past, scholars argue that the notion of what could have been nevertheless informed visions for the future of successor states. Studies also demonstrate that for some young adults in the region, remembering Yugoslavia signaled a desire to overcome strained ethnic relationships; for others, it reflected an investment in socialist ideals like equality and solidarity.[8]

The Youngest Yugoslavs builds on existing scholarship to highlight this generational group's distinct engagement with the past, giving voice to its globally mobile members. The Yugoslav wars caused massive displacement of people, and conditions in the aftermath of state collapse drove young adults to seek opportunities abroad. Everyone interviewed in this collection lived outside the region at some point. Some emigrated during or after the Yugoslav wars, while others left for varying intervals in pursuit of education or employment. Some returned to the region, and others remained abroad. As a result, they remembered childhood and related to the Yugoslav past differently than individuals who only experienced living in the successor states. The interviews in *The Youngest Yugoslavs* offer novel insights into the meaning individuals invest in Yugoslav socialism and multinationalism from without. Their collective voices broaden our understanding of this generational experience and give us a richer lens for exploring the impact Yugoslavia had on its youngest cohort of former citizens.

In its focus on the global network of former Yugoslav citizens, this volume serves as an important resource for studying the role of diaspora on postsocialist memory. Migration out of the region precipitated the formation of place-based and virtual diasporic communities. Most existing scholarship studies the nationalization and radicalization of new diasporas, which mobilized individuals abroad in the interests of successor states or nations.[9] Scholars argue that traumas such as civil war and displacement triggered the development of strong nationalist orientations in both place-based and virtual diasporas of the former Yugoslavia.[10] However, the multinational Yugoslav diasporic communities that those interviewed in this volume mentioned have not yet been researched. *The Youngest Yugoslavs* offers a chance to consider how globally mobile members of Yugoslavia's youngest cohort engaged with one

---

8. Maksimović, "Unattainable Past, Unsatisfying Present," 1073; Lavrence, "Making Up for Lost Time," 89.

9. Jurić Pahor, "Diaspora and Diasporisation"; Koinova, "Four Types of Diaspora Mobilization"; Winland, "The Politics of Desire and Disdain."

10. Halilovich, "Reclaiming Erased Lives"; Hasić, "Diaspora as Digital Diplomatic Agents"; Kriještorac, *First Nationalism Then Identity*; Stubbs, "Virtual Diaspora?"

another abroad despite newly drawn or redrawn national lines at home. For some of the individuals interviewed here, such communities were integral to their sense of self as Yugoslav or post-Yugoslav; for others, they were peripheral touchstones of belonging. At the very least, most interviewees expressed an awareness of Yugoslav diasporic communities not limited to those built around the national identities of successor states, meaning that these communities shaped how interviewees conceived of the Yugoslav past.

This volume ultimately shows that many globally mobile members of the youngest Yugoslav generation find immense value in the legacies of socialism and multinationalism. Individuals identified several common experiences as distinct inheritances of their former homeland. They spoke about a sense of belonging at the neighborhood, state, and cultural community level. They associated Yugoslavia with safety, well-being, and opportunity. And they identified specific ideological pillars of former Yugoslav society that continue to be relevant to their lives. Their memories are markedly different from the nostalgia, often termed Yugonostalgia, of older generations. While the members of the youngest Yugoslav generation sometimes reminisced about aspects of childhood, they more often thought critically about the factors that led to the end of Yugoslavia and their lives in it. No individual included here expressed hope for the reunification of Yugoslavia when we spoke; they instead closely considered the futures that could have been but never were. Many held their connection to the past closely, and those with children were often eager to share it. The youngest cohort's persistent engagement with Yugoslavia suggests that the state's ideals remained compelling for those who lived in the region as much as those who resettled abroad. Interviewees embraced the promises of their former homeland and asked if these promises could still be realized, showing that Yugoslavia left a lasting impact on their lives and continues to be a captivating vision for the future.

Methodology

My approaches to sampling, interviewing, editing, and formatting shape *The Youngest Yugoslavs*. The sociopolitical moment in which I conducted the interviews likewise impacts it.

The eight oral histories included here were chosen from thirty-five interviews conducted between 2021 and 2023. I identified most interviewees through chain-referral sampling. I contacted the first interviewees through my personal network; I asked them and all subsequent interlocutors to put me in touch with colleagues, friends, and family members born in Yugoslavia between 1971 and 1991. I then reached out to those individuals to scout their willingness to speak with me.

The project's inherent sampling bias is that those who agreed to participate were likely more invested in Yugoslavia than those who declined or did not respond. Those who agreed were also disproportionally educated.[11] Many demonstrated a nuanced understanding of Yugoslavia's complex twentieth-century history and contextualized their own bottom-up narratives with the state's top-down ones. Interviewees generally shared positive memories of childhood in Yugoslavia, negative sentiments related to state collapse, war, and postcommunist transition, and critical perceptions of the region's successor states. Most were familiar with the concept of Yugonostalgia and thoughtful about their engagement with it. This volume is thus a collection of perspectives of individuals who continued to critically reflect on Yugoslavia and its lasting impact on their lives. Instead of an exhaustive portrayal of this generation's memory of Yugoslavia or post-socialism in general, *The Youngest Yugoslavs* gives insight into how an educated contingent of this globally mobile cohort negotiated the Yugoslav past and recollections of it.

I selected the eight interviews included in this volume to highlight the multiplicity of individuals' experiences during and after Yugoslavia. I wanted to showcase several variables that likely impacted childhood and, thereafter, recollections of the past.

- Gender: The volume represents individuals who identified as men and women. Four of the interviewees were women, and four were men.
- Place of birth: The interviews capture a diverse sample of hometowns. The eight interviewees were born in five of the six constituent Yugoslav republics, which shaped their everyday

---

11. There are not many oral histories of former Yugoslav citizens, and few of those prioritize the voices of working-class, rural, or uneducated individuals. One fascinating collection is Zorka Milich's *A Stranger's Supper: An Oral History of Centenarian Women in Montenegro*, which brings together ten interviews with women from the Montenegrin highlands. Milich conducted these interviews in the 1990s with women who had lived almost all their lives in the interwar or postwar Yugoslav state. While she was primarily interested in interviewees' experiences of marriage and family life, it is notable that the women almost never mentioned Yugoslavia, major leaders like Tito, or major national or international events. They often referenced "Turkish," "Austrian," "German," "Albanian," and "Bulgarian" conflicts, showing an awareness of broader political context with topics relevant to the women insofar as they might have triggered a disruption of everyday life or loss of a family member. These interviews are an indispensable lens into twentieth-century rural life in Yugoslavia; they also show that the subjects interviewed were not equipped with the privileged tools to reflect on society beyond their own communities (Milich, *A Stranger's Supper*).

life, experience of dissolution and war, and perspectives on successor states. Among those interviewed, unfortunately, none were born in Montenegro.

- Place of residence: Everyone included in this volume was globally mobile, with experience studying, working, or otherwise living in at least one country outside the region. Two individuals fled with their families in the 1990s, one as a refugee and one as an émigré; they both permanently resettled abroad. Three interviewees moved abroad as adults, either in pursuit of education and employment opportunities or due to dissatisfaction with quality of life. Three individuals were based in the region at the time of their interview.
- Ethnicity: The interviewees highlight the ethnic diversity of the former state. Some grew up in ethnically homogenous families, and others had ethnically intermarried parents or ethnically mixed families. Of the eight individuals, six identified fully or partially as members of Yugoslav constituent nations (included here are Serbs, Croats, Macedonians, and Slovenes), and two identified as members of state-recognized nationalities (included here are Hungarians and Albanians).
- Class: While all the interviewees included in this volume were educated, that was not necessarily the case for their families. Interviewees had a spectrum of class experiences during the time of Yugoslavia. Some discussed their privilege, but many also spoke about their family's process of upward mobility during the postwar years as a benefit of socialist initiatives in education, work placement, and housing accommodations. Among their relatives, interviewees enumerated factory workers, administrators, business owners, teachers, journalists, engineers, military personnel, and a host of other professions. Almost all had relatives in villages or rural regions.
- Other forms of difference: The volume represents other vectors such as bilingualism, queerness, and parenthood that shaped interviewees' experiences and memories of Yugoslavia.

The Youngest Yugoslavs makes no claims to be a definitive portrait of this generational group. The volume's sample is illustrative, not representative or exhaustive. There were far too many forms of diversity among the population of the unified state and variables to capture in any one place. As a result, this collection offers only a slice of the diversity of Yugoslav and post-Yugoslav lives.

To preserve the complexities of postwar Yugoslav identities, *The Youngest Yugoslavs* steers away from essentializing individuals into singular identities. I asked participants to share with me their place of birth, and I noted that information in the introduction of each interview. It allows us to map the regional distribution of interviewees across Yugoslavia and tells us in which present-day country each location now stands. But place of birth does not necessarily correspond with national, ethnic, religious, or any other identity at the time of Yugoslavia or after its collapse. Unless the interviewee self-identified as such, readers should not make assumptions about identity based on information like name or family background. An openness to ambiguity is important for understanding a past in which Yugoslav citizens could espouse a combination of identities that seem incompatible in the nationalized region today. It is also important for guarding against the erasure of Yugoslavia, a rare twentieth-century European state founded on the model of multinationalism.

This is not to say that identity did not matter in Yugoslavia or that it does not matter in the post-Yugoslav world. On the contrary, identity is consequential in any discussion of modern history, but it is more frequently imposed on individuals than claimed by them. In these interviews, I offered participants an opportunity to define their identity on their own terms and discuss how it evolved. I asked everyone the following question: How do you identify nationally, ethnically, or culturally today? I wanted the question to be broad enough to allow interviewees to self-describe their identity in a way that suited them. Some elected to identify with a national or ethnic identity mapped onto a present-day nation state, some chose a composite identity reflecting their family's mixedness, and some declared themselves Yugoslavs or post Yugoslavs. Many interviewees pushed back against the question altogether. They told me, for instance, that they thought of themselves as Europeans, as cosmopolitans, as urbanites, as anarchists, or as humans. Resistance to simplified identities can be interpreted as a legacy of Yugoslavia, a multinational country that was home to ethnic, religious, linguistic, and cultural diversity.

The interviews in *The Youngest Yugoslavs* are semistructured. I asked each interviewee to share their memories about five broad topics: hometown, friends and family, conflict and state collapse, life after conflict and state collapse, and present-day reflections on Yugoslavia. I briefed interviewees about the overarching topics ahead of time but did not provide specific questions to prepare. I relied on common questions for each section of the interviews, and I asked follow-up questions based on each interviewee's responses. I aimed for neutral and open-ended questions, resulting in interviews that resemble conversations centered on the individual's reflections and encourage candid engagement with their memories. My questions are reproduced in the interviews in this volume so that readers can understand the responses in relation to the questions. Interviews ranged in length from one to two hours and were held over a video conferencing platform. Although most interviewees were fluent in at least one language spoken in former Yugoslavia, I conducted interviews in English for the sake of consistency.

Seven research assistants at SUNY Geneseo transcribed the interviews, and I edited them for clarity. Scholars debate how to best transform aspects of spoken language such as hesitation, repetition, and unfinished thoughts into writing. While these aspects of speech might offer additional insights into an interview, I followed the best practices of editing outlined by historian Donald Ritchie in *Doing Oral History*: I preserved the content, tone, vernacular, and verbal rhythm of each conversation but cut out inconsequential filler words, false starts, and fragmented sentences in the interest of readability. When an interviewer expressed nonverbal sounds and gestures, I noted that in brackets.[12] "Editing and rearranging interviews for clarification and cutting away tangential material are appropriate so long as the original meaning is retained," Ritchie writes. "The goal is to sharpen the focus without putting words in the interviewee's mouth or altering the essence of what was said."[13] Volumes like Mark Cave's and Stephen M. Sloan's *Listening on the Edge: Oral History in the Aftermath of Crisis* showcase the diversity of methodological approaches scholars take when editing oral history.[14] My approach aimed to preserve authenticity and create clarity. When I finished editing the interviews, I shared them with each interviewee and gave them the opportunity to make adjustments, as Ritchie suggests.[15] Seven interviewees agreed to have their full names published in this collection. The eighth interviewee worried that the interview might have negative repercussions on their family, so we worked together to develop a pseudonym that approximated their name. I noted this adjustment in the introduction to their interview.

Each interview in this collection is preceded by a short introduction that provides biographical information about the interviewee and an overview of main themes. To supplement the glossary of key concepts, each interview also contains annotations, which include full names, dates, and basic biographical information for people of note and expand interviewees' references with historical background on concepts, events, and places. The transcripts of the

---

12. Ritchie, *Doing Oral History*, 129–32.
13. Ritchie, *Doing Oral History*, 130.
14. Cave and Sloan, *Listening on the Edge*.
15. Ritchie, *Doing Oral History*, 132.

interviews are otherwise unmediated so that they can be freely interpreted. I follow the model of historian Donald Raleigh's oral history collection *Russia's Sputnik Generation: Soviet Baby Boomers Talk about Their Lives*. Raleigh explains that he does not offer direct or synthetic analysis of individual interviews in order to guard against "suggesting what conclusions should be drawn from these narratives because that would limit what readers might otherwise see."[16] *The Youngest Yugoslavs* provides contextual grounding but similarly invites readers to engage with the voices of the youngest Yugoslav generation on their own terms.

It is important to note that the layers of sociopolitical context in which these interviews were collected informed how individuals remembered their childhood and the Yugoslav past. When I collected the interviews in 2021–2023, it had been thirty years since the start of Yugoslavia's dissolution. That meant the youngest Yugoslav cohort had lived more than half their lives in a world without a unified Yugoslav state. Memory is malleable, shaped by individual life trajectories and collective social and historical narratives; in some cases, it fades, weakens, or erodes. Moreover, the trauma of experiences such as war, genocide, and emigration may have impacted how the youngest Yugoslav cohort remembered the past. During our conversations, interviewees occasionally noted that they could not be sure about the origin of a particular memory—whether they were remembering a personal experience, a story told by someone else, or a conflation of recollections. At times, they plainly stated that they could no longer recollect certain facts or events. The interviews thus give an insight into what individuals remember over time and, less directly, what they blur, forget, or erase from memory. Existing studies explore the memory of Yugoslavia ten or twenty years after the onset of state collapse, so *The Youngest Yugoslavs* offers a lens not just into the memories of the youngest cohort but also into understanding how recollections of Yugoslavia continue to evolve over time. On a macro level, this volume stands beside a growing scholarly initiative to remember Yugoslavia in the face of nationalist revisionist projects that seek to erase it. The writer Dubravka Ugrešić terms this dual assault on memory as the "terror of forgetting" Yugoslavia and the "terror by remembering" a nationalist past one does not actually remember.[17] *The Youngest Yugoslavs* offers an access point for understanding former citizens' unfolding reflections on the last decades of socialism and multinationalism.

---

16. Raleigh, *Russia's Sputnik Generation*, 22. Raleigh later published a monograph that analyzes the interviews he had collected earlier, including those published in *Russia's Sputnik Generation*. See Raleigh, *Soviet Baby Boomers*.

17. Ugrešić, *Culture of Lies*, 70.

The volume also captures the memories of the youngest Yugoslav generation on the heels of two global events. One is the COVID-19 pandemic, which isolated people from one another and reshaped how we live, work, and interact. This project emerged from my own need to connect with others and conduct meaningful research at a time when I was not able to travel abroad to work in archives, and it was enabled by the growing popularity of videoconferencing communication. It is possible that interviewees too were seeking a sense of community and that this impacted how they looked back on the Yugoslav past.

The other global event was Russia's invasion of Ukraine, the first major armed conflict in Europe since the Yugoslav wars. Interviewees made explicit comparisons between their experiences of war and those of Ukrainians. They noted that recent events had recentered their own or their relatives' memories of war and displacement. As the conflict continues, witnessing another war in Eastern Europe—this time as adults—may impact interviewees' childhood memories of the Yugoslav wars and the time before. Current events might retraumatize them and alter their memories. Evolving narratives about war, politics, and national identity may prompt them to reconsider their understanding of their experiences. Scholar Christine Lavrence suggests that the collapse of the unified Yugoslav state engendered a reevaluation of socialist identities. "The Yugoslav wars make it easy to forget that Yugoslavia was a powerful category of identity for many people, rather than just an empty ideological trope," Lavrence writes. "It is easy to forget that as postcommunist subjects grapple with large-scale political and social transformation they are also dealing with the loss of personal identity."[18] Transformations triggered by the conflict in Ukraine stand to precipitate a crisis of memory and prompt rearticulation of socialist and post-socialist identities. *The Youngest Yugoslavs* thus captures memories that seem precarious due to both the passage of time and the state of the contemporary world.

Oral History

The Youngest Yugoslavs is an addition to a growing body of scholarship that relies on oral history as a methodology to access voices, experiences, and narratives not easily heard in socialist and post-socialist history.

Recent scholarly and popular texts note the significance of oral history as a lens that circumvents propaganda and state narratives when studying life before, during, and after the collapse of socialism.[19] In the introduction to their

---

18. Lavrence, "Making Up for Lost Time," 88.
19. Molloy, *The Lost World of Communism*; Shapiro and Shapiro, *The Curtain Rises*.

compilation of narratives about Czechoslovakia's 1989 revolution, Miroslav Vaněk and Pavel Mücke suggest that this methodology allowed them to get at the voices of ordinary people while decoupling and decentering top-down history.[20] Scholars Natalia Khanenko-Friesen and Gelinada Grinchenko make a similar case in their edited collection *Reclaiming the Personal: Oral History in Post-Socialist Europe*. They argue that oral history is an effective tool for uncovering repressed socialist history and alternative socialist pasts; voices of everyday historical actors have the capacity to destabilize traditional academic discourse that relies on archival and written sources. Oral history, Khanenko-Friesen and Grinchenko stress, has the "intrinsic ability to reclaim and reposition the individual from and within the social processes of history."[21] In their excellent book *Gulag Voices: Oral Histories of Soviet Incarceration and Exile*, scholars Jehanne M. Gheith and Katherine R. Jolluck suggest that oral history is now considered more reliable than official sources as an access point for the study of socialism.[22] Even the inevitable inaccuracies, contradictions, and omissions, they argue, offer clues to guide scholars to richer historical understanding.

Oral history has been used to study the East European socialist and post-socialist past. Scholars have relied on interviews to explore aspects of life that might not have been well documented or socially sanctioned, such as expressions of gender and sexuality.[23] Through oral history, they have unearthed experiences of persecution and dissent silenced by totalitarian regimes.[24] And they have found a useful entry point for documenting life under socialism in general.[25] Soviet and post-Soviet historiography is particularly robust when it comes to oral history. Scholars have called on this methodology to research the experiences of a broad range of Soviet citizens, from politicians and scientists to migrants and nuclear disaster survivors, whose voices might not otherwise be included in history.[26]

---

20. Vaněk and Mücke, *Velvet Revolutions*, 1–2.
21. Khanenko-Friesen and Grinchenko, *Reclaiming the Personal*, 13.
22. Gheith and Jolluck, *Gulag Voices*, 8.
23. Lemke, *Gay Voices from East Germany*; Massino, *Ambiguous Transitions*.
24. Long, *Making History*; Philipsen, *We Were the People*; Todorov, *Voices from the Gulag*.
25. Koleva, *Memory Archipelago of the Communist Past*; Rejmer, *Mud Sweeter Than Honey*; Thomas, *Local Lives, Parallel Histories*.
26. Alexievich, *Secondhand Time*; Alexievich, *Voices from Chernobyl*; Cohen and vanden Heuvel, *Voices of Glasnost*; Edgar, *Intermarriage and the Friendship of Peoples*; Engel and Posadskaya-Vanderbek, *A Revolution of Their Own*; Gerovitch, *Voices of the Soviet Space Program*; Messana, *Soviet Communal Living*; Raleigh, *Russia's Sputnik Generation*; Raleigh, *Soviet Baby Boomers*; Rogacheva, *Soviet Scientists Remember*; Sahadeo, *Voices from the Soviet Edge*.

In studies of Yugoslavia, scholars use oral history to examine the experience of war, transition, and reconciliation. For instance, several recent texts rely on survivor narratives to write about persecution in the Bosnian genocide.[27] Others harness interviews with members of specific demographics, such as men who served in the Yugoslav National Army or individuals who were youth activists in the 1980s, to explore how former citizens remember socialist Yugoslavia.[28] Scholars interested in the process of societal rebuilding after the Yugoslav wars have similarly turned to oral histories of particular groups, such as residents of Mostar in the decades after war and young adults in 2000s Serbia.[29]

Most of all, oral history has been a critical methodology for the study of memory in post-socialist societies. However, because socialist states encouraged production of homogenous collective histories through media and other forms of propaganda and, at times, deliberate erasure of the past, scholars of Eastern Europe frequently encounter missing memories when conducting interviews. Dalia Leinarte suggests that "silence or amnesia in interviews is an important component of *oral history* because the refusal and/or inability of respondents to talk can reveal unexpected aspects of history."[30] Leinarte believes that suppressed or forbidden memories can be reconstructed, but she also believes that their absence can be interpreted as part of historical record. For instance, if an interviewee makes no mention of an experience of persecution, their silence might signify trauma causing them to suppress the memory, fear of discussing the experience conditioning them to silence it, or shame about the episode pushing them to forget it. Scholars acknowledge that contradictions, incompleteness, and fragmentation are part of memory, especially when that memory pertains to times of stress.[31]

Historiography

The Youngest Yugoslavs makes important contributions to our understanding of East European socialism and post-socialism, Yugoslav history, and memory

---

27. Leydesdorff, *Surviving the Bosnian Genocide*; Petrila and Hasanović, *Voices from Srebrenica*; Wehr, *Making It Through*.
28. Petrović, "Nostalgia for the JNA?"; Spaskovska, *The Last Yugoslav Generation*.
29. Greenberg, *After the Revolution*; Greenberg, "On the Road to Normal"; Palmberger, *How Generations Remember*.
30. Leinarte, "Silence in Biographical Accounts and Life Stories," 13.
31. Leydesdorff, *Surviving the Bosnian Genocide*, xv.

studies. Particularly through its methodological embrace of oral history, this volume grows our access to everyday experiences of socialist and post-socialist societies as well as individuals' memories of—and, on occasion, nostalgia for—them.

First, *The Youngest Yugoslavs* contributes to the historiography of East European socialist and post-socialist studies. While scholarship produced immediately after the collapse of socialism focuses on shortcomings and negative long-term impacts the period had on East European societies, recent work is uncovering a more nuanced story. Scholars take a wide range of approaches to studying East European socialist societies, chief among them the lived experience of socialism. This rich subfield explores a variety of topics such as gender, consumption, tourism, leisure, and culture in individual countries as well as comparatively.[32] Positioning *The Youngest Yugoslavs* within this historiography helps identify the diversity of experiences among socialist societies. There were certainly many similarities between Yugoslavia and other East European socialist states. However, after Tito broke with Stalin in 1948, Yugoslavia charted its own socialist path apart from the Eastern bloc; its citizens lived under significantly different political, social, economic, and cultural conditions. For instance, Yugoslavs were able to travel to zones dominated by the US and USSR when Yugoslavia repositioned itself between the two Cold War blocs in the 1950s, and they were able to work and travel to most European and nonaligned states without visas by the 1960s. The collapse of socialism in Yugoslavia was coupled with the violent breakup of the state itself, so the experience of war, genocide, and dislocation in the former Yugoslavia are uniquely paired with the experience of post-socialist transition. *The Youngest Yugoslavs* is therefore a resource for understanding the particularities of Yugoslav socialism and post-socialism in dialogue with the East European region.

Second, this volume builds on our evolving understanding of Yugoslavia's rich history. During and immediately after Yugoslavia's collapse, scholars were

---

32. Bren, *The Greengrocer and His TV*; Bren and Neuburger, *Communism Unwrapped*; Dragostinova, *The Cold War from the Margins*; Fidelis, *Women, Communism, and Industrialization in Postwar Poland*; Ghodsee, *Muslim Lives in Eastern Europe*; Ghodsee, *The Red Riviera*; Gorsuch and Koenker, *Turizm*; Guistino, Plum, and Vari, *Socialist Escapes*; Kenney, *Rebuilding Poland*; Mëhilli, *From Stalin to Mao*; Neuburger, *Balkan Smoke*; Scarboro, *The Late Socialist Good Life in Bulgaria*; Scarboro, Mincyté, and Gille, *The Socialist Good Life*; Taylor, *Let's Twist Again*.

preoccupied with explaining how and why the state had fallen apart.[33] They often pointed to top-down events such as the Croatian Spring of 1971, economic crisis, Tito's death in 1980, and rising nationalism among political leaders as critical junctures that led to the state's downturn. In many instances, scholarly accounts billed Yugoslavia as a failed experiment and told its history backward, starting from the 1990s.[34] Others tackled this question by studying violence in the region across the twentieth century.[35] In more recent scholarship, however, scholars are newly invested in critical evaluations of socialist society on its own terms, especially when it comes to politics, class, race, and gender.[36] Moreover, they are taking an increasingly broad interest in cultural practices that structured everyday life for former Yugoslav citizens, from art, music, and sports to tourism, labor, and consumption.[37] Like *The Youngest Yugoslavs*, some scholars investigate how Yugoslavia is remembered—or forgotten—in the post-Yugoslav world.[38] Much of this scholarship offers bottom-up narratives that center the experiences of ordinary citizens and everyday life. *The Youngest Yugoslavs* builds on this work by narrowing attention on a generational group whose experience of Yugoslavia has not been thoroughly studied. The interviewees included in this volume were deeply shaped by Yugoslavia and its collapse during their childhood. In the three decades since, they have grappled

---

33. For instance, Banac, *The National Question in Yugoslavia*; Cohen, *Broken Bonds*; Cohen and Dragović-Soso, *State Collapse in South-Eastern Europe*; Djokić, *Elusive Compromise*; Djokić, *Yugoslavism*; Dragović-Soso, 'Saviors of the Nation'; Jović, *Yugoslavia*; Pavković, *The Fragmentation of Yugoslavia*; Pavković, "Yugoslavism"; Pavlowich, *The Impossible Survivor*; Perica, *Balkan Idols*; Ramet, *The Three Yugoslavias*.

34. For a synthesis of the historiography following the Yugoslav wars, see Jović, "The Disintegration of Yugoslavia."

35. For instance, Calic, *A History of Yugoslavia*; Greble, *Sarajevo, 1941–1945*; Prusin, *Serbia under the Swastika*; Yeomans, *Visions of Annihilations*; Zakić, *Ethnic Germans and National Socialism in Yugoslavia in World War II*.

36. For instance, Baker, *Race and the Yugoslav Region*; Archer, Duda, and Stubbs, *Social Inequalities and Discontent in Yugoslav Socialism*; Lóránd, *The Feminist Challenge to the Socialist State in Yugoslavia*; Štiks, *Nations and Citizen in Yugoslavia and Post-Yugoslav States*; Stubbs, *Socialist Yugoslavia and the Non-Aligned Movement*.

37. For instance, Brentin and Zec, *Sport in Socialist Yugoslavia*; Grandits and Taylor, *Yugoslavia's Sunny Side*; Jakovljević, *Alienation Effects*; Kim, *The Partisan Counter-archive*; Le Normand, *Citizens without Borders*; Le Normand, *Designing Tito's Capital*; Luthar and Pušnik, *Remembering Utopia*; Patterson, *Bought and Sold*; Praznik, *Art Work*; Tumbas, "I Am Jugoslovenka!"; Videkanić, *Nonaligned Modernism*; Vučetić, *Coca-Cola Socialism*; Vuletic, *Postwar Europe and the Eurovision Song Contest*.

38. Gorup, *After Yugoslavia*; Horvat and Štiks, *Welcome to the Desert of Post-Socialism*; Petrović, "'When We Were Europe'"; Spaskovska, *The Last Yugoslav Generation*.

with the legacy of Yugoslavia near and far from the region, showing a complex engagement with the past, present, and future of the idea of Yugoslavia. Their interviews are an invaluable addition to our growing understanding of Yugoslavia's history and legacy.

The third historiographical field *The Youngest Yugoslavs* engages with is memory studies, particularly focusing on nostalgia. The work of Svetlana Boym suggests that nostalgia is "a longing for a home that no longer exists or has never existed... but it is also a romance with one's own fantasy."[39] When people long for childhoods or lives untouched by war, violence, or displacement, they are often seeking refuge from the present in memories of the past. Boym identifies two types of nostalgia: "reflective nostalgia," which dwells on the ambivalences of longing, and "restorative nostalgia," which seeks to recover a mythologized past.[40] Most expressions of post-socialist nostalgia, including Yugonostalgia, fall into the reflective category; scholars often study post-socialist nostalgia as a coping mechanism for grappling with the post-socialist transition.[41] As historian Maria Todorova suggests, East Europeans did not want socialist regimes to return, but they turned to nostalgia to mourn the loss of a specific form of sociability these regimes had provided.[42] By comparison, national revivals that make competing claims on history by calling to rebuild a past thought to be unjustly lost are better understood as restorative nostalgia.[43] Although reflective and restorative forms of nostalgia lay claim to different moments in history, they often compete for memory narratives in post-socialist Eastern Europe.

Yugonostalgia is expressed in several ways. At times, it is kitschy, satiric, and commercial; scholars interpret this type of nostalgia as wistful longing for cultural artifacts like music, television, and consumer products. Scholars also point to the ubiquitous use of socialist symbols to sell and advertise products in post-Yugoslav spaces, noting the irony of utilizing socialist emblems for capitalist profit.[44] At other times, expressions of Yugonostalgia are political, overt rejections of nationalism. Scholars have shown that expressions of nostalgia frequently correlate with negative views of particular successor states.[45] Others

---

39. Boym, *The Future of Nostalgia*, xiii.
40. Boym, *The Future of Nostalgia*, 41.
41. Velikonja, "Lost in Transition," 546.
42. Todorova, "Introduction," 7.
43. For instance, 1990s Serbian nationalist appeals to revive the glory of the medieval kingdom, prioritize rural life, and center religion in society are examples of restorative nostalgia (Lawrence, "Making Up for Lost Time," 83).
44. Volcic, "Post-Socialist Recollections," 188.
45. Kolstø, "Identifying with the Old or the New State."

have argued that reflective, self-critical, or even ambivalent Yugonostalgia can be an antidote to its restorative, ahistorical, and nationalistic counterpart.[46] This claim is viable foremost because Yugoslavia's ideals of antifascism, solidarity, and brotherhood and unity during the postwar years were antithetical to nationalism. Scholar Maja Maksimović sees the political type of Yugonostalgia as a path toward regional reconciliation because "the past represents a utopian desire for a better tomorrow and gives people hope that a different world is possible."[47] She believes that the shared experience of nostalgia can help residents move toward cooperation and normalization. While the impact of nostalgia on political change is difficult to measure, its mere presence reflects a dissatisfaction with the state of present society.

The Youngest Yugoslavs offers an exploration of post-socialist memory that stretches well beyond nostalgia. Interviewees certainly expressed a nostalgic longing for favorite foods, carefree summer holidays, and popular culture. But more often, they reflected critical forms of memory that engage with the Yugoslav past in complex ways. Unlike members of older generations, interviewees did not necessarily have enough lived experience in Yugoslavia to romanticize positive aspects of socialist sociability while filtering out difficult memories of state dissolution. Instead, they examined childhood recollections though perspectives they gained as they reached middle age, settled across the world, and reckoned with their relationship to former and current homelands.

By centering the voices of a generational cohort that continues to find meaning in the Yugoslav past as a lived experience and set of ideals, this volume adds necessary texture to memory studies. Many of those interviewed recognized that their childhood memories were happy precisely because they were children; they understood that they did not have extensive recollections of shortages, restrictions, or surveillance because adults had shielded them from the hardships of everyday life. However, relative to their parents or grandparents, members of the youngest cohort were also more emotionally detached from Yugoslavia because they had not experienced it as adults. This distance allowed them to be more critical but no less invested in their memories of Yugoslavia. *The Youngest Yugoslavs* dialogues with existing research to show how this generation of former citizens grappled with the legacy of the unified state's brief, turbulent history and how they understood the value of Yugoslav ideals in their past, present, and future.

---

46. Lindstrom, "Yugonostalgia."
47. Maksimović, "Unattainable Past, Unsatisfying Present," 1073.

A Brief History of Yugoslavia

Yugoslavia has a rich history both defined and marred by diversity. The state existed in several different articulations between 1918 and 2008; at each instance, it experienced political challenges. In recent reevaluations of Yugoslavia's history, scholars have moved away from examining the past through a lens of inevitable state failure and have instead considered the myriad possibilities that existed at the time of Yugoslavia itself. *The Youngest Yugoslavs* aims to contribute to this growing understanding of the lived experience of Yugoslavia across history.

The Kingdom of the Serbs, Croats, and Slovenes was created after World War I as a unified home for southern Slavs who had previously been either subjects of the Habsburg and Ottoman empires or citizens of the independent kingdoms of Serbia and Montenegro. Its creation was spurred by the Illyrian movement, which advocated for the ethnic and linguistic unification of Slavs in Austria-Hungary and the pooling of resources to create a large state in southeastern Europe that could compete politically in the postimperial world order. The major founding problem of the Kingdom of the Serbs, Croats, and Slovenes was that it adopted the political infrastructure of the prewar Kingdom of Serbia, including its royal family, legal framework, and capital city. This made it unwelcoming for citizens of different national, ethnic, religious, and linguistic identities, and their political representatives often criticized the state's Serbian hegemony. In response to mounting discord, King Alexander I Karadjordjević (1888–1934) declared a dictatorship in 1929 to force state centralization. Among his executive actions, he renamed the state the Kingdom of Yugoslavia, redrew internal borders, and banned national political parties, but he ultimately failed to solve the core of the problem. The state struggled to balance the demands of major recognized groups—Serbs, Croats, and Slovenes—and granted almost no protections to minorities. Several years later, separatists assassinated King Alexander I during a state visit to Marseilles. The king's underage son Peter II Karadjordjević (1923–1970) succeeded the throne; the king's cousin Prince Paul Karadjordjević (1893–1976) served as head of the regency council. Historian Dejan Djokić argues that Yugoslav politicians had approached compromises that might have made the Kingdom of Yugoslavia viable as a federal state in the late 1930s.[48] Historian John Lampe also suggests that there was potential to economically integrate the state's dissipate regions.[49] However, at the onset

---

48. Djokić, *Elusive Compromise*.
49. Lampe, *Yugoslavia as History*.

of World War II, Yugoslavia was not unified enough to overcome the onslaught of foreign and domestic fascism.

The Kingdom of Yugoslavia collapsed during World War II. As Hitler conquered Europe, Prince Paul signed the Tripartite Pact with the Axis powers in 1941 in hopes of keeping Yugoslavia out of war. But when military officials who opposed the pact launched a coup, the Axis immediately invaded and split the administration of occupied Yugoslavia into sections. German forces occupied parts of Serbia, Bosnia, and Slovenia; the domestic fascist group Ustaša, led by Ante Pavelić (1889–1959), established the Nazi puppet Independent State of Croatia in parts of Croatia, Bosnia, Serbia, and Slovenia; and Italy, Bulgaria, and Hungary occupied the rest of the country. The wartime occupation of Yugoslavia was violent, particularly in regions governed by the Ustaša. The regime waged targeted attacks on Serbs, Jews, and Roma though forced assimilation, expulsion, and genocide in the interest of creating a racially pure Croatian state. Two notable groups mounted homegrown resistance to fascist occupation: the Serbian royalist group Četniks, led by Dragoljub "Draža" Mihailović (1893–1946), and the communist Partisans, led by Josip Broz (1892–1980), commonly known as Tito. The two groups briefly worked together but clashed ideologically and soon turned against each other. The Allies initially supported the Četniks, but they abandoned this alliance once it became plain that Mihailović was collaborating with local fascists, receiving Axis supplies, and agitating for his own racially motived persecution of Croats and Muslims. By the end of the war, the Allies transferred their support to Tito, who had by then grown a massive guerrilla resistance army that attracted nationally, ethnically, and religiously diverse members. The Partisans ultimately liberated Yugoslavia and reformed it as a socialist state.

Yugoslavia became the Federal People's Republic of Yugoslavia in 1945, and it was renamed the Socialist Federal Republic of Yugoslavia in 1963. Its constitution, initially modeled on that of the Soviet Union, established the state as a federation of six republics and two autonomous provinces with three official languages (Serbo-Croatian, Macedonian, and Slovene). Yugoslavia recognized constituent nations, nationalities, and national minorities and promised them all equal rights under its ideology of brotherhood and unity. Much of postwar Yugoslavia's identity was founded on Partisan resistance to and victory over foreign and domestic fascist forces. After the war, the state called on the spirit of the Partisans to mobilize citizens into so-called voluntary work actions, federal programs to rebuild infrastructure after World War II. These work actions, for instance, built the Brotherhood and Unity Highway that stretched across the territory of Yugoslavia and connected four republics and some major cities. Yet unity felt precarious because the state developed few strategies to resolve and reconcile wartime conflict among citizens who again found themselves living in the same country.

Yugoslavia remained allied with the Soviet Union in the first years after World War II, but it charted its own way after Tito split from Stalin in 1948. The state quickly distanced itself from the Soviet sphere: it violently purged alleged Stalinists, withdrew from the Eastern bloc, and started nurturing relationships with the West. In 1961, Yugoslavia served as a founding member of the Non-Aligned Movement, a global consortium of states unified in opposition to Cold War bloc politics. In the 1960s, the state began practicing greater decentralization, expanding the autonomy of its constituent republics and Serbia's two autonomous provinces (Kosovo and Vojvodina), and extending the rights of various minority groups. It also increased civic liberties and access to the West. Yugoslavs could work and travel abroad, purchase Western goods, and engage in global cultural trends. In response to the calls for reform after the 1968 student protests and the Croatian Spring in the early 1970s, the state ratified a new constitution in 1974 that aimed to address the de facto Serbian hegemony by granting even more rights to individual republics and autonomous provinces. Over time, Yugoslavia set itself apart from other socialist states through relatively mild authoritarianism, economic robustness, and ideological promises of worker solidarity. For a portion of the postwar years, historian Patrick Patterson argues, Yugoslavs were living the "good life."[50]

Over the course of the 1970s and 1980s, however, economic crises and the broader collapse of socialism dovetailed with rising nationalism. Yugoslavia accumulated foreign debt, experienced massive hyperinflation, and saw troubling unemployment and shortages. The crises highlighted regional economic inequalities and exasperated tensions between wealthier northern republics and poorer southern ones. Tito's death in 1980 further fractured Yugoslavia's federalism by creating a political vacuum in which nationalist leaders, notably Slobodan Milošević (1941–2006), gained a more prominent platform. When the Albanian majority in Kosovo demanded the transformation of the province into a republic in 1981, Serbian leaders retaliated with repressive measures. Milošević reduced the rights of Serbia's autonomous provinces during the Anti-Bureaucratic Revolution, stoked the flames of ethnic nationalism, and eliminated political alternatives from public and private life. When the first democratic multiparty elections were held in individual republics, nationalist parties won almost all of them. In response to Serbia's attempt to recentralize,

---

50. Patterson, *Bought and Sold*.

delegates from Slovenia and Croatia walked out of the Fourteenth Extraordinary Congress of the League of Communists of Yugoslavia in 1990; the two republics declared independence in 1991.

Starting in 1991, Yugoslavia disintegrated in a series of wars and conflicts that killed 140,000 people, precipitated a genocide, and displaced millions. The Yugoslav National Army waged the brief Ten Day War against Slovenia immediately after the republic seceded from Yugoslavia in 1991. The Croatian War of Independence (1991–1995) was more complicated because the republic was home to a Serbian minority population that felt targeted by Croatia's new nationalist policies and rejected the secession. The Yugoslav National Army opposed Croatia's independence, while Croatian Serbs formed the proto-state Republic of Serbian Krajina, which advocated for autonomy within Croatia and unification with other regions with sizable Serb populations. Croatia ultimately established control over most of its territories—at the cost of violence, ethnic cleansing, and substantial infrastructural damage. The Bosnian War (1992–1995) was similarly complicated by the diversity of the former republic's population. Following Bosnia and Herzegovina's declaration of independence, Bosnian Serbs and the Yugoslav National Army mobilized to secure the territories inhabited by ethnic Serbs. Fighting occurred among the forces of the Republic of Bosnia and Herzegovina, Republika Srpska (supported by Serbia), and the Republic of Herzeg-Bosnia (supported by Croatia), leading to large-scale destruction, violence, assault, displacement, and Serb-instigated genocide of Bosnian Muslims.

In the late 1990s, in response to rising Serbian nationalism and oppression of Albanians in the rump of Yugoslavia, particularly in Kosovo, the guerrilla group Kosovo Liberation Army attacked Serb civilians, Serbian law enforcement, and the Yugoslav military. In the Kosovo War (1998–1999), Serbia redoubled its repression of Kosovar Albanians and increased the presence of regular forces and paramilitary units in Kosovo to systematically expel Albanians from the province. NATO initiated a bombing campaign of Yugoslavia in 1999 to pressure the withdrawal of troops from Kosovo and end the war. The declaration of Macedonian independence was the only instance of Yugoslav secession in the 1990s that did not end in war. However, because Macedonia discriminated against its Albanian population during the time of Yugoslavia as well as in its aftermath, the ethnic Albanian National Liberation Army eventually led an armed insurgency in 2001. The last remnant of unified Yugoslavia, a union between Serbia and Montenegro named the Federal Republic of Yugoslavia in 1992 (renamed Serbia and Montenegro in 2003), officially dissolved in 2006 when citizens of Montenegro voted for a referendum to secede. Two years later, in 2008, Kosovo leaders declared independence from Serbia. Serbia responded by immediately contesting the Republic of Kosovo's legality and refusing to recognize its sovereignty. Although many countries across the world have since diplomatically recognized the Republic of Kosovo, Serbia, alongside major global players like China, India, Mexico, and Russia, still has not.

Scholar Milica Bakić-Hayden conceptualizes the collapse of Yugoslavia as the collapse of a "neutralizing framework" that supported multinationalism. "As a political entity, the former Yugoslavia encompassed traditional dichotomies such as east/west and their nesting variants (Europe/Asia, Europe/Balkans, Christian/Muslim), largely neutralizing their usual valorization," she writes. "With the destruction of this neutralizing framework, the revalorization of these categories, now oppositions rather than simply differences, has resulted in the destruction of the living communities that had transcended them."[51] Yet despite its undeniable destruction, the idea of Yugoslavia continued to resonate with former citizens. The interviews included in *The Youngest Yugoslavs* are indicative of the durability and desirability of Yugoslav-era social ideals relative to the capitalist, nationalistic, and democratic world in which most former citizens live today. Members of this cohort viewed the social pillars of Yugoslavia as a foundation that could serve them in the present, offering benchmarks for kinder societies and helping reclaim the past from dominant narratives of war, dislocation, and emigration. Many of those interviewed saw powerful potential in the Yugoslav ideals they were raised with but never had the chance to experience as adults. For some, those ideals were rooted in socialism. For others, they were rooted in multinationalism. For most, they were found at the intersection of the two.

How to Use This Book

This volume is designed to be an English-language primary source collection that gives scholars and students access to the history of everyday life in East Europe in general and in Yugoslavia in particular. It is intended as a resource for understanding socialist and post-socialist lived experiences and memory and the practice of oral history as a methodology.

Several aids accompany the interviews. A glossary of key political, social, and cultural concepts commonly referenced by the interviewees follows this general introduction. Each interview has a brief introduction that provides biographic information about the interviewee and identifies key themes discussed.

---

51. Bakić-Hayden, "Nesting Orientalism," 930–31.

Each interview also contains annotations specific to the interview itself that supplement the glossary. General and comparative discussion questions to prompt conversation appear after the interviews.

The individual interviews can be read on their own or in dialogue with one another. When read together, the interviews unearth patterns, contradictions, and insights no singular experience can offer on its own. As historian Donald Raleigh suggests in his own volume of interviews, considering the entire set gives readers an opportunity to "construct their own narrative out of the fragments."[52] *The Youngest Yugoslavs* invites readers to draw conclusions from individual interviews or from comparisons among them.

---

52. Raleigh, *Russia's Sputnik Generation*, 10.

Glossary of Key Concepts

This glossary includes concepts commonly discussed or referenced in the interviews that follow. It is intended to aid readers in understanding the broader political, economic, social, and cultural context of the interviews. The glossary is not meant to be an encyclopedia or textbook. It does not include all Yugoslav history or reflect a universal representation of its past.

Armed Insurgency in Macedonia (2001): Following Macedonia's independence in 1991, the state's relationship to its Albanian minority (22 percent of the population, according to the 1994 census) was peaceful but uneasy. Albanian parties participated in the government as coalition partners and played an active role in political dialogue. However, Albanians faced systematic discrimination in Macedonia, such as limited access to Albanian-language education and media, restrictions on public display of the Albanian flag, underrepresentation in police, military, and government, and voter suppression. Macedonian Albanians demanded political rights and representation throughout the 1990s. Albanian discontent increased after thousands of Kosovar Albanians took refuge in Macedonia during the Kosovo War. In 2001, the militant group Albanian National Liberation Army led an insurgency that culminated in the Ohrid Agreement. In the agreement, the Macedonian government pledged to extend political, cultural, and economic rights to the ethnic Albanian community and other communities in the country.

Atheism: Before World War II, Yugoslavia reported that 0.01 percent of citizens were atheist or nonreligious. According to a 1953 census, 12.6 percent of those surveyed identified as atheist or nonreligious, and on a 1987 census, 31.6 percent identified as such. In the early 1990s, however, religious identification increased across the region. Scholar Reinhard Henkel suggests this increase was due to two major changes: the collapse of socialism and the superimposition of religion onto the national identities of Yugoslav successor states. Although citizens did not necessarily become more involved with religious institutions, religion did gain a more prominent place in society. This shift left less room for citizens to identify as atheist or nonreligious. From survey data collected in the early 2000s, Henkel calculated that only 2.7 percent of citizens across the former Yugoslavia identified as atheist or nonreligious (Henkel, "Religions and Religious Institutions in the Post-Yugoslav States between Secularization of Resurgence").

Bajram: The Muslim holiday Eid al-Fitr is commonly known as *Bajram* in the region. In Bosnia it is known as *Ramadanski bajram*, and in Macedonia it is known as *Ramazan bajram*. The holiday is celebrated to mark the end of month-long Ramadan fasting.

Bosnian War (1992–1995): In 1991, Bosnia's population was 43.4 percent Bosnian Muslim or Bosniak, 31.2 percent Serb, 17.3 percent Croat, and 7.9 percent Yugoslav, with smaller communities of Montenegrins, Roma, and Albanians. Following Bosnia and Herzegovina's declaration of independence from Yugoslavia, ethnic Serbs proclaimed six autonomous Serbian oblasts had merged into the breakaway parastate Republika Srpska in March of 1992. Over the course of the war, fighting occurred among the forces of the Republic of Bosnia and Herzegovina, Republika Srpska (supported by Serbia), and the Republic of Herzeg-Bosnia (supported by Croatia), producing extensive destruction, displacement, ethnic cleansing, and genocide. Incidents included the killing of eight thousand Bosniak men and boys in Srebrenica, a major crime in the Bosnian genocide, and the Siege of Sarajevo that lasted nearly four years. The Bosnian War ended with the Dayton Peace Agreement in 1995, which divided Bosnia into two ethnically homogenous substate entities: Republika Srpska and the Federation of Bosnia and Herzegovina.

Brotherhood and Unity (*Bratstvo i jedinstvo*): The Socialist Federal Republic of Yugoslavia used the slogan "Brotherhood and Unity" to promote cooperation and peaceful coexistence among its population of recognized nations, nationalities, and national minorities. The slogan was popular among citizens during the time of Yugoslavia, and it is a core symbol of Yugoslavia's multinationalism.

Četniks: The Četniks (sometimes spelled Chetniks) was a Serbian royalist and nationalist guerrilla group known for its participation in World War II. The Četniks initially mounted a resistance to occupation but later collaborated with the Axis powers with the intent of forming an ethnically homogenous greater Serbia after the war. Leaders of socialist Yugoslavia banned the Četniks and executed its major leaders, including Dragoljub "Draža" Mihailović (1893–1946). On the eve of the Yugoslav wars, Serb nationalists began rehabilitating, reviving, and reclaiming the legacy of the Četniks and their ethno-nationalist legacy. As a result, "Četnik" is also a derogatory term for ethnic Serbs.

Croatian Independence (1991): The Croatian Parliament held a referendum about Croatia's independence from Yugoslavia on May 19, 1991. There was an 83.5 percent voter turnout, and 93.2 percent voted in favor of independence. Croatia and Slovenia both declared independence on June 25, 1991, and recognized each other the same day. The European Economic Community hesitated to recognize the new states, fearing unrest in the region, so both states agreed to place a three-month pause on the decision with the Brioni Agreement. Lithuania was the first state to recognize Croatia that summer. Several others, including Germany and Iceland, followed in 1991, and many other major states, including all members of the European Economic Community, recognized Croatia in 1992. After declaring independence, Croatia faced a one-third drop in GDP, high inflation, and an economic crisis. The Croatian War of Independence moreover caused damage to infrastructure, created housing needs for displaced people, and derailed the robust tourist industry. Scholars Vojmir Franičević and Evan Kraft suggest that Croatia's economy stabilized in its first years after secession, but it had yet to address privatization, banking, taxation, the external sector, and investment (Franičević and Kraft, "Croatia's Economy after Stabilization").

Croatian War of Independence (1991–1995): The same day Croatia declared its independence, ethnic Serbs (12.2 percent of the population of Croatia in 1991) opposed to secession from Yugoslavia proclaimed the parastate Serbian Autonomous Oblast of Eastern Slavonia, Baranja, and Western Syrmia. Two additional autonomous Serbian oblasts in Croatia (Krajina and Western Slavonia) eventually joined and merged into the Republic of Serbian Krajina. Scholar Vjeran Pavlaković suggests that the Republic of Serbian Krajina lacked clear political vision but mobilized the memory of Serbian persecution at the hands of Croatian Ustaša during World War II, rejecting all possibility for interethnic cooperation in independent Croatia (Pavlaković, "Symbols and the Culture of Memory in Republika Srpska Krajina"). The Yugoslav National Army also mobilized against Croatia's independence. Croatia eventually established control over most of its territories at the cost of violence, ethnic cleansing, and substantial infrastructural damage.

Day of the Republic (*Dan republike*): The Day of the Republic was a Yugoslav national holiday celebrated on November 29. The day commemorated the 1943 declaration of the Anti-Fascist Council for the National Liberation of Yugoslavia (ANVOJ) as the state's future government and the 1945 declaration of Yugoslavia as a democratic, federal, socialist state with the transfer of power from King Peter II to Tito. During Yugoslavia's existence, the Pioneers annually inaugurated new generations of schoolchildren into their ranks on November 29. The Day of the Republic was a two-day state holiday and a popular day for weddings (Ninković Slavnić, "Celebrating Yugoslavia," 69). The other two-day state holidays were May Day, or International Workers' Day, and New Year's.

Day of Youth (*Dan mladosti*): Tito was born on May 7 in Kumrovec (now Croatia). Yugoslavia institutionalized the Day of Youth on May 25 to honor his birthday, as May 25 was the date of birth listed on his forged wartime documents as well as the date the Nazis launched the air and ground attack Operation Rösselsprung in 1944 to capture or kill Tito. The state celebrated the Day of Youth with a relay race called Relay of Youth (*štafeta mladosti*), a ritual in which young adults carried a baton through all major Yugoslav cities and regions and delivered it to Tito at a celebration in Belgrade on May 25. Scholars suggest that the Day of Youth was a manifestation of Yugoslavia's cult of revolutionary action and of Tito himself (Božić, "Conversations with Bosnian Youth," 747). The Relay of Youth was discontinued after a 1987 controversy: the organizing committee selected a promotional poster made by the art group Neue Slowenische Kunst that was based on Richard Klein's 1936 painting *The Third Reich* and compared the Yugoslav state ritual to fascist rallies. In the aftermath of the Yugoslav wars, the Day of Youth became a benchmark of nostalgia for former citizens. Today, thousands of visitors gather in Kumrovec to celebrate the Day of Youth, and there are official and unofficial commemorations in other successor states as well. When Tito passed away in 1980, a large state funeral was held at Belgrade's House of Flowers, a structure built as a winter garden for Tito, where he is still buried. Tito's spouse Jovanka Broz (1924–2013) was also buried at the House of Flowers after her death. The building is now a mausoleum and a memorial museum. It is located next to the Museum of Yugoslavia, an institution built in the 1960s to showcase gifts Tito received from foreign dignitaries as well as batons from Relay of Youth celebrations.

Economic Debt (1970s and 1980s): Western banks and monetary organizations offered Yugoslavia favorable loans due to Tito's nonalignment during the Cold War. These loans were important to jumpstarting Yugoslavia's industrialization and economic growth. However, when the 1974 constitution gave

Yugoslav republics and autonomous regions the ability to borrow money from abroad without approval from the central government, they began taking out loans uncontrollably, exacerbating the overall debt of the state. Yugoslav debt increased gradually in the first postwar decades and then astronomically starting in the 1970s. In 1971, the state's debt was $3.2 billion; in 1980, it was $18.9 billion. The debt crisis precipitated inflation and unemployment. Moreover, historian John Lampe suggests that the debt crisis perpetuated regional disparity and disconnection because wealthier republics like Slovenia and Croatia resented paying disproportionately higher percentages of the debt. "That was the real Faustian bargain the Titoist regime made, not with Western lenders for economic advantage, but with republic and local party leaders to preserve their common political monopoly," Lampe writes (Lampe, "The Two Yugoslavias as Economic Unions," 194).

Economic Disparity: The Yugoslav economy developed unevenly, creating substantial regional disparities. Wealthier republics like Slovenia and Croatia brought substantially more capital to Yugoslavia through industry and trade and, in turn, contributed disproportionately higher percentages of the national budget. While Yugoslav investment policies favored less developed republics like Macedonia and Bosnia, they failed to even out disparities across the state. As economic conditions worsened in the 1980s, these disparities contributed to wealthier republics' arguments for independence from Yugoslavia. For instance, Slovenia accounted for 8 percent of the Yugoslav population but contributed 22 percent of state public revenue and 25 percent of export. As a result, citizens in Slovenia were resistant to Yugoslav economic integration and compelled by the arguments of the liberal, reformed-minded leadership of the Slovene Communist Party. When Milan Kučan (1941–) became leader of the party in 1986, he initiated a wave of liberalization reforms that clashed with the agendas of Serbia's Slobodan Milošević. Slovene opposition groups also vocally criticized the Yugoslav National Army in the media. They called for domestic reforms, such as an alternative to military service, and foreign relations reforms, such as cuts to the export of arms to the Third World. These voices unified Slovene public opinion against the Yugoslav National Army as well as Yugoslavia itself. See Lampe, *Yugoslavia as History*, 349–52, and Velikonja, "Slovenia's Yugoslav Century," 95–97.

Economic Sanctions (1990s): In response to the Yugoslav wars, the international community imposed a series of economic sanctions on the region. The European Economic Community imposed the first sanctions against Yugoslavia in late 1991. The United Nations placed Serbia and Montenegro, then still known as the Federal Republic of Yugoslavia, under an embargo during the Croatian War of Independence and the Bosnian War. The United Nations Security Council banned all international trade, cooperation, and exchanges with Yugoslavia in 1992, and later resolutions banned shipments to and from Yugoslavia. The Yugoslav dinar experienced a period of hyperinflation. Average income dropped, and residents faced shortages of gas, oil, and everyday goods. The United Nations, European Union, and United States again sanctioned Yugoslavia during the Kosovo War. Sanctions froze trade, professional cooperation, cultural exchange, and travel and caused hyperinflation. Although there was no warfare in Serbia and Montenegro, wartime sanctions greatly impacted everyday life. Residents had severely limited access to food, heat, electricity, gasoline, medicine and medical care, and commercial goods. Sanctions also triggered the proliferation of an underground, black-market economy.

Ekavica / ikavica / ijekavica **variants:** Three spelling and pronunciation variants of Serbo-Croatian based around the transformation of a vowel were commonly used in Yugoslavia, roughly corresponding to territorial regions. The two most commonly used were *ekavica* and *ijekavica*, and the third was *ikavica*. *Ekavica* was mostly used in Serbia, seen in the words for "milk," *mleko*, and "white," *belo*. *Ijekavica* was mostly used in Croatia and Bosnia, as in the words for "milk," *mlijeko*, and "white," *bijelo*. After the Yugoslav wars, language policies in the successor states aimed to distinguish Serbian, Croatian, Bosnian, and Montenegrin from one another. Linguists redefined phonology, grammar, and basic vocabulary, standardizing the variants of Serbo-Croatian into national languages. Scholar Catherine Baker explains how the use of *ekavica* and Cyrillic script became markers of Serbian language and, by extension, Serbian ethnicity. By the same token, 1990s Croatian language policy distinguished Croatian by the use of *ijekavica* (Baker, "Cultural Space and Meaning in the Phenomenon of 'Cro-dance,'" 315). Linguist Ranko Bugarski explains that "in a semi-official drive for purification and Croatization, the public language was purged of anything smacking of Serbian or of Yugoslavia, and replacements were introduced by reviving Croatian archaisms, institutionalizing regionalism, and creating neologisms" (Bugarski, "What's in a Name," 12). Anthropologist Špela Drnovšek Zorko reiterates that these spelling and pronunciation variants have become "political tools of differentiation"—all the more in Bosnia, a successor state divided into two autonomous regions by the Dayton Peace Agreement that ended the Bosnian War in 1995. In Republika Srpska, an autonomous region with a predominantly Bosnian Serb population, *ekavica* is commonly used. In the Federation of Bosnia and Herzegovina, the population of which is predominantly Bosnian Croat and Bosniak, *ijekavica* is more common (Drnovšek Zorko, "See(m)ing Strange," 87–88).

Eurovision Song Contest: The Eurovision Song Contest started in 1956 as a stage for Western European cultural, economic, and political integration after World War II. Yugoslavia participated in Eurovision almost every year from 1961 to 1992. It was the only East European state to submit contestants during the Cold War, signaling its membership to the Western cultural sphere. Performers from all Yugoslav republics except Macedonia and the autonomous provinces, Kosovo and Vojvodina, represented Yugoslavia in Eurovision at some point. More than half the performers representing Yugoslavia came from Croatia. In 1989, the group Riva from Zadar (now Croatia) won Eurovision, and Yugoslavia hosted the contest in 1990 in Zagreb. Historian Dean Vuletic writes that "Eurovision had a huge audience among the country's citizens: it provided entertainment for millions of them who each year followed the preliminary contest for the Yugoslav entry, its preparation for Eurovision and then the final itself, when many of them would gather around television sets with their family and friends to watch it. They found Eurovision enticing as it had the status of a Western product, and because it was the West that initiated the most attractive global trends in popular music during the Cold War" (Vuletic, "European Sounds, Yugoslav Visions," 122–23). Also see Vuletic, "The Socialist Star."

Holiday with Pay: Socialist Yugoslavia instituted the Holiday with Pay program from its first years, and the federal Labor Act of 1958 mandated that all citizens be entitled to twelve to thirty days of vacation annually. The Labor Act of 1965 extended the minimum leave to fourteen days. Federal and regional governments, trade unions, factories, firms, and associations invested in subsidized holiday centers (*odmarališta*) because they believed that leisure and rest contributed to job productivity, health, and consumption. These subsidized centers allowed citizens to take vacations at deeply discounted rates; the state further incentivized travel with rail and air vouchers. As scholar Igor Duda shows, holiday centers played an important role in the development of domestic tourism, particularly on the coast of the Adriatic Sea (Duda, "Adriatic for All," 290–93).

Housing Policy: Yugoslavia's housing policy, like its economy and politics, moved away from centralized state socialism in the postwar years. A social sector of housing concentrated in urban areas was administered by enterprises and municipalities, while a largely informal private sector was concentrated in rural areas. Scholars Jasna Mariotti and Daniel Baldwin Hess suggest that urban housing in Yugoslavia was meant to prioritize equality, access to amenities, and standardization of units. "Centralized provision of neighborhood amenities was a critical aspect of socialism, and the allocation of housing to occupants was intended to establish an egalitarian society," they write (Mariotti and Hess, "Enlargement of Apartments in Socialist Housing Estates in Skopje under Transition," 43). Scholar Peter Troch suggests that Yugoslavia's development gap—higher industrialization and investment in northern parts of the country and lower in the southern parts—also impacted housing. In his study of housing in Kosovo, he found a lower proportion of social-sector housing in the province than in Yugoslavia as a whole and that it was less accessible to ethnic Albanians (Troch, "Of Private and Social in Socialist Cities," 51–52). Moreover, scholar Josip Mihaljević shows that class contributed to the unfair distribution of social-sector housing. Enterprises were less likely to distribute housing to poorly educated, low-qualified, low-income workers, just as the state was less likely to give these citizens housing loans. While Yugoslavia proclaimed commitment to "housing for everyone," Mihaljević argues that its housing policy was not egalitarian in practice (Mihaljević, "Social Inequalities from Workers' Perspective in 1960s Socialist Yugoslavia," 34–35).

Kosovo: Kosovo's majority Albanian population experienced discrimination in Yugoslavia throughout the twentieth century. Interwar Yugoslavia initiated a large-scale expulsion of Muslims and recolonization by Serbs. Tensions between the Yugoslav government and the Albanian population were high after Tito split with Stalin in 1948 because the state feared that Kosovo harbored sympathizers of Albanian leader Enver Hoxha's (1908–1985) Stalinist regime. Conditions improved with Yugoslavia's decentralization in the 1960s, when the state granted Serbia's autonomous provinces (Kosovo and Vojvodina) more rights and recognized Muslims as a nation. The 1974 constitution granted Kosovo higher levels of self-rule: it had its own administration and assembly as well as constitutional, legislative, and judicial autonomy. However, the Albanian population still experienced discrimination, and its leaders rallied for the province to become a constituent republic. In 1981, protests about conditions at the University of Pristina grew into protests about the status of Albanians in the state as a whole. Yugoslav leaders blamed the protests on nationalist radicals and declared a state of emergency. After military and police forces suppressed the protests, the state rescinded many of the rights it had granted the Albanian population. Around the same time, Kosovo's minority Serb population reported discrimination at the hands of the majority Albanian population, which led to increased ethnic tensions in the region. The 1990 constitution of the Republic of Serbia stripped Kosovo of most of its rights as an autonomous province. Kosovar Albanians responded with nonviolent separatism, developing parallel civic structures in Serbia to serve Albanians; the guerilla group Kosovo Liberation Army sought armed separation from Serbia, eventually triggering the Kosovo War.

Kosovo War (1998–1999): In response to rising Serbian nationalism and the oppression of Albanians in Kosovo during the 1980s and 1990s, the guerrilla group Kosovo Liberation Army began attacking Serb civilians, Serbian law enforcement, and the Yugoslav military in the late 1990s. The group sought independence from Yugoslavia and unification with Albania. In response, Serbia redoubled its repression of Kosovar Albanians and increased the number of regular forces and paramilitary units in Kosovo to systematically expel Albanians from the province. NATO initiated a bombing campaign of Yugoslavia in 1999 to pressure the withdrawal of troops from Kosovo. When the Republic of Kosovo declared independence in 2008, Serbia contested its legality and refused to recognize its sovereignty. Although many countries across the world have diplomatically recognized the Republic of Kosovo, Serbia—alongside major global players like China, India, Mexico, and Russia—still has not.

Language Policy: Socialist Yugoslavia's decentralized language policy allowed recognition of official languages at federal, republic, and communal levels. Official languages were meant to be equally accessible and used in official documents, judicial and administrative proceedings, and education. The constitution of the Yugoslav federal state recognized three languages: Serbo-Croatian, Slovene, and Macedonian. However, as scholar Vanya Ivanova suggests, "Serbo-Croatian functioned as the *lingua franca* of Yugoslavia. It was used in the Yugoslav army and by the federal administration staff in its communications with all republican governments. All pupils in the primary schools in Slovenia and Macedonia had to learn Serbo-Croatian but there was no reciprocity required regarding the learning of Slovene and Macedonian in Serbo-Croatian speaking districts" (Ivanova, "Language Policy and National Equality in Socialist Yugoslavia (1945–1974)," 85–86). Constitutional reforms in 1968 and 1974 granted individual republics and autonomous provinces the right to define official languages beyond those recognized by the federal state. From there, decisions about use of and access to language were made at the communal level based on the particularities of the population. Scholar James Tollefson provides two examples from Slovenia, a republic that recognized Italian and Hungarian as additional languages. In Ljubljana, where the population was overwhelmingly Slovene, city administration used Slovene in all official capacities and provided access to translators when necessary. In Piran, home to a majority Italian population, the city functioned on a bilingual model that implemented equal use of Slovene and Italian, including in schools (Tollefson, "Language Policy and National Stability in Yugoslavia," 509–14).

League of Communists of Yugoslavia: The League of Communists of Yugoslavia (known as the Communist Party of Yugoslavia until 1952) ruled Yugoslavia as a one-party state from 1945 until 1990. It was expelled from Cominform in 1948 after its leader, Tito, broke from Stalin. Thereafter, the League of Communists charted Yugoslavia's independent path toward socialism, sometimes called Titoism.

Macedonian Independence (1991): The first multiparty elections in Macedonia were held on November 11, 1990, and the Macedonian government was formed the following year. On September 8, 1991, citizens voted on an independence referendum to separate from Yugoslavia. There was a 75.7 percent voter turnout (ethnic Albanian and Serbian communities boycotted), and the referendum was approved by 96.4 percent of voters. After Macedonia declared independence, it established its own armed forces. In response, the Yugoslav National Army withdrew all its troops, equipment, and arms from Macedonia, even stripping and destroying facilities. Macedonian officials saw this as overly aggressive because the former republic had consistently contributed resources to the Yugoslav National Army. As a preventative measure, the United Nations Protective Force (UNPROFOR) deployed a peacekeeping mission to Macedonia in 1992 to ensure the former republic's independence would not escalate into conflict. It was tasked with monitoring Macedonia's border with Albania and rump Yugoslavia, strengthening security and stability, and tracking potential threats. Peacekeepers remained in Macedonia until 1999; there was no armed conflict in the state during the peacekeepers' stay. While declaring independence did not precipitate war in Macedonia like it did in other regions of Yugoslavia, the Albanian National Liberation Army led an armed insurgency in 2001 in response to continued discrimination against the country's Albanian population.

Macedonian Name Dispute: After Macedonia gained independence from Yugoslavia, Greece contested its use of the name "Republic of Macedonia," arguing that it would be confused for Greece's own region of Macedonia and ancient kingdom Macedon. The dispute lasted from 1991 to 2019, during which time Macedonia was known internationally as the Former Yugoslav Republic of Macedonia (FYROM). At a moment of particular discord in 1994, Greece imposed an eighteenth-month-long trade embargo on Macedonia that blocked its access to the Thessaloniki Sea port and froze its north-south trade routes (there was a US embargo on the rump of Yugoslavia, Macedonia's northern border, at the same time). Scholar Ilija Milchevski suggests that the dispute added an obstacle to Macedonia's political and economic transition, international recognition, and NATO and EU membership (Milchevski, "A Requiem for a Dream"). In 2019, Greece and Macedonia agreed that Macedonia be named the Republic of North Macedonia. The state joined NATO in 2020, but it has not yet been admitted into the EU.

Milošević, Slobodan (1941–2006): Slobodan Milošević rose to power in the late 1980s on a platform of nationalist, populist, and centralist views. When he was elected president of the Socialist Republic of Serbia in 1989, he scaled back the rights of Serbia's two autonomous provinces, Kosovo and Vojvodina, and silenced domestic opposition. Milošević rejected the independence of seceding Yugoslav republics that were home to sizable Serbian communities, particularly Croatia and Bosnia. He deployed the Yugoslav National Army in the Croatian War of Independence and the Bosnian War to fight against both states' independence. The International Criminal Tribunal for the former Yugoslavia charged Milošević with war crimes in these two conflicts as well as the Kosovo War. Many Serbians criticized the authoritarianism, nationalism, censorship, electoral fraud, and police brutality of Milošević's rule in the 1990s. Many also complained that his leadership brought a series of international sanctions that severely impacted quality of life. In addition to mass protests, including notable student protests during the winter of 1996–1997, Serbians opposed Milošević by deserting their Yugoslav National Army service and emigrating abroad. In 2000, the student group Otpor! led a successful campaign to overthrow Miloščvić and install a democratic government. Scholar Florian Bieber argues that Serbia's delayed democratic transition was due in part to Milošević's authoritarianism and Serbia's fragmented opposition (Bieber, "The Serbian Opposition and Civil Society").

Mostar Bridge: The Mostar Bridge, known as Stari most (Old Bridge), was a sixteen-century stone arch bridge in Mostar (now Bosnia) commissioned by Suleiman the Magnificent during the Ottoman Empire's rule of the region. It stood across the Neretva River and joined the two sides of Mostar. On November 9, 1993, the Croat Defense Council, the main military force of the Croats of Bosnia and Herzegovina, destroyed the bridge as it fought the Army of the Republic of Bosnia and Herzegovina. Although the International Criminal Tribunal for former Yugoslavia deemed the bridge a military target, it declared the bridge's destruction a war crime (this decision was later revised). The bridge was reconstructed with major international investment and reopened in 2004.

NATO Bombing of Yugoslavia: NATO bombed the Federal Republic of Yugoslavia in 1999 in response to the ethnic cleansing of Albanians during the Kosovo War. NATO ceased bombing once an agreement was reached for the withdrawal of Yugoslav armed forces and the establishment of a United Nations peacekeeping mission in Kosovo. NATO bombings killed about one thousand members of the Yugoslav military and five hundred civilians. The bombings destroyed military infrastructure, government facilities, bridges, roads, railways, factories, businesses, hospitals, schools, and monuments.

Naš jezik (**Our Language**): *Naš jezik* refers to the closely related languages of Bosnian, Croatian, Montenegrin, and Serbian. During the time of Yugoslavia, the languages were considered one language called Serbo-Croatian. Today, the languages are sometimes called BCS (Bosnian/Croatian/Serbian) or BCMS (Bosnian/Croatian/Montenegrin/Serbian). Many people from Yugoslavia who speak one of these languages refer to it as *naš jezik*, or "our language," to underline their shared linguistic inheritance in spite of national splintering. While this gesture is intended to level differences, it implicitly excludes former Yugoslavs whose first language is not Bosnian, Croatian, Montenegrin, or Serbian and who might not claim, or might not feel they can claim, *naš jezik* as their own.

Non-Alignment Movement: The Non-Alignment Movement was founded in 1961 by Yugoslavia's president, Tito, India's prime minister, Jawaharlal Nehru (1889–1964), and Egypt's president, Gamal Abdel Nasser (1918–1970). The organization was intended to offer states an alternative to the bipolarity of bloc politics during the Cold War. The principles of the Non-Alignment Movement were mutual support of territorial integrity and sovereignty, nonaggression, noninterference in domestic affairs, mutual benefit, and peaceful coexistence. The Non-Alignment Movement today has 120 member states and additional observers. See Niebuhr, "Nonalignment as Yugoslavia's Answer to Bloc Politics."

Partisans: The Yugoslav Partisans, officially known as the National Liberation Army and Partisan Detachments of Yugoslavia, formed as a resistance group during the Axis occupation of Yugoslavia in World War II. The Partisans started as communist-led antifascist guerillas but developed into an organized resistance movement that liberated Yugoslavia. After the war, the Partisans were reorganized into Yugoslavia's armed forces.

Pioneers: The Union of Pioneers of Yugoslavia, also known as Tito's Pioneers, was a state-sponsored group for children aged seven and older that most Yugoslav children de facto joined with their school groups. It was founded in 1942 as a subgroup of the League of Socialist Youth (known as the League of Communist Youth before Tito's break from Stalin in 1948) and was formally dissolved in 1992. The last generation of Pioneers was inducted in 1989, the year children born in 1982 turned seven. Inductions typically took place at schools on November 29, Yugoslavia's Day of the Republic. Children were expected to wear a uniform that reflected the colors of the Yugoslav flag to the ceremony: a white shirt, a red scarf, and a blue cap known as a *Titovka* that often bore a red star on the front. Many Yugoslavs recall their inauguration fondly because joining the Pioneers was a political rite of passage that marked their belonging in socialist society. The word "pioneer" (*pionir*) was an acronym of characteristics that underlined the ideological traits of an ideal socialist citizen. Members were expected to be honest (*pošten*), sincere (*iskren*), brave (*odvažan*), progressive (*napredan*), persistent (*istrajan*), and hardworking (*radišan*). To engage members after inauguration, the organization printed a children's periodical, planned extracurricular activities, and sponsored group trips (Erdei, "'The Happy Child' as an Icon of Socialist Transformation," 157).

Pioneer Pledge: Many Yugoslavs recall the pledge they recited at their Pioneer inauguration. The pledge read: "Today, as I become a Pioneer, I give my Pioneer's word of honor. That I shall study and work diligently, respect parents and my seniors, and be a loyal and honest comrade/friend. That I shall love our homeland, self-managed Socialist Federal Republic of Yugoslavia. That I shall spread brotherhood and unity and the principles for which Comrade Tito fought. And that I shall value all peoples of the world who respect freedom and peace!"

Refugees from the Yugoslav Wars: According to the United Nations High Commissioner for Refugees, the Yugoslav wars displaced 3.7–4 million people in Yugoslavia itself. Of those, 2.2 million were displaced in Bosnia and Herzegovina; the rest primarily went to other former republics. *Deutsche Welle* reported that Serbia, for instance, received about 540,000 refugees, mostly from Bosnia and Croatia, over the course of the wars. Refugees faced housing insecurity, low wages, unemployment, and discrimination when economic conditions in Serbia worsened in the 1990s (Rujevic, "A Home for Forgotten Balkan Refugees"). About 600,000–800,000 people fled to other European countries like Austria, Germany, Denmark, France, Italy, the Netherlands, Norway, Sweden, Switzerland, and Turkey. Additionally, 10,000–15,000 found refuge overseas in countries like the United States, Canada, and Australia. Many states offered temporary protection to refugees unable to return to their home countries safely. These protections often suspended asylum procedures and conferred temporary residential rights to refugees. Germany, for example, offered refugees from Yugoslavia *Duldung* status: temporary protection or, more explicitly, a suspended deportation permit. However, Germany revoked refugees' protection status and forced them to leave when the Bosnian War ended. By 2000, most refugees had been repatriated to a successor state of the former Yugoslavia. Like Germany, European states that received large numbers of refugees lacked political and economic incentives to offer refugees permanent residency. They also resisted providing a permanent home due to high rates of asylum seekers and xenophobia (Bahar, Hauptmann, Özgüzel, and Rapoport, "Migration and Post-conflict Reconstruction," 3–4).

Republika Srpska: After Bosnia and Herzegovina declared independence from Yugoslavia in 1992, Bosnian Serb separatists established the breakaway parastate Republika Srpska. The state was led by Radovan Karadžić (1945–) and supported by the Serb-dominated Yugoslav National Army and Serb paramilitary groups. Republika Srpska's political aims were to seize territory and ethnically cleanse it of non-Serb populations. During the Bosnian War, the forces of Republika Srpska fought those of the Republic of Bosnia and Herzegovina and the Republic of Herzeg-Bosnia, a quasi state representing Croatian nationalist interests in Bosnia. When the Bosnian War ended in 1995, the Dayton Peace Agreement recognized Republika Srpska and the Federation of Bosnia and Herzegovina as the two entities of present-day Bosnia and Herzegovina. Today, due to ethnic cleansing and population movements, Republika Srpska has a majority Bosnian Serb population.

Roma: The 1981 Yugoslav census counted 148,604 Romani residents, about 0.7 percent of the total population. The majority of Yugoslavia's Roma lived in Serbia, where 110,959 were counted. However, Roma census records were wildly underreported because the community feared being counted would lead to discrimination and pressure to assimilate (Surdu, "Why the 'Real' Numbers on the Roma Are Fictitious," 497). Census data also creates ethnic categories, which, for the Roma, meant essentializing different communities into a single group that has been consistently racialized, criminalized, and marginalized in all European states. Scholar Judith Latham argues that socialist Yugoslavia extended some social, economic, and political opportunities to the Roma but that these did not translate to major improvements in living conditions in Yugoslavia or its successor states. Latham writes that "the successor states of the former Yugoslavia, where Roma have traditionally been part of the underclass and where 'nationality' and ethnicity are everywhere more important than 'citizenship' or idealistic notions of a pan-Yugoslav identity, the Roma have been major losers. With collapsing economies, rampant unemployment, and faltering societal safety nets, the largely unskilled and poorly educated Roma are unable to compete with other populations. Lacking political organization and strong leadership, the Roma are—despite their numbers—an unseen and virtually ignored minority" (Latham, "Roma of the Former Yugoslavia," 217–18). Scholar Zoltan Barany suggests that postwar socialist states attempted to assimilate the Roma as "useful" members of society without addressing systematic social inequalities like access to education: "In a plethora of publications the conditions of the Roma were painstakingly described and decried, but the causes of these conditions were rarely investigated" (Barany, "Living on the Edge," 327).

Slovenian Independence (1991): The first democratic elections were held in Slovenia in April 1990. The new government held a referendum in December in which 88.2 percent of voters supported independence from Yugoslavia. Slovenia declared independence on June 25, 1991, precipitating the Ten-Day War between the Yugoslav National Army and the Slovenian Territorial Defense and the Slovene Police in late June and early July 1991. Participants reached a peace agreement with the Brioni Agreement, and the Yugoslav National Army left Slovenia by October. Slovenia was internationally recognized soon after. Milan Kučan served as president until 2002.

Student Protests in 1968: Yugoslavia's student movement gained momentum in the late 1960s and precipitated massive demonstrations in the state's major cities in June 1968. Like protests around the world in 1968, Yugoslav student demonstrations were motivated by issues ranging from grievances about university conditions like funding, health care, accommodation, and libraries to critiques of the state's commitment to socialism. As historian Madigan Fichter suggests, students did not have an official venue for voicing grievances with the university system, which they viewed as a failure of Yugoslav self-management. Student leaders demanded opportunities to participate in the educational, administrative, and political processes of universities. At the same time, students criticized Yugoslav socialism as overly bureaucratic, socially unequal, and repressive. They did not call for an overthrow of the state but demanded a return to its revolutionary roots. State officials suspected that student demonstrations were driven by foreign influence or domestic enemies; they responded by co-opting the movement as an expression of student loyalty to the system. Fichter suggests that while the League of Communists of Yugoslavia published a series of guidelines and implemented some measures to improve university living conditions, "the much deeper debates about social inequality and participatory government at the universities and beyond was not addressed in any serious way" (Fichter, "Yugoslav Protest," 119).

Textbooks: All successor states revised textbooks after the collapse of Yugoslavia to reflect new national narratives. As scholars Irena Stefoska and Darko Stojanov show in their study of textbooks from Macedonia, this process often prioritized a linear national history and an "intentional forgetting of socialist Yugoslavia and its legacy" (Stefoska and Stojanov, "Remembering and Forgetting SFR Yugoslavia," 207). Whereas history textbooks in Macedonia in the 1970s and 1980s devoted 53 percent of their content to Yugoslavia, they offered just a few pages on the topic by the early 2000s.

Tito, Josip Broz (1892–1980): Josip Broz, known as Tito, was the communist revolutionary leader of the Yugoslav Partisans during World War II and leader of Yugoslavia until his death.

Tudjman, Franjo (1922–1999): Franjo Tudjman was a Croatian politician who participated in the Croatian Spring, advocated for Croatian independence in the 1980s, led Croatia in its war for independence, and served as first democratically elected president of Croatia from 1990 until his death. While Tudjman is celebrated as the architect of Croatian sovereignty, writer Sven Milekic explains that his legacy is marred by interventions in the Bosnian War, historical revisionism, corruption, and undemocratic practices (Milekic, "Franjo Tudjman").

Ustaša: The Ustaša (sometimes spelled Ustasha) was a Croatian fascist and nationalist group formed by politician Ante Pavelić (1889–1959) in the interwar years; it is most often studied for its leadership of the Axis puppet state Independent State of Croatia (NDH) during World War II. The Ustaša advocated for the creation of a racially pure greater Croatian state, persecuting Serbs, Jews, and Roma and establishing and operating the death camp Jasenovac. After the Allied defeat of the Axis powers, the Independent State of Croatia collapsed. Some Ustaša leaders were massacred by the Yugoslav Partisans, and others fled abroad. Historian Ulf Brunnbauer explains that many Yugoslav refugees who had left the state before or during World War II were aligned with nationalist groups like the Ustaša and opposed the Partisans' new socialist order. During the Cold War, these refugees formed separatist ethno-nationalist émigré communities framed as anticommunist communities abroad (Brunnbauer,

"'The People of Our Blood, Who Are Citizens of Foreign Countries'"). For an examination of the radicalization of émigré communities, see Tokić, "Avengers of Bleiburg."

Vojvodina: Before World War I, Vojvodina was part of the Austro-Hungarian Empire. In the 1910 census, 28.1 percent of its 1.5 million residents were Hungarian. However, the Hungarian population steadily decreased over the twentieth century due to emigration, mixed marriages, social declassing, and assimilation. According to the 1981 Yugoslav census, Vojvodina was home to 2 million residents: 54.4 percent Serb, 18.9 percent Hungarian, 8.2 percent Yugoslav, 5.4 percent Croat, 3.4 percent Slovak, 2.3 percent Romanian, 2.1 percent Montenegrin, and an undisclosed percentage of Roma. Constitutional reform in 1968 granted Vojvodina higher levels of legislative self-rule as the Socialist Autonomous Province of Vojvodina, including the right to recognize official languages. In addition to Serbo-Croatian, one of the three officially recognized languages of Yugoslavia, the Socialist Autonomous Province of Vojvodina recognized four minority languages: Hungarian, Romanian, Rusyn, and Slovak. In the postwar years, when it was part of Yugoslavia, Vojvodina bordered Hungary and Romania. Today, as part of Serbia, it also borders Croatia and Bosnia. Vojvodina is one of Europe's most heterogeneous regions.

Workers' Self-Management: After Yugoslavia's ideological split from the Soviet Union in 1948, it moved away from the Soviet model of planned economy and state ownership. Yugoslav socialism distinguished itself through a combination of market socialism and workers' self-management. Self-management dictated that factories be organized on the principle of egalitarianism and run by worker-elected representatives. By the early 1960s, Yugoslavia's economy was based on social ownership, a system scholars Anna Calori and Kathrin Jurkat describe as neither public nor private but rather "nobody's and everybody's with management given over to workers' and citizens' collectives" (Calori and Jurkat, "'I'm Both a Worker and a Shareholder,'" 659). The model intended to transfer power from state central planning to autonomous workers' councils and give workers the power to influence the policies that governed them and share in revenue earnings. It was meant to forge Yugoslavia's "third way" between socialist and capitalist models. Historian John Lampe suggests that during Yugoslavia's early years, workers' councils tended to redistribute revenue toward bonuses for skilled workers rather than toward overall investment (Lampe, *Yugoslavia as History*, 256). In later years, scholars suggest, Yugoslavia reshaped self-management by introducing market principles that "denuded self-management of any radical edge," sometimes making it inefficient or corrupt (Martin, Daguerre, and Ozarow, "Spectrum, Trajectory, and the Role of the State in Workers' Self-Management," 63).

Youth Work Actions (*Omladinske radne akcije*): Youth Work Actions were Yugoslav federal programs created to rebuild infrastructure after World War II. The actions brought together able-bodied youth from across the state to reconstruct damaged infrastructure and build new roads, highways, railways, and housing. Although participants later romanticized these postwar actions as voluntary, scholars suggest that state agents pressured and sometimes coerced participants into labor. Yugoslavia revived Youth Work Actions in the 1970s as prestigious volunteer programs that were, by then, part of national mythology. Agents handpicked participants and emphasized socialist education. Scholar Anna Matthiesen writes that "being a part of the brigades offered a chance to meet and socialize with people from the country's various republics, and to embody the Yugoslav ideal of 'brotherhood and unity' through bonds of shared experience, collegiality, and friendship" (Matthiesen, "Shifting Resources, Shifting Forms," 257). Many former citizens look back on the actions as symbols of socialist solidarity and Yugoslav unity.

Yugoslav National Anthem: The Yugoslav national anthem was "Hey, Slavs" ("Hej, Slaveni"). The lyrics were written by Slovak poet Samo Tomášik (1813–1887) in 1834 as the anthem of the pan-Slavic movement and titled "Hey, Slovaks." The song has been at times adopted as the anthem of various states, including Poland, the First Slovak Republic, Yugoslavia, and Serbia and Montenegro. In Yugoslavia, the song was adopted as an unofficial anthem after World War II. It was formally adopted as the state's anthem in 1988.

Yugoslav National Army (JNA): Yugoslav National Army, also known as the Yugoslav People's Army, was the military of the Socialist Federal Republic of Yugoslavia. Between 1945 and 1991, all healthy men aged eighteen to twenty-seven served a mandatory military term of one to two years. Most recruits were placed in a Yugoslav republic other than their own. Everyone received basic military training and instruction in state history, socialist ideology, personal hygiene, and other topics. Depending on placement, some recruits also received specialized training. Recruits often performed state-building tasks, like rebuilding rail networks, constructing housing, and teaching. The recruits of the Yugoslav National Army were ethnically representative of the Yugoslav population, but Serbs disproportionally occupied leadership positions (Lampe, *Yugoslavia as History*, 345). Over the course of their service, men developed a high degree of comradery, which many look back on nostalgically. In her study of men who served in the Yugoslav National Army, scholar Tanja Petrović identifies three common themes in men's memories: male friendship, "school of life," and subversive strategies that made service easier (Petrović, "Nostalgia for the JNA?").

Yugoslav Passport: Many former citizens fondly remember the passport of the Socialist Federal Republic of Yugoslavia. The booklet itself was red, and the passport was colloquially referred to as a "red passport" (*crveni pasoš*). Many recall that the postwar Yugoslav passport allowed holders to travel almost anywhere without a visa. Anthropologist Stef Jansen explains that travel to US- and USSR-dominated zones became possible after Yugoslavia repositioned itself between the two Cold War blocs in the 1950s. By the 1960s, Yugoslavia had signed mutual agreements for visa-free entry for work and travel with most European and nonaligned states. Jansen estimates that about half of Yugoslav citizens had an issued passport and traveled "whether as tourists (especially amongst so-called urban 'middle layers'), as *gasterbajteri* (guest workers—especially from specific [semi]rural regions), or as shoppers (with Trieste as favourite destination)." Jansen contextualizes nostalgia for the Yugoslav passport: "After the end of Yugoslavia, the fondness with which the previous possibility to travel was recalled seemed largely unrelated to whether one had actually crossed borders with some frequency. Instead, now that visa regimes made travel very difficult even for those who could afford it, what counted was the retrospective knowledge that the Yugoslav passport had once certified one as worthy of easy border-crossings" (Jansen, "After the Red Passport," 823).

1

INTERVIEW WITH
Luka Lisjak Gabrijelčič

Luka Lisjak Gabrijelčič was born in Šempeter pri Gorici (now Slovenia) in 1980 and grew up in nearby Nova Gorica (now Slovenia). While he has studied and worked in other parts of Europe, today Lisjak Gabrijelčič is a historian, political analyst, and essayist based in Slovenia. When we spoke over a video call in early 2023, he was participating in a workshop in Bergen, Norway. In our conversation, Lisjak Gabrijelčič discussed memories of growing up on the border with Italy, a space that deeply mediated his experience of Yugoslavia. On the one hand, he was raised with the same socialist and multinational values as most of the youngest Yugoslav generation. On the other, he lived with the inescapable presence of the border with a Western state. As we talked, Lisjak Gabrijelčič explained how he conceived of his Slovene identity today and how he rediscovered his Yugoslav identity long after the collapse of the unified state.

In many ways, Lisjak Gabrijelčič had a typical Yugoslav childhood. His grandparents had been members of Yugoslavia's Partisan movement, his family lived in a planned socialist city, and he participated in the Pioneer organization as a child. In school, Lisjak Gabrijelčič learned about the pillars of Yugoslav society. He understood that the state was vast and diverse. Thinking back on his classmates in grade school, he recalled that "a quarter or a third of the class was from other republics. We had many Serbs, Bosnians, both Bosnian Muslims and Serbs, also one Croat, and then one Macedonian." Lisjak Gabrijelčič underlined that in Slovenia, Yugoslavia's most homogenous republic, ethnicity was a visible marker of difference, in addition to wealth and religion, but that social particularities were a mere fact of life. Lisjak Gabrijelčič also recalled being an earnest Yugoslav patriot during his young years. When he sensed tensions in the late 1980s, he immediately started thinking about how they might be overcome. "It was clear that this country was in deep shit and that something was happening," he told me. "When I was around eight, I said, 'What if Yugoslavia was attacked by Albania, wouldn't that be nice?' [I thought that] if we were attacked by Albania, there would be a sense of patriotic unity, and we would forget all the differences. [I reasoned that] Albania is such a small country, and we would easily defeat it." As for most members of the youngest Yugoslav generation, Yugoslavia—and its permanence—was an unquestionable part of Lisjak Gabrijelčič's childhood worldview.

Yet his childhood worldview was also shaped by the visibility of the border and the military guarding it. Soldiers from the Yugoslav National Army were stationed all along the border, including in Nova Gorica. "We had a lot of soldier stations because [we lived in] a border town," he remembered. "Apart from large barracks, we also had many of these small barracks, which were like border guards." He told me the military was "very present in life." Soldiers visited his school to talk about their work, and students toured guards' barracks with school groups. For Lisjak Gabrijelčič, these visits were "something that was exciting and positive because that was another world that was always among us . . . a moment in which you can kind of peek into a separate reality." He recalled that Yugoslavia's World War II mythology was integrated into public spaces, from the names of buildings to displays of weapons at his school, and recognized that his childhood had been saturated with "very militaristic imagery." He pointed out that he saw similar imagery when he visited family on Italy's side of the border, which meant that the military loomed over his everyday life at every step.

Growing up on the border also impacted Lisjak Gabrijelčič's experience of Yugoslavia because he was able to regularly cross it to visit family members who lived in another country. By the 1960s, the Yugoslav border was relatively open; citizens could travel to most European and nonaligned states without visas. Those who lived close to borders often held supplementary passes that allowed more frequent entry or extended stays abroad. "We would cross the border constantly to visit the sisters of my granddad or my cousins on the other side," Lisjak Gabrijelčič told me. "I have vivid memories of moving from one space to another and moving between different languages." Considering his childhood, Lisjak Gabrijelčič identified frequent border crossings as defining of his Yugoslav experience. He not only engaged with spatial, cultural, and linguistic diversity within Yugoslavia but also had a first-person view into the West and its "very different economic and political systems." The border—or, more accurately, its permeability—lent Lisjak Gabrijelčič access to a world beyond Yugoslavia.

Lisjak Gabrijelčič ultimately described himself as "a person of the border" and explained that this childhood positionality was formative in defining the layers of his identity. First, he identified as Slovene. "I very unproblematically identify as a Slovenian," he said. "I have come to develop a very strong regional and local identity because I realized that living in that place gave me a very specific perspective on the world"—a perspective of belonging to both Eastern and Western societies as well as local and global spaces. Second, Lisjak Gabrijelčič espoused a generational identity anchored by his time in Yugoslavia and in Slovenia. "Being a Slovenian of my generation means being the last generation to still experience Yugoslavia," he explained. "That's absolutely still very important to me. I cannot imagine myself not having that part of my identity or memory. I'm very much conscious of how this impacted my self-awareness and my way of thinking about the world." Last, Lisjak Gabrijelčič thought of himself as post-Yugoslav, a relatively flexible identity he conceived of as an access point to a diverse community of people with a shared historical legacy. He only began to think of himself as a post-Yugoslav later in life, after he had left the region. "When I was abroad, one of the things I understood was how deeply I was impacted by Yugoslav pop culture," he narrated. "This is one of the things that my generation experienced. First, there was that experience itself, and then you had another one when meeting people from the post-Yugoslav republics abroad and realizing how much you had in common. I rediscovered a part of my Yugoslav identity through common pop culture references because all the post-Yugoslav kids would know *Ko to tamo peva* or [Goran] Bregović or Bijelo Dugme." Long after Yugoslavia ceased to exist, it continued to carry meaning for many former residents. For Lisjak Gabrijelčič, post-Yugoslav identity signified belonging to a cultural legacy unbound by time and space. This afterlife is rather fitting for a state that encompassed multiplicity and enabled—even encouraged—its citizens to cross borders.

INTERVIEWER: What are your earliest memories of your hometown—the neighborhood, your home, or school?

LISJAK GABRIJELČIČ: I have a lot of early memories. To summarize it, I would say it is memories of moving in between different spaces. I grew up in a very typical late 1970s and early 1980s apartment block, with the particularity that you could see Italy from the window of my room. My hometown was built in the postwar period, and it was really a socialist project intended to be a window toward the West to project the idea of an ideal socialist town.[1] I think that aspect impacted my childhood because the border [between Yugoslavia and Italy] was open. It was even more open for us who lived on the border because we had this special permit, or *propusnica*, with which we would cross twice or three times a week.[2] We would cross the border constantly to visit the sisters of my granddad or my cousins on the other side. Our family members were part of the Slovenian minority in Italy, [and they had] different ways of conceiving of identity. They wore different clothes. The buildings looked totally different. I have vivid memories of moving from one space to another and moving between different languages.

But it was not just about moving between socialism to capitalism across the border. It was also about moving within Yugoslavia, even within our small region. Of course, some of our family members lived in the countryside. I was in love with the smell of the countryside, when you went to the village and you smelled cows, for example. Some of my early memories are the ones that I really have, and some are the ones which are perpetuated by my parents telling me [stories] over and over again. This is one of those [latter ones]. I remember it, but I've also been told so often that wherever we went to the village to visit family members, I was always like, "Oh, we have to stop, we have to check out the farm animals." I also remember the differences in speech and dialect. I still

---

1. Lisjak Gabrijelčič grew up in Nova Gorica, a planned town established in 1947 after the Paris Peace Treaty defined the border between Yugoslavia and Italy. The treaty transferred much of the Slovene-inhabited province of Gorizia, previously held by Italy, to Yugoslavia. The town of Gorizia itself, however, remained on the Italian side. The Yugoslav state commissioned the Slovene architect Edvard Ravnikar (1907–1993), a student of modernist architect and urban planner Le Corbusier (1887–1965), to design an urban center to unify the newly annexed region on the Yugoslav side of border. Much of Nova Gorica was built in the 1950s and 1960s. See Jerman, "Border Town of Nova Gorica and Its Role in Forming a New Urban Center," 103–18.

2. During the socialist period, particularly from the mid-1960s onward, Yugoslavs commonly traveled abroad for leisure, recreation, and shopping. They visited nearby countries like Italy, Austria, Greece, Turkey, and Hungary but also traveled further afield. While it was common for Yugoslavs to cross the border up to twice per year just for shopping, scholar Maja Mikula explains that those who resided close to the border sometimes crossed much more frequently. These Yugoslavs held border passes called *propusnica* or *iskaznica* that allowed them privileges other citizens did not have (Mikula, "Highways of Desire," 222). Border passes were country specific, for instance entitling those who lived on the Italian border special privileges when visiting Italy. The passes mandated a set number of border crossings for a set number of days but allowed the bearer to petition for extensions in cases of marriage, birth, death, or other family circumstances. The passes designated an area radius in the other country to which the bearer was confined.

have aunts of my father who spoke in a thick, rural dialect, which was very different from the way I spoke. We somehow had families all along the region.[3]

We went every weekend to a different village, and everything was a little bit different on the coast, in the Alps, or across the border. Even though it was a small child's worldview, it had a lot of diversity. And when I think back, I think that this had a very important impact on my identity and development: realizing from very early on, and internalizing from very early on, and reflecting from very early on that there were different *lebenswelt*, or different worlds, where you move in and out of. [There were] different conventions of behaving and [there were different standards of] what was acceptable.

INTERVIEWER: Do you remember often traveling to visit family or traveling otherwise?

LISJAK GABRIJELČIČ: Both, actually. My great-grandfather was from a village on the Slovenian coast which is not so far away, but to get there, the roads were bad. We always crossed through Italy, and we still do that now. We spent most of our summers and a lot of time [otherwise] there in northern Istria.[4] Of course, during the summer, we would always go to the seaside in Croatia, to the Croatian islands.

---

3. The Slovene minority in Italy was primarily located in the provinces of Friuli (Venezia Giulia), Trieste (Trst), Gorizia (Gorica), and Udine (Videm). Because many Slovenes had supported antifascist groups and the Yugoslav Partisan movement during World War II, the Slovene minority in Italy faced discrimination, marginalization, and othering during the postwar period (McConnell, "International Disputes in the Italian-Yugoslavian Borderlands," 117–34). A series of international treaties (the Paris Peace Treaty in 1947, the London Memorandum in 1954, and the Osimo Agreement between Yugoslavia and Italy in 1975) defined the protection of minority rights, including the right to use Slovene in public and the right to a Slovene-language education. According to scholars Lucija Čok and Susanna Pertot, the Slovene spoken among the minority in Italy had many dialectical variants. "The colloquial variant," they write, "which could be defined as a 'local' variant despite not being a dialect, differs in some measure from the colloquial variety used in Slovenia and the proper Slovene standard" (Čok and Pertot, "Bilingual Education in the Ethnically Mixed Areas along the Slovene-Italian Border," 67).

4. Istria is a peninsula in the Adriatic Sea shared between Slovenia, Croatia, and Italy. Istria was part of the larger border zone between Italy and Yugoslavia called Julian March (Julijska Krajina in Slovene and Venezia Giulia in Italian). After World War II, almost all of Istria was ceded from Italy to Yugoslavia. While Italian fascists had targeted Slavs in the region in the 1920s and 1930s, the Partisans attacked Italians in a wave of violence known as the Foibe massacres during and after World War II. These attacks spurred an Italian migration out of Yugoslav territory referred to as the Istrian exodus. About 350,000 Italians were displaced from Yugoslavia in the postwar years due to fear of persecution, resistance to nationalization, rejection of communism, and desire to practice Catholicism. Many were repatriated to Italy, but others settled further afield. Italians who left Istria often romanticized the region as "pure" Italian land, while those who remained saw it as a "hybrid" space (Ballinger, *History in Exile*, 11).

And one of my early memories was when I was six and visited Bosnia. We went for holiday to the Dalmatian island Korčula [now Croatia], and on the way back, we went through Počitelj [now Bosnia], Mostar [now Bosnia], Jajce [now Bosnia], Bihać [now Bosnia], and then back to Slovenia. I remember this first really long trip vividly, and I still have memories of crossing the old Mostar Bridge. That trip was very exotic for me. When you're a kid, you sort of absorb all these stereotypes of what the adults say, and in Slovenian discourse at the time, around 1986, "Bosnia" was a general term for migrants from Yugoslavia.[5] Bosnia had been almost like a nonspace for me. For a kid, it was difficult to imagine that it was not just a general word for the space out there but that it was a space where people lived. I think it must have affected me very strongly because some of the most vivid memories I have as a child from any trip are those from that trip to Bosnia.

INTERVIEWER: Do you remember attending school in Yugoslavia?

LISJAK GABRIJELČIČ: I remember a lot. I think I remember all of the important things from my school years. I remember most of my schoolmates. I remember what the first, second, and third grade [classrooms] looked like. When I was in third grade in 1990, we went to *šola v naravi* [school in nature], [a program in which students spent] one week or ten days at the beginning of the school year observing marine life and nature with their schools. I remember we went to the Croatian [part of] Istria that year. I think we were literally the last generation that went to another republic of Yugoslavia.

I think I was, if not the last, then one of the two last generations of the *pioniri* [Pioneers]. I went through that in 1987. I remember quite clearly that the next year, 1988 or maybe 1989, was the last year in which we celebrated the anniversary of Tito's death. On May 4, at the hour of Tito's death, there was an alarm, and everybody had to stand still for one minute. I remember very clearly the last time we did that because we had a teacher who was very much

---

5. Within Yugoslavia, Slovenia was the wealthiest republic; it had the most industrial development, the highest standard of living, and the lowest unemployment rate. Moreover, after the settlement of border disputes with the London Memorandum in 1954, international trade with Italy and other Western states boomed. During the 1960s and 1970s, internal migration from poorer Yugoslav republics to Slovenia increased, and migrants settled in cities like Ljubljana or towns with mines or iron factories. These migrants were noticeable among Slovenia's homogenous population. According to the Yugoslav census, Slovenes constituted 95.6 percent of the Slovene population in 1961, 95 percent in 1971, 90.8 percent in 1981, and 88.3 percent in 1991. As Lisjak Gabrijelčič mentioned at a different point in the interview, internal migration during the socialist period and later during the Yugoslav wars led to the rise of nationalism and xenophobia in Slovenia that targeted people from other parts of the former state.

a believer in the official narrative, and she insisted that we do it very, very strictly. Many of us kids started laughing, and she was very upset. Looking back, the world was crumbling in front of her eyes.

INTERVIEWER: You mentioned that you were inaugurated as a Pioneer. Was that important to you?

LISJAK GABRIJELČIČ: I think it was. From the very beginning it was a very big deal. All of us had to wear a specific outfit. We didn't have official uniforms, but we were told to dress in the same way. If I remember correctly, it was a white shirt, blue trousers, and a red scarf. I'm not sure about all the colors, but I'm pretty sure about the blue trousers or skirts and the white shirt. Each [student] would buy [the clothes] by themselves, but I remember one kid who mixed it up and got a blue shirt instead of a white one.

There were preparations toward [the inauguration]. We had to learn things like the Pioneer pledge. I think this might have been before we could really read or after we had just learned to read, so we had to rememorize it. All the parents came to the big ceremony, and it was meant to feel that it was a big deal. But I do remember that somebody else's parents in that ceremony said, "You know, this is pointless. We're going to get rid of this soon." Maybe these were not the exact words but something like that. Somebody voiced skepticism about the ceremony. It was not my parents. I think that they thought the same way, but they didn't voice it.

We also had [older] kids coming to explain [Pioneer principles to us]. I remember that we went through what the name of the country, Socialist Federal Republic of Yugoslavia, meant. Everyone understood "Yugoslavia," but they explained the three other adjectives to us. I remember very clearly that the way [the older kids] described "socialism" and the way they described "republic" didn't make any sense to me. They used the same description for both, and they said it was about equality. So [I wondered], "Okay, then why do we need two words that mean the same thing?" [Laughs] Then we learned that Yugoslavia was composed of six republics and two autonomous regions. I remember that we had a map, and we had to color each in its own color. We even had a discussion [about] which republic should be which color. I still remember what we chose.

INTERVIEWER: I'm so curious—which colors did you choose for which republics?

LISJAK GABRIJELČIČ: Croatia was blue because it had a sea, and all the kids went to the sea in Croatia. Slovenia was green because it had a lot of forests.

[We decided that] Macedonia should be purple because we had a student from Macedonia, and she always wore purple sweaters. Bosnia, I think, was brown because we were always told that there were lot of coal mines there. And the other [republics were] the colors that remained. Montenegro was red. I vividly remember that Serbia was yellow, and I don't remember the rationale. I think the reason was that we just didn't have any other colors left. [Laughs]

INTERVIEWER: Do any other Yugoslav or state-sponsored youth activities come to mind? Did you participate in a choir or go on any organized trips?

LISJAK GABRIJELČIČ: Not really. For one year or two years, I was part of a scout group, *taborniki*, but I never got anywhere, though. I remained at that stage where we just basically learned the theory or how to make a knot, but we never went on any real trips. I mean, I remember many school activities, like trips, but I don't really recall activities based on any youth organizations.

I do remember very well that there was a day of the army; I don't know when it was, sometime in September or November.[6] It was the anniversary of something. I don't know, but I do remember that every year we would collect stuff for the soldier stations. We had a lot of soldier stations because [we lived in] a border town. Apart from large barracks, we also had many of these small barracks, which were like border guards. We would always collect stuff like cigarettes and chewing gum, and then we would send delegations to them.

A soldier also came to [visit] our school once to tell us what his life was like. I don't remember anything he said, but I remember the uniform. Once we also went to visit one of those border barracks just near the border [when they had] opened the doors to the kids from the school. They would give us *pasulj* [cooked beans] and show us around. Of course, all of the boys, me included, were checking out the arms they showed us. This I remember quite vividly.

INTERVIEWER: And was that coded as something exciting or positive for you?

LISJAK GABRIJELČIČ: It was for me. I remember it as something that was exciting and positive because that was another world that was always among

---

6. Lisjak Gabrijelčič is referring to the Day of the Yugoslav National Army (*Dan Jugoslovenske narodne armije* or *Dan armije*), the anniversary of the founding of the Yugoslav National Army. The anniversary was celebrated on December 22, the day the predecessor of the Yugoslav National Army, the People's Liberation Army of Yugoslavia, was founded in 1941. Yugoslav National Army units and organizations marked the day with award ceremonies that recognized their important contributions to the defense of Yugoslavia.

us. [Visits to the barracks were] a moment in which you can kind of peek into a separate reality.

I have this memory of the military being very present in life, but it was a separate reality. Even our school was named after a military unit, *deveti korpus* [IX Corps]; then it changed its name in 1991. In the school, which was built in the late 1970s, we had a huge display window with weapons from World War II. This is something that is difficult now to imagine. It was very militaristic imagery. I think for me, it was sort of cool. Even back then, I think I was a little bit interested in military history. Now looking back, I think it was really militaristic, and I think some people don't even want to remember or don't realize how militaristic certain imagery in that period was.

On the other side of the border, it was the same. Even now, if you go to Gorizia [in Italy], there are lots of military monuments, and some of them are really gruesome. Near one of my favorite ice cream shops in Gorizia, right near a small square, there is [a statue] of a hero—maybe from the Italian Wars of Independence, maybe World War I, I really don't know. But it's very vivid. It shows a soldier without a foot throwing a crutch.[7] But back then, I was so impacted by this. I saw that you had military presence on both sides, and this is something that I do remember as a kid.

I didn't realize this then, but I learned later that [the late 1980s was] precisely when there was a huge counter-push in civil society in Slovenia against the military [the Yugoslav National Army].[8] The political mobilization against the military presence was something that brought together different oppositional groups and currents within the ruling party.

---

7. Lisjak Gabrijelčič is referencing the statue of Italian soldier Enrico Toti (1882–1916) made by sculptor Mario Montemurro and installed at the Piazza Cesare Battisti in 1958. Toti was rejected as a volunteer for the Italian army at the onset of World War I because his left leg had been amputated after he had an accident while working as a stoker for the railway. Toti was an avid bicyclist, and when he was rejected from service, he rode to the frontlines and served as an unregistered volunteer. While serving with the Third Bersaglieri Bicycle Battalion, Toti was fatally wounded in 1916 at the Sixth Battle of the Isonzo. He posthumously received Italy's Gold Medal of Military Valor. Subsequent governments used Toti to symbolize Italy's territorial losses, its "mutilated victory," in World War I. See Griffiths, "Enrico Toti," 341–54.

8. Slovene opposition groups vocally criticized the Yugoslav National Army in the media. They called for domestic reforms, such as an alternative to military service, and reforms to foreign relations, such as cuts to the export of arms to the Third World. As Lisjak Gabrijelčič suggested, these voices unified the Slovene public opinion against the Yugoslav National Army as well as Yugoslavia itself. See Lampe, *Yugoslavia as History*, 349–52, and Velikonja, "Slovenia's Yugoslav Century," 95–97.

INTERVIEWER: You mentioned that you had a classmate who was Macedonian. Was there a lot of diversity in your school group? Do you remember other classmates who were from elsewhere?

LISJAK GABRIJELČIČ: Yes. In terms of diversity, in terms of people from other parts of Yugoslavia, for sure. I think that a quarter or a third of the class was from other republics. We had many Serbs, Bosnians, both Bosnian Muslims and Serbs, also one Croat, and then one Macedonian. The vast majority were Serbs and Bosnians in my class.

INTERVIEWER: Were you aware of that difference among your classmates?

LISJAK GABRIJELČIČ: There was already a lot of racism in that period. If you went to school, there was a lot of, "He's Bosnian," which meant that [the student was] from one of the other republics of Yugoslavia. There was this kind of racist element that was present from day one [in school] onward. There was a tendency to think that everybody whose surname ended in "-ič" was not Slovenian, which is not true.[9] Many Slovenian surnames end in the same way. One of my two surnames ends in "-ič," and I was sometimes accused of being Bosnian. [In situations like this], you then had to prove your own pedigree. In the schools, the teachers were strongly against this, and it was not sanctioned if you were caught being racist to [other] students. But when we played outside, there was a lot of this racism going on.

INTERVIEWER: How did kids treat each other differently based on how they perceived others?

LISJAK GABRIJELČIČ: I'm not too pessimistic about human nature, but there is something about this that's like the *Lord of the Flies*. Especially among boys, I remember from my kindergarten years, there was this tendency for the whole class to split into two factions. [It was] not at all along ethnic lines then but just personalities. It was necessary that you belong to one of these factions, and we immediately had this sort of civil war. There were only two of us who refused to join one of the factions. I never particularly liked it. When we went from kindergarten to elementary school, the factions [became] partially

---

9. Last names that end in "-ič" are indeed common in Slovenia. They are derived from the patronymic practice of assigning a parent's first name as a child's last name. For instance, the last name Markič suggests "son of Marko." Other Slovene last names are derived from professions, trades, characteristics, or regions of origin, and have a variety of different endings. The "-ič" ending is also common among Croatian names, and "-ić" appears among Serbian and Croatian ones. In Bosnia, the most diverse of the former Yugoslav republics, a wide range of last names was used.

split by ethnic lines. [Students would say], "Okay, we don't want to have Bosnians among us." In the end, every group was heterogeneous, but there was a lot of evocation of ethnic differences.

Kids are very good at spotting vulnerabilities. If they want to be cruel, they can mobilize whatever they hear from parents or whatever might hurt you. This ethnic difference thing, as I remember it, was used against others quite often. At least in my school, if you were from the former Yugoslavia, it was very unlikely that you wouldn't have heard a racial slur directed at you or your ancestry. Kids who came from other parts of Slovenia who had funny ways of doing things, had a rural accent, or didn't dress as nicely were also subject to the same sort of bullying. But if you were not from our republic, it was almost certain that you would experience it one day or another. That I remember very clearly.

INTERVIEWER: Do you remember any other kinds of difference or anything that would have made someone stand out as different, other than where they were from?

LISJAK GABRIJELČIČ: Before 1990, I would say that differences in status and wealth were interlocked or almost always related to differences of geographical origin. If someone was poorer, in that context it usually meant they were either from another republic of Yugoslavia or from eastern Slovenia. [There were also differences in] rural versus urban [origin] as well. There were other status things that started to come out. For example, [there were] the kids who could afford to have a bottle of Coca-Cola on their table for their birthday and [there were] those who couldn't. I was quite aware of that. Of course, in my family we discouraged [judging others based on class], so, whenever these things came up, we would actively say, "No, you should not say this."

I also remember clearly that there was a difference between those kids who went to church and those who didn't. In our class, in our school, the majority of kids were not religious, did not go to church, and did not go to religion classes after school. But other differences I think were differences of personality and character, which remained individual.

INTERVIEWER: Did religion play any role in your childhood in Yugoslavia?

LISJAK GABRIJELČIČ: One of my grandmothers was religious, so my father was baptized, took communion, and received religious schooling. Although he is not particularly religious, he is officially Catholic. My mother is not [religious]. Religion didn't play any particular role in my childhood, but I was taught to respect the church and other people's beliefs. I had a religious education in the sense that my father read me stories from the Bible alongside ancient myths and Greek myths, as they were part of the cultural [canon].

INTERVIEWER: Can you tell me a little bit more about who you grew up with?

LISJAK GABRIJELČIČ: I'm an only child. I think in my generation there were more only children than there were before, and there was a difference between those who had brothers and sisters, those who didn't, and those who had many.[10]

Both of my parents were basically the first generation born in [Nova Gorica] after it was built in 1947 following a peace treaty with Italy. My father was an electrical engineer; he worked in the state electrical company. He designed power plants. We were the center for the hydropower plant from the river Soča, which was being electrified in the 1980s. My mother worked as a sales manager in a big state shop where they sold clothes. I had the chance to meet all four of my grandparents. They were from very Partisan families. Both of my grandfathers were Partisans. One of my grandmothers came from an antifascist family, too. The other grandmother came from a relatively bourgeois and religious family, which was less politicized. The others were not particularly religious; they were agnostic or atheist. They were all from the western region of Slovenia, which was part of Italy before World War II.

INTERVIEWER: Were you aware of any mixedness in your family background?

LISJAK GABRIJELČIČ: Looking back now, we were a very homogenous family. I mean, the only difference we had was that after World War II, a lot of the family remained or moved to the Italian side of the border while the others were in Slovenia. I think that half of my grandfather's siblings and most of my other grandmother's cousins were on the Italian side of the border. This was the main difference that impacted how my family developed.

If I think in terms of class—not [of] my parents because they were kids of socialism, and it was a classless society—there were differences in education and status. My grandparents came from relatively well-to-do families from before World War I, which got proletarized in the interwar period. Their kids radicalized into communism or very radical streams of antifascism. I think

---

10. The fertility rate in Slovenia steadily decreased from the 1960s. In 1981, the year after Lisjak Gabrijelčič was born, 37 percent of families had only one child. That year, the fertility rate in Slovenia dropped below the replacement rate (2.10). Yugoslavia's fertility rate was 2.09 in 1981; it steadily decreased in the 1980s.

it is a typical story. I think I come from a very typical family from my region. Nothing particularly stands out.

INTERVIEWER: What kind of discourse was there around Yugoslavia at home? Did your family members talk about it?

LISJAK GABRIJELČIČ: For a very long time, I thought of politics as something that was not for kids, almost like sex. [Laughs] So I was always trying to listen in to what the adults were saying, but I didn't fully understand it. I don't have any political memories before 1989 or 1990. For example, [I know that] in the summer of 1988, four journalists were arrested in Ljubljana and that there were huge protests and mobilizations.[11] [I also know that] my father took part in them. But I have zero recollection of those events. Afterward, I remember [Slobodan] Milošević and Slovenian political leaders on television.

One of my granddads did not talk about his Partisan war years at all. I knew that he was a former officer in the Yugoslav navy, and my father always told me, "Remember, your grandparents were Partisans. This is something to be proud of." But my father says that he never heard anything more [about this experience] from him either when he was a kid. I heard some stories from him [my grandfather] much later, when I was around fifteen, when I went with him to celebrate the anniversary of fifty years after the end of World War II. We went to a big celebration in Ljubljana, and I went with the bus full of former Partisan veterans. That's when I heard a story of his near-death experience for the first time. I think that story was the only story I ever heard, though. When he died, we discovered some of his writings and an autobiography, so we reconstructed his war years from there.

My other granddad died when I was five. I remember many things about him but nothing about his war years. I know that he was drafted by the Italian

---

11. Under the leadership of Milan Kučan, Slovenia expanded its freedom of the press. However, when the magazine *Mladina* published critical articles based on meeting notes from the central committee of the League of Communists of Yugoslavia that detailed plans to arrest dissidents in Slovenia, the federal government retaliated by arresting four journalists. The state claimed that the journalists had betrayed military secrets and tried them in a military trial known as the JBTZ trial (the name came from the initials of the defendants: Janez Janša, Ivan Borštner, David Tasić, and Franci Zavrl). Slovene public opinion supported the journalists; Slovenes demonstrated in mass against the trial, which was held in chambers and in Serbo-Croatian. All four journalists were sentenced to imprisonment, with sentences ranging from six months to four years. The trial unified Slovene political opposition and the argument for independence from Yugoslavia.

army and that he fought in northern Africa.¹² Later, we discovered some war memorabilia in the house that I knew was from the war period. He had this canister for water, and we still have it.

Both of my grandmothers experienced war in Italy. One of my grandmothers spent most of her childhood and teenage years in Brescia, a town in Lombardy, because her father was employed in the state railways in Italy. She would tell us stories from the wartime in Lombardy, in Brescia. My [other] grandmother was in southern Italy during the war. Her father was arrested during the fascist years, and he was sent to southern Italy to be kept in confinement. She and her mother [followed] him. She was always telling us about how she lived through those war years in Italy and how she crossed from southern Italy to Dalmatia. [She also told us] her stories from Dalmatia during the last months of the war. The family stayed in contact with the family that hosted them in the war period in southern Italy. In 1991, we went to visit them. That was a very, very emotional experience.

INTERVIEWER: Tell me a little bit about the way your parents related to Yugoslavia.

LISJAK GABRIJELČIČ: When I was eleven or twelve, I started to understand that the generation of my grandparents was very much pro-Yugoslav, pro-Communism, and pro-Tito.¹³ My parents were not. Neither of them was a member of the Communist Party, which was already a statement. My grandfather wanted my mother to become a member, but she refused. She voted for the opposition party in 1990. That was something that started coming up in family conversations, and I remember there were some tensions and fights. I remember especially one argument very clearly because it went very, very badly. My parents were defending the independence of Slovenia and

---

12. Once Italy declared war in June 1940, it set its sights on capturing British and French colonies in Africa. The Italian army, however, met many setbacks due to poor preparation, lack of equipment, and the difficult desert terrain. The Italian army collapsed by early 1941, at which point it contributed troops to the Nazi Afrika Korps. The Allies defeated the Axis in northern Tunisia in May 1943, prompting the Allies to launch the Italian campaign that led to the collapse of Mussolini's fascist regime several months later.

13. The grandparents of Lisjak Gabrijelčič, like those of many members of the youngest Yugoslav generation, were born before World War II. Anthropologist Monika Palmberger terms members of this generation the "first Yugoslavs." She suggests that their experience was defined by World War II, the struggle against fascism, and participation in the Partisan movement. Members of this generation were generally committed to the idea of Yugoslavia because they came of age in the postwar years of physical, social, and economic security (Palmberger, *How Generations Remember*, 127–59).

[saying that we needed to] move beyond socialism and reestablish democracy. Their uncles, who were more conservative, sort of socialist conservative, responded, "No, this is stupidity; this will bring disaster." The arguments my parents had with their parents were less confrontational, but it was very clear there was a generational difference there.

When Yugoslavia was falling apart, some members of the family that lived in Italy, in Trieste, had a very different perspective of what was happening. They were more pro-Yugoslav because they didn't live in Yugoslavia. [Laughs]

INTERVIEWER: Was there a fissure between the family members who lived in Yugoslavia and the ones who lived in Italy?

LISJAK GABRIJELČIČ: I think the people who lived in Italy moved after World War II for economic opportunities, not ideological reasons. They were not necessarily nostalgic for Yugoslavia. One of the sisters of my grandfather who lived in Italy decided not to school her children in Slovenian schools. These cousins still spoke Slovenian—but not standard Slovenian—but their children did not. In 1991 and 1992, when the border opened and there was additional value for shopkeepers to speak Serbo-Croatian or Slovenian, my grandmother didn't miss a chance to comment on that. Especially when my second cousins had to take Slovenian [language] courses, my grandmother would never miss a chance to ask, "So how come she had to take a Slovenian course? Oh, that's so interesting. Oh, what a pity she didn't learn it in the family." There were many fissures like this.

INTERVIEWER: When was the first time you were aware of political tension in Yugoslavia?

LISJAK GABRIJELČIČ: I remember the Rally of Truth in December of 1989 and the "Yogurt Revolution" in Vojvodina.[14] One of those rallies of

---

14. The Rally of Truth (sometimes known as the Meeting of the Truth or the Anti-Bureaucratic Revolution) was a series of protests organized by supporters of Slobodan Milošević in 1988 and 1989 aimed at overthrowing governments in Yugoslav republics and autonomous provinces and installing allies of Milošević in their place. The protests, motivated by nationalist discourse in Serbia that opposed political liberalization and decentralization, overthrew governments in Montenegro, Kosovo, and Vojvodina. In Vojvodina, the two-day rally that forced leadership to resign became known as the "Yogurt Revolution" because protestors threw packages of yogurt at the provincial committee building in Novi Sad (now Serbia). After local politicians were ousted, Milošević purged leaders who supported Vojvodina's autonomy and installed his allies. Scholar Marko Grdešić suggests that "this event was one of the largest and more dramatic protests of the entire antibureaucratic revolution," due

pro-Milošević groups was supposed to take place in Ljubljana in December 1989. I remember that the climate was ominous; this is one of my first memories. It did not happen because it was prevented by the Slovenian police. They blocked the borders, and the participants could not cross. But I remember very clearly that climate of extreme anxiety in society.

After that, I remember everything. There was the Slovenian democratic election in April 1990. I remember very clearly the names of the candidates and some of the speeches. At that point, some kids would say, "In our family, we will vote for this candidate," or, "We will vote for that candidate."

INTERVIEWER: Do you remember the war in Slovenia starting?

LISJAK GABRIJELČIČ: Oh yes. Very, very clearly. My mother's birthday is June 30 [five days after Slovenia declared its independence], and she was preparing a picnic. My grandmother was cautiously saying, "Do you think we should invite our family from Italy?" My mother said, "But why?" My grandmother said, "Well, because something might happen." My parents responded, "Oh, what could happen? Nothing will happen." And then, of course, the war broke out.

I remember the air raids. It was like a grotesque movie or somewhat of a parody. Did you watch this Croatian movie *How the War Started on My Island*?[15] It was sort like that, sort of like a comedy. It really had many comedic instances. During the air raids, we would go to the cellar or to the raid shelters. In my grandmother's house, we went to the cellar because there was no proper refuge. I remember my grandmother had a fixed protocol of what she had to do when the alarm [sounded]: switch off the gas, open all the windows or maybe close the windows, and take this, this, and this. And I remember she would say, "Run to the cellar, and I will get everything ready." But before she got everything ready, the alarm was over. [Laughs] It was very funny.

---

in part to the actions of political elites and in part to the popular mobilization of ordinary citizens (Grdešić, "Looking Back at Milošević's Antibureaucratic Revolution," 615). Additional protests were planned but were not successful. In Slovenia, for instance, authorities banned the protests, and Milošević retaliated with an economic blockade of Slovene goods to Serbia. In turn, Slovene representatives walked out of the last meeting of the Congress of the League of Communists of Yugoslavia in January of 1990. See Grdešić, "Thirty Years of Yugoslavia's 'Antibureaucratic Revolution,'" and Vladisavljević, *Serbia's Anti-bureaucratic Revolution*.

15. *Kako je počeo rat na mom otoku* (*How the War Started on My Island*) is a Croatian black comedy film directed by Vinko Brešan (1964–) and released in 1996. The film is set on an unnamed Croatian island in 1991; it tells the story of residents' interactions with Yugoslav National Army soldiers stationed at nearby garrisons after Croatia declared independence from Yugoslavia.

Then, from the same day, I remember another, almost apocalyptic scene. Later that day, my grandma said, "For the next air raid, you have to cross the street and go to your school." My school had a big, proper antiraid shelter. On that day, there were three air raids. I did precisely [what she told me], and I ran across the meadow to the school. Everybody was also going to that shelter from all the houses and the apartment blocks in the vicinity, and it was a very strong image of all the people gathering in the meadow. But when we were in the shelter, it was again a comedy. There was a very fat lady sitting right in front of me, and the benches that were made for kids broke under her weight.

It didn't feel like a real war, although there was a lot of anxiety around. Nothing really happened, but there was also a lot of anxiety about the "what if." I remember that I heard the term "fifth column" for the first time. Somebody said, "You know, what I'm really afraid of is the fifth column." I said, "What is the fifth column?" I thought it was a large or fierce army unit. I have memories of the TV program being interrupted because of the first air raid and the anchor telling us to go to air shelters. I remember the images of the generals on television. I never really felt [that I was] in danger, but seeing these generals on television felt threatening.

Everybody knew that independence was something serious as a political project, but it was only when the war started that people realized this was a serious thing. People really became mobilized, radicalized—even those who were like, "Okay, we are for independence, but we know we have to figure things out." When the war started, everybody was so anti-army and anti-Yugoslav immediately. I could feel that strong, patriotic, fervent feeling when the war started. I didn't feel it before.

INTERVIEWER: What do you remember changes in your everyday life after Slovenia declared independence?

LISJAK GABRIJELČIČ: School adapted the slowest. I remember that we had Yugoslav schoolbooks for years to come, and some teachers were still teaching the old way. We had to remind them that there was no more Yugoslavia. I'm so glad that we still had one year of Serbo-Croatian language even when Slovenia was independent.[16] Our teacher fiercely defended the necessity of keeping it. Most kids were saying it was not important anymore, but she was pushing back even though she of course knew that it was coming to an end.

---

16. For children in the Republic of Slovenia, instruction in Slovene and Serbo-Croatian was compulsory. After independence, Slovenia continued to offer instruction in Italian and Hungarian as recognized minority languages, but it did not implement instruction in any of the languages once encompassed by Serbo-Croatian (Bosnian, Croatian, Montenegrin, or Serbian). See Stebej, "Size Isn't Everything," 13–30.

Okay, I didn't learn much, but I did learn Cyrillic in the second half of the course, and I can still read Cyrillic because of that. The first new textbook I clearly remember was from history in eighth grade.

I remember that the currency changed—twice. This was a big thing. First, we had the currency without a name. It was just numbers.[17] Then, I remember the introduction of the new Slovenian currency, the tolar. The way it looked was exciting. It was a stable currency.[18]

Generally, I think that the feeling was that there was no radical change. I feel the way the war ended was sort of anticlimactic. It just slowly waned. I didn't think of it as a big break in anything.

INTERVIEWER: Do you remember if the shift in the boundaries of the actual state where you lived changed anything for you? How did your ability to cross borders change?

LISJAK GABRIJELČIČ: Yeah, that's absolutely one of the big changes. Before the war, we always went to Croatia, very often to Dalmatia. In the early 1990s, we went to Istria. All the towns there like Rovinj [now Croatia], Novigrad [now Croatia], and Umag [now Croatia] that were usually filled with tourists were so empty in the early 1990s. There was such a spectral feeling there. I remember that very vividly. We stopped going to Croatia because it was so eerie, and there was this coat of arms being put suddenly everywhere where Tito was before. I remember very clearly that images of Tito [had been] everywhere—from shops to every office—and they disappeared from one day to another. The shadows of the frames were sometimes still there. That was a big difference.

---

17. After Slovenia declared independence from Yugoslavia, the Bank of Slovenia replaced the National Bank of Yugoslavia, and the Parliament called for introduction of a new currency: the Slovenian tolar. The state had secretly printed provisional currency tokens in 1990, and it put these notes into use for three months (October–December of 1991) while it issued Slovenian tolar banknotes and coins. This provisional currency had neither a printed designation nor a name (Minniti and Polutnik, "Currency Conversion and the Role of Expectations," 10–11).

18. Stagnation, increasing prices, and hyperinflation characterized the Yugoslav economy in the 1980s. As the state transitioned from a socialist to a market economy, most republics experienced monetary instability. Slovenia set out to decouple from the Yugoslav economy after it declared independence. The state phased out the Yugoslav dinar in 1991 and introduced the Slovenian tolar as national currency that "was to be convertible from the beginning and was to trade freely against the dinar and other international currencies" (Minniti and Polutnik, "Currency Conversion and the Role of Expectations," 13). The inflation rate in Slovenia steadily dropped in 1992 after the tolar was put into circulation, while it continued to increase in the rump of Yugoslavia. As Lisjak Gabrijelčič noted, the Slovenian tolar was a stable currency; it contributed to quickly building public support of the new independent state and its leadership.

Having to wait at the border of Croatia was also a big change. I think that we were all shocked that this was real, that this was a border now. It was even stricter than the border with Italy we were used to. We actually had to queue at the border. That was a shock.

INTERVIEWER: Did your family travel elsewhere instead of in the former Yugoslav regions?

LISJAK GABRIJELČIČ: There were couple of years when we couldn't afford [to travel abroad], so we mostly started going to [places in] Slovenia. We visited our friends and family in the countryside. My mother sometimes went to these spas in Slovenia. Vacationing in Slovenia was a new thing for us: one of my childhood memories was that Slovenia was for spas and skiing but not for summer holidays. Croatia was for summer holidays.

We still crossed the border into Italy, of course. We started going to the West—to Paris, London, and so on—from the early to mid-1990s. I went to Paris for the first time in May 1993. This was like "wow" for me. I was dreaming about Paris, and when I first saw it, it was like "wow." I remember when we went to a *brasserie*, and the waiter asked us, "Where are you from?" We said "Slovenia, former Yugoslavia." He went pale. These were precisely the years when the images from the war in Bosnia were flooding Western media.

INTERVIEWER: Were there any other changes that you remember experiencing as Slovenia came into its independence?

LISJAK GABRIJELČIČ: There was a big economic disruption in the early 1990s. A lot of firms from my hometown closed down. Most of the industry closed down. I knew kids whose parents lost their jobs. Unemployment was becoming an issue. Yugoslavia had a relatively high unemployment rate in the 1980s, but Slovenia did not. There was a big disparity [across] different areas. But suddenly unemployment became an issue in Slovenia in the 1990s, and there was a sense that some people were becoming more fortunate and others less fortunate. My dad moved from one firm to another, but my mother lost her job. She was unemployed for a while. Afterward, she worked for a colleague and struggled to get her own shop open. I think she managed that in 1998 or 1999, and it was a big deal that she had her own shop.

The images from the war in Croatia and Bosnia were devastating, especially for my parents. I didn't know the other Yugoslav republics well, but my parents knew these places and had friends there. It was traumatic for them. My mother cried very rarely, but I remember that she cried when she saw the Mostar Bridge falling down. I remember my father saying, "People are dying.

Why are you crying about a bridge?" My mother replied, "You're right, but bridges are not supposed to fall down. This was supposed to last." I remember that bridge very, very well.

[The wars] were far, but they felt very present. [A lot of information] came from the media. I remember this image of when the bomb fell on the market in Sarajevo because the Slovenian television warned [viewers] that they were going to show graphic images because they were important for the public to see, but they advised that kids should [not watch].[19] My parents didn't allow me to watch *Schindler's List* because they did not want to expose me to [images of suffering], but they decided that I could stay to see this. I will never forget these images of corpses of women lying with bags of groceries scattered on the ground. I couldn't sleep at night.

[A lot of information] also came from refugees who were coming in. I remember that friends who were from Bosnia and hosted family members in their homes had stories about what was happening in the war. I had many kids in my class who were from Bosnia, so the war in Bosnia impacted the lives of many of my friends. The military barracks in our town were also emptied out from 1991, and many of them were transformed into refugee centers.

When I was fourteen or fifteen, I remember the last phase of the wars. I followed it very closely. I read all the newspapers. I followed all the plans, like [the] Vance peace plan.[20] I was cutting out maps from newspapers. I remember very well Oluja because it happened the day I traveled with

---

19. There were two major massacres at the Markale market in Sarajevo. The first attack was on February 5, 1994, and it killed sixty-eight people and wounded two hundred. The second attack was on August 28, 1995; it killed thirty-seven people and wounded eighty. In their study of how responsibility was assigned for civilian attacks during the Bosnian War, scholars Benjamin Rusek and Charles Ingrao suggest that the two market attacks, in addition to the Breadline Massacre on May 27, 1992, which killed twenty and wounded one hundred, were important because they drew significant media attention to the violence during the Siege of Sarajevo (April 1992–February 1996). Bosnian Serb leaders denied responsibility for these attacks, but evidence indicates that "there is a very high probability" that the Army of Republika Srpska was behind them (Rusek and Ingrao, "The 'Mortar Massacres,'" 827–52).

20. The Vance plan was a two-part peace agreement negotiated by US secretary of state Cyrus Vance (1917–2002) in late 1991 and early 1992, at the beginning of the Croatian War of Independence (1991–1995). The plan was intended to prompt a ceasefire, demilitarize parts of Croatia under the control of the Yugoslav National Army, and resettle refugees. Even though representatives from the Yugoslav National Army, Serbia, and Croatia signed the agreement, it was not implemented. Vance later attempted to negotiate the failed Vance-Owen peace plan in 1993 to divide Bosnia into ten separate regions.

my father to Croatia.[21] I remember very clearly all of the phases of the Yugoslav wars.

INTERVIEWER: It sounds like the Yugoslav wars were very present for you in the media and in your everyday life through interaction with people. Do you remember discussing them in school in any way? Was this something that came up in lessons?

LISJAK GABRIJELČIČ: No, I don't think so. But there were things that happened that would not have happened before. In Yugoslavia before 1990, teachers kept racism out of the classroom, but somehow this sort of stopped after 1991. Some teachers felt emboldened to share their racist or nationalist bias. I remember the first year we had history [as a subject], I was around thirteen, and we had a teacher who was so inappropriate. She was quite orientalist, looking back on it now. When we were talking about Islam, she said to a student, "Albijana! You are from Bosnia, aren't you?" The student was like, "No, I'm from here." And the teacher was like, "Well, your family is from Bosnia. Do you know what a mosque is? Do you go to a mosque?" And the student was like, "Well . . ." I don't even know if she was a Muslim. She may have very well been a Bosnian Serb. It felt very uncomfortable. The teacher was pushing her in a very insensitive way. All the kids realized that this was so fucking inappropriate. Afterward, we always made fun of that teacher by parroting her saying, "You are Bosnian!" There was at least one other teacher who used racial slurs or sayings when he was very angry.

INTERVIEWER: Did your own sense of self shift in independent Slovenia?

LISJAK GABRIJELČIČ: That's interesting. I don't think so. It was so natural in my family that we didn't really talk about identity at home. It was not an issue.

I remember that when I was a kid—that must have been around 1987 or 1988—I was a Yugoslav patriot because I had learned all about Tito in school. At the same time, I was sensing that things were not going well—especially in 1988 and 1989, when Milošević was the *bête noire* for everybody in Slovenia.

---

21. Oluja, known as Operation Storm, was a decisive victory for the Croatian army in the Croatian War of Independence in August 1995. Croatian forces reasserted territorial control and made significant territorial gains against Croatian Serb insurgents, eventually displacing the Serbian population from the region. Oluja was also a strategic victory for the Army of the Republic of Bosnia and Herzegovina in the Bosnian War that led to the Dayton Peace Agreement that same year. See Ashbrook and Bakich, "Storming to Partition," 537–60.

It was clear that this country was in deep shit and that something was happening. When I was around eight, I said, "What if Yugoslavia was attacked by Albania, wouldn't that be nice?" [I was thinking that] if we were attacked by Albania, there would be a sense of patriotic unity, and we would forget all the differences. [I reasoned that] Albania is such a small country, and we would easily defeat it. [Laughs]

INTERVIEWER: You were a political mastermind at age eight!

LISJAK GABRIJELČIČ: It's like that film *Wag the Dog*.[22] It's an American film with Dustin Hoffman from the 1990s. There is an American president whose ratings were falling because of sexual scandals. The illusion was planted, and then they fabricated a war in Albania. So I came to the same idea before them.

One of the first political memories I have is actually not connected at all to Yugoslavia. It was the fall of [Nicolae] Ceaușescu.[23] I remember it very well because I discovered that Romania existed. [Laughs] We were watching this Italian show *Zecchino d'Oro* that was popular in Yugoslavia. It was a children's singing contest. It was also quite popular in the Eastern bloc, so they often had kids from [places like] Poland or Hungary. The revolution must have happened around the time I was watching *Zecchino d'Oro*. There was a girl who was supposed to come to the competition from Romania, but she could not come because of the border restrictions from Romania. I remember my grandmother telling me, "This is a very bad man who wouldn't even let a child cross the border to sing for this competition." I remember very clearly the images that aired on television of Ceaușescu's last speech, and I remember the images of Ceaușescu being killed.

Later on, I remember [talking to] my father about Ceaușescu and how bad he was, and my father said something life shattering. He said, "Tito

---

22. *Wag the Dog* is an American black comedy produced and directed by Barry Levinson (1942–) and released in 1997. It stars Dustin Hoffman and Robert De Niro. It was adapted from Larry Beinhart's novel *American Hero* (1993) and released the year of the Clinton-Lewinsky scandal, two years before the NATO bombing of the rump of Yugoslavia intended to force withdrawal of Yugoslav forces from Kosovo during the Kosovo War.

23. Nicolae Ceaușescu (1918–1989), general secretary of the Romanian Communist Party from 1965 to 1989, is considered among the most repressive dictators of the Cold War era. Ceaușescu curtailed human rights, censored the media, and mismanaged the economy. Scholar Dan Draghia shows that the Romanian border was strictly monitored from the early postwar years due in part to Soviet pressure to implement totalitarian border measures with Yugoslavia after the Tito-Stalin split in 1948 (Draghia, "Bordering Tito," 243–60). During the revolutions of 1989, the military captured Ceaușescu, tried him, and sentenced him to death.

was not very different from Ceaușescu," or maybe it was, "Tito was a friend of Ceaușescu." This was the first time that I discovered that my father was against the system. I didn't know this before. The idea that somebody could think that Tito was not a good person—that *my father* would think that Tito was not a good person—was just "wow." This was December 1989, the same period as the failed Rally of Truth in Ljubljana. That was when I discovered that there was a public sphere and a world happening outside. By the summer 1991, I already had a nuanced political consciousness.

INTERVIEWER: I know that you went to high school and then university in Slovenia and then that you also went abroad for school and various other engagements. How did you explain Yugoslavia or where you were from when you were abroad?

LISJAK GABRIJELČIČ: I presented myself as Slovenian. But by the time I was in college, I had a much more developed identity. When I was abroad, one of the things I understood was how deeply I was impacted by Yugoslav pop culture. This is one of the things that my generation experienced. First, there was that experience itself, and then you had another one when meeting people from the post-Yugoslav republics abroad and realizing how much you had in common. I rediscovered a part of my Yugoslav identity through common pop culture references because all the post-Yugoslav kids would know *Ko to tamo peva* or [Goran] Bregović or Bijelo Dugme.[24] They would know the lyrics. If no one at a party knows the lyrics of "Djurdjevdan," there's something missing there.

I also see now with the war in Ukraine that I can make references to the Yugoslav wars, and people [from the region] pick up on them. It's a geographical thing because people from France and Germany just don't pick up on them the same way. It's also generational because I see young kids in Slovenia

---

24. *Ko to tamo peva* (*Who's Singin' over There?*) is a Yugoslav dark comedy film written by Dušan Kovačević (1948–), directed by Slobodan Šijan (1946–), and released in 1980. The film follows a diverse cast of Yugoslav passengers traveling on a bus through Serbia on the eve of the Axis invasion of Yugoslavia in 1941. Goran Bregović (1950–) was guitarist and songwriter of acclaimed Yugoslav rock band Bijelo Dugme, active from the mid-1970s to the late 1980s. Cycling through several vocalists, the band blended folk, rock, and new-wave sounds. After Bijelo Dugme disbanded, Bregović went on to have a successful career writing film scores and performing with other musical projects. He often collaborated with Yugoslav filmmaker Emir Kusturica (1954–). "Djurdjevdan," the song Lisjak Gabrijelčič mentioned subsequently, appeared on Bijelo Dugme's last record, *Ćiribiribela*, released in 1988. The song is based on a Romani melody called "Ederlezi" that also appears in other works of East European pop culture, including in Kusturica's 1988 film *Dom za vešanje* (*Time of the Gypsies*). As scholar Eliot Borenstein suggests, "Ederlezi" can be interpreted as "national appropriation and reappropriation in an age of global cultures" (Borenstein, "Our Borats, Our Selves," 5). Bijelo Dugme remains popular among former citizens of Yugoslavia.

Figure 1.1. Portrait of Luka Lisjak Gabrijelčič. *Courtesy of N1 (Slovenia).*

who just don't know [the references to the wars]. For them, it's like speaking about the war of succession in America.

INTERVIEWER: How you relate to the Yugoslav diaspora today?

LISJAK GABRIJELČIČ: It's quite a strong [connection], almost like an epiphany. It's something that happens in most places. I remember when we went to Munich with our high school German class to try to improve our broken German—it so happened that in almost every shop and in almost every bar, you can get by with Serbo-Croatian.[25] Or in a group of students [abroad] when there's someone from Yugoslavia, we immediately start hanging out

---

25. Of the European countries, Germany admitted the most asylum seekers during the Yugoslav wars. Many were attracted to Germany because it had hosted Yugoslav guest workers during the postwar years (see Molnar, "Imagining Yugoslavs," 138–69). In 1994, when Lisjak Gabrijelčič was starting high school, there were about 930,000 registered residents from Yugoslavia in Germany.

together. Maybe it's not with everybody because there's always somebody you like and dislike, but a group always forms naturally. There is a linguistic reference. All the kids [from the former Yugoslavia] have some—good or bad—knowledge of Serbo-Croatian. Of course, I understand everything in Serbo-Croatian. I read and everything, but I'm so self-conscious when I speak it because I hate hearing my accent. There are cultural references as well. As I saw at CEU [Central European University] in Budapest, there was a [similar] post-Soviet sphere: Ukrainians hanging out with Russians and Kazakhs because of their common [Soviet] experience. It's like, "We understand each other in a way that others do not." This was very present for my generation of post-Yugoslavs.

INTERVIEWER: How do you identify today, whether nationally, ethnically, or culturally?

LISJAK GABRIJELČIČ: It's very unproblematic for me. I remember being a Yugoslav patriot in my childhood, but basically, I very unproblematically identify as Slovenian. I have come to develop a very strong regional and local identity too, because I realized that living in that place gave me a very specific perspective on the world. I lived between two economic systems. I also developed a generational identity. Being a Slovenian of my generation means being the last generation to still experience Yugoslavia. That's very important to me. I cannot imagine myself not having that part of my identity or memory. I'm very much conscious of how this impacted my self-awareness and my way of thinking about the world.

INTERVIEWER: Is there a context in which you would identify as Yugoslav?

LISJAK GABRIJELČIČ: I am post-Yugoslav in the same sense as [someone might be] post-Habsburg, in the sense of a certain shared historical legacy.[26] There is a duty to know more about these spaces or what is happening in these spaces. I am a historian. I've worked on the interwar period, which means I'm working on a period of Slovenian history that's [set in] a different space and [a different] country. I know that most of the experts who come from the field are not necessarily experts on Yugoslav matters. I treat [Yugoslavia] as something that has a very important historical legacy.

INTERVIEWER: To what extent do you think your childhood in Yugoslavia shaped who you are today, whether it's something about Yugoslavia or

---

26. Austria-Hungary was a large, multinational empire in central Europe ruled by the Habsburg monarchy that collapsed after World War I. When former residents found themselves in separate states after World War I, some looked back fondly on the culture they had shared. There is extensive scholarship on Habsburg nostalgia.

something about socialism? What are those inheritances that you carry with you today?

LISJAK GABRIJELČIČ: Socialism in Yugoslavia was different than in the Eastern bloc countries, but the differences among the members of the Eastern bloc were just as big. Being a kid in Romania was not the same as being a kid in Hungary or Russia or Kazakhstan or Poland or East Germany. In the former Yugoslavia, we sometimes overestimate these differences from the Eastern bloc because we tend to essentialize the Eastern bloc as one big, homogenous entity and [think about] Yugoslavia as separate. I think this is not correct. Having experienced socialism and the transition in the 1990s, even as a kid, brings me closer to other Eastern Europeans. I feel close to [people who grew up in] other post-socialist countries.

The experience of living right on the border is also really important to me. I cherish it as a personal experience. I think of myself as a person of the border. I realized the way I think is really mediated by this experience of a border which was, on the one hand, open—but, on the other hand, a border with two very different economic and political systems. It was tangible on a daily level. Even as a kid, I could understand that [it separated] different worlds.

My childhood was not typical of Yugoslavia. I think somebody who was born in Tuzla [now Bosnia] or Srebrenica [now Bosnia] had a much different experience. Our childhoods ended in a radically different way. My teenage years from around thirteen, fourteen, or fifteen were more similar to somebody who was born in Hungary or Poland than somebody who was born in Sarajevo [now Bosnia] or Pristina [now Kosovo] or Belgrade [now Serbia]. In terms of daily experience, and really in terms of everything, the 1990s meant something very different for somebody who lived in Belgrade or Sarajevo [now Bosnia] than they meant to me. I'm very aware of that. When I speak about the 1990s, my 1990s are very different from how others in Yugoslavia [experienced them]. I do share this idea of the 1990s as a period of unrestrained optimism, successes, and upward mobility of the nouveau riche [coupled with] economic disparages and also war. But for me, the latter was nevertheless in the background. The war that I experienced was very short and radically different. I can say I have fond memories of the war, and this is not something that somebody in Croatia, Bosnia, or Serbia could say!

INTERVIEWER: What does Yugoslavia mean to you today?

LISJAK GABRIJELČIČ: That's a tough question because I don't think I have one answer. I do think primarily that I am not a big fan of Yugonostalgia. I think it can be toxic, as every nostalgia can be. I'm prone to nostalgia as a person because I like indulging in the past. I had a nice childhood, and I think that most of us start studying history because we are fond of the past. Liking the past has always had this sort of antiquarian element to it. But if you want to be a historian, then you have to pass [through] this phase because history is not about antiquarianism or nostalgia. If it is, it's bad history. I try to be critical and try to avoid Yugonostalgia in terms of creating a myth out of a historic experience. I'm also against whitewashing or disregarding negative historical aspects.

I think Yugoslavia was a very important historical experience in its seventy years of various political experiments. I really think it has to be treated as [Leopold von] Ranke would say, "[Jede Epoche ist] unmittelbar zu Gott"—as one of the epochs of our historical experience.[27] In that sense, I would say that for me personally, it's more important than Austria-Hungary or something like this. In terms of historical experience, I think we should really put it on equal footing with others. Although it was a state that existed through most of the twentieth century as characterized by [Eric] Hobsbawm as the short twenty-first century,[28] this was a very transformative period, so it had an important impact. The bottom line is that I try to think critically about it, which means neither glorifying it nor disparaging it.

INTERVIEWER: Is there anything that you miss about Yugoslavia? It doesn't have to be nostalgia necessarily, but is there anything from your childhood in Yugoslavia that you wish was still around?

LISJAK GABRIJELČIČ: No, when I think about it, I don't think I miss anything. I cherish memories of that experience. Maybe I miss the people that were alive in that period that are not alive anymore. That's all, really.

INTERVIEWER: Thank you for sharing these memories with me, Luka. I really appreciate it.

LISJAK GABRIJELČIČ: Thank you.

---

27. German historian Leopold von Ranke (1795–1896) delivered his first historical lecture to Maximilian II of Bavaria and declared that "all eras are equally God's children." Known as the founder of evidence-based history, Ranke suggested that every era ought to be interpreted on its own terms rather than ahistorically from the present.

28. Eric Hobsbawm (1917–2012) was a British Marxist historian who studied capitalism, socialism, and nationalism. He coined the historicization of the "long nineteenth century" in his trilogy *The Age of Revolution* (1962), *The Age of Capital* (1975), and *The Age of Empire* (1987) and "the short twentieth century" in his text *The Age of Extremes* (1994).

2

INTERVIEW WITH
Krisztina Rácz

Krisztina Rácz was born in Senta (now Serbia) in 1981 and spent most of her childhood in Zrenjanin (now Serbia). She remained in the region until her early twenties and then intermittently worked and studied in other parts of Europe. When we spoke over a video call in early 2022, she was living in Mali Idjoš (now Serbia), known as Kishegyes in Hungarian, and working as a researcher in Belgrade (now Serbia). In the interview, Rácz shared memories of growing up as a member of the Hungarian community in Yugoslavia, learning Serbo-Croatian at school and negotiating her minority identity. While Rácz criticized contemporary iterations of Yugonostalgia, she nevertheless underlined the comfort found in sharing cultural inheritances with other members of the last Yugoslav generation.

Many of Rácz's memories of Yugoslavia, including her earliest ones, were shaped by her Hungarian identity. She was born to Hungarian parents in Vojvodina, an autonomous region in northern Serbia with a historically sizable Hungarian minority. Rácz's first language, the one she spoke at home, was Hungarian. While the Yugoslav constitution mandated access to education in the minority languages recognized by each republic and autonomous region, minority-language education was often only available in districts with a certain number of students. Rácz recalled that her parents had driven her older sister to a Hungarian-language kindergarten but enrolled Rácz in a Serbo-Croatian one closer to home. This was a jarring, formative experience. Rácz described how she was not able to communicate with classmates and feared not being able to let her teacher know if she had an emergency. She remembered soothing herself on the way to school by practicing phrases she thought might be useful to know in Serbo-Croatian, such as "I don't feel well." Once she started grade school, Rácz attended classes in Hungarian. Her school was not bilingual: Serbian students studied in Serbo-Croatian, and Hungarian students studied the same material in Hungarian. Hungarian students, however, took Serbo-Croatian language classes, while their Serbian peers did not study Hungarian. As she thought back on her elementary education in Yugoslavia, Rácz recalled other forms of inequality. She noted, for instance, that teachers did not always include Hungarian students in extracurricular activities. "I had less opportunities," she said. "I remember things like going to summer schools. They were available for us as well, of course, but they were not advertised enough or our teachers didn't really encourage [Hungarians] to take part in these events, which were in Serbian. To be fair, it has to be added that we had some other opportunities that Serbian kids didn't, such as camps, school trips, competitions, etcetera in Hungary, that were part of the program of Hungary to help diaspora Hungarians." Rácz recognized that marginalization was part and parcel of living as a Hungarian in Yugoslavia.

Reflecting on her identity, Rácz explained that she never identified as a Yugoslav. She considered herself a Hungarian from Vojvodina or, alternatively, from Serbia. She insisted that the regional modifier was important. "It's also a big difference whether you identify as Hungarian or Hungarian from Vojvodina because, at least in our community, when you say Hungarian, it just means ethnic Hungarian from Hungary," she explained. "Very few people would identify simply as Hungarian, and it would be mostly nationalists, what we'd call them." In addition to clarifying what she was and was not, the regional modifier helped Rácz claim a defining part of her identity. She found neither "Yugoslav" nor "Hungarian" to be reflective of her sense of self, but adding "from Vojvodina" helped articulate the particularity of her experience—she was a member of a distinct Hungarian minority in a region of a multinational Yugoslav state where Serbs constituted the majority. Of all the places she had lived, Rácz told me, her hometown of Zrenjanin and the Vojvodina region more broadly still felt most like home. Yugoslavia was not necessarily inclusive for all its citizens—foremost those who were not Slavs—but it nevertheless created space for other identities to exist within its boundaries.

Rácz noted that while many former citizens were nostalgic for Yugoslavia, she was ambivalent about the state's legacy. "I don't see it as a valid identity anymore," she said. "You can say of course that you would like to live in a different time, in a different state that is now nonexistent, but I think it simply makes no sense to claim an identity of a country that doesn't exist. Of course I understand what it means. It's an ideological statement and in a way a grievance for lost privileges, but it's just not my thing, probably partly because I never had some of those privileges." Rácz's critical view of Yugonostalgia aligns with that of many other members of the youngest Yugoslav generation. She recognized that nostalgia highlights the positive potential of Yugoslav socialism and multinationalism without necessarily recognizing its negative outcomes. While Rácz did not dismiss the ideological pillars of the Yugoslav idea, she underlined that her own experiences were evidence that these pillars were not always realized. Moreover, she noted that some post-Yugoslav spaces replicate Yugoslavia's exclusionary practices even when attempting to rectify them. Rácz cited again the example of language. Since the Yugoslav wars, individual successor states have nationalized language: Bosnian, Croatian, Montenegrin, and Serbian are the official languages of record rather than Serbo-Croatian. When people want to reiterate their shared linguistic inheritance, they often say they speak "our language," *naš jezik*, rather than naming one of the nationalized variants. "After the wars in the former Yugoslavia," journalist Slavenka Drakulić writes, "the term became a kind of code indicating good intentions. We are not enemies, *naš jezik* implies. We can still understand one another in spite of everything."[1] Yet as Rácz pointed out, these good intentions are misguided: she considered neither Serbo-Croatian nor any of the nationalized variants to be her language. When other former Yugoslavs would suggest speaking "our language," Rácz would sometimes point out that it was, in fact, "your language" (*vaš jezik*). She explained that "often it's only if I make this joke, 'shall I call it *vaš?*' that these otherwise very smart people become aware of these language hegemonies ... this language is not ours, it's theirs." Nostalgic attempts to erase contemporary differences among former Yugoslavs ultimately fell flat for her because they reiterated her marginalization from Yugoslavia and its legacy.

Yet Rácz told me that her Yugoslav childhood remained formative for her. She noted that she shared many cultural touchstones with others who grew up in last decades of socialist Yugoslavia and was usually able to relate to them on multiple levels. While conversations might start with reminiscences about popular culture or activities such as Pioneer inaugurations and seaside excursions, they would continue on the grounds of similar sensibilities. Rácz, like many others with whom I spoke, identified humor as a lens through which she could connect with others. Ultimately, Rácz told me that she gravitated toward individuals from the former Yugoslavia in social situations. "It's always somehow this Yugo crowd that I end up with," she stated. "I always end up with the Serbs or Croats or whatever." Many of those people did not share the

---

1. Drakulić, "Letter from Vienna."

experiences of Yugoslavia that Rácz had as a Hungarian from Vojvodina, but they did take part in a common culture accessible to citizens across the former country regardless of individual identity. This common culture was not the perfect iteration of Yugoslav socialism and multiculturalism, as members of the youngest Yugoslav generation were often quick to point out, but it was the foundation of an experience many continue to find meaningful more than three decades after Yugoslavia's collapse.

INTERVIEWER: I would like to get started thinking about your earliest memories from childhood. What do you remember about everyday life, about your surroundings, or about your childhood?

RÁCZ: I was born in Senta [now Serbia] by accident because my mom was pregnant in a close by town and I was born prematurely. I grew up in Zrenjanin [now Serbia], and I consider that my hometown. My earliest memories are obviously from Zrenjanin, where I lived with my mom and dad and older sister. I don't really have many recollections of growing up with my sister because she is thirteen years older, so she was basically out of the house by the time I have some memories. All my first memories are related to living in Zrenjanin, which is a midsize town by Serbian standards. I wouldn't say it was idyllic, but it was typical small-town life. My first memories are from the period I was in kindergarten, which was when I was five.

I remember neighborhood things, kindergarten things, and also one of the main things that features in these early memories is actually already connected to the topic we are here to talk about implicitly, and that is that I remember not being able to speak Serbian because Hungarian is my first language. I remember wanting to do the same things as the other kids, like playing with them and socializing with them, and not having the words for it. With today's knowledge, I would say it's quite traumatic, but I guess at that time it was just the way it was. And then my parents decided to enroll me in Serbian kindergarten because it was close by. My sister used to go to Hungarian kindergarten, and they drove her every day, but with me, they were a bit more lazy. So they did the sink-or-swim thing when I was five.

I remember being in kindergarten. I think I understood what was going on because I don't remember not understanding. But again, I remember not being able to say what's happening to me, and I remember asking my parents phrases that I thought were important for getting by in kindergarten. I was always afraid that I would be sick. One of my first memories is of me walking to the kindergarten—it was two blocks away—and practicing aloud,

"Vaspitačice, meni je zlo" ["Teacher, I feel sick"] because I was afraid that I wouldn't be able to say so if something happened. My first memories are really connected to this language thing. And then later, in the second year of kindergarten, I learned Serbian because I don't remember these things anymore.

INTERVIEWER: Were any of the schools you attended bilingual?

RÁCZ: [They were] not officially called bilingual. There are no bilingual schools in Serbia, and there were no official bilingual schools in Yugoslavia. I think there were in Slovenia, but that was a completely different thing. My school and most of the schools in Vojvodina had separate streams, so you learned the same things, but you went to a Hungarian class or the Serbian class. I went to the Hungarian class in elementary school. In Zrenjanin, there were maybe ten elementary schools, and one of them had a Hungarian class. In grammar school, I also went to the Hungarian class of the grammar school, but it was not really Hungarian because there was a shortage of teachers who spoke [Hungarian], especially for philosophy or psychology or art history. So I learned those in Serbian even though officially I had my education in Hungarian.[2]

INTERVIEWER: Do you remember being different from the other children?

RÁCZ: No, I wouldn't say so because most of my friends were here in Vojvodina, and these situations were quite usual. It's a bit different language wise, but somehow that's part of life that you have these separate language streams at school and that sometimes you struggle with a language. Eventually you learn the language. Much later, when I started like really consciously thinking about these things, I felt that because I was going to the Hungarian

---

2. The interwar Yugoslav state nearly dismantled the Hungarian education system (Ferdinand and Komlosi, "The Use of Hungarian and Serbian in the City of Szabadka/Subotica," 3–4). By World War II, scholars Lajos Göncz and Ottó Vörös show, there were only two Hungarian high schools in Vojvodina; they enrolled 337 Hungarian students, but even at these schools, some class instruction was delivered in Serbo-Croatian. Conditions for Hungarian education improved somewhat in the first decades of socialist Yugoslavia. Students had more opportunities to attend school in their first language, but access varied by region and age level. Beyond elementary school, Hungarian students often only had access to some classes in Hungarian. Moreover, unlike Serbo-Croatian, Hungarian as a subject was not usually compulsory—most Hungarians in Vojvodina were bilingual out of necessity, whereas most Serbs were monolingual (Göncz and Vörös, "Hungarian in the Former Yugoslavia (Vojvodina and Prekmurje)," 202–3).

stream, I had less opportunities. For instance, I remember things like going to summer schools. They were available for us as well, of course, but they were not advertised enough or our teachers didn't really encourage [Hungarians] to take part in these events, which were in Serbian. To be fair, it has to be added that we had some other opportunities that Serbian kids didn't, such as camps, school trips, competitions, etcetera in Hungary, that were part of the program of Hungary to help diaspora Hungarians. I think we were a little bit like a ghetto. But in Zrenjanin, this was not so harsh because it's a town which is mostly Serbian, so [Hungarians] had to take part in most of the things, like it or not. I think I had a bit less encouragement to do some extracurricular stuff and things like that, so that's the only thing I would say was a bit different.

INTERVIEWER: Do you remember any kids in school who were different from you, who might not have been treated equally, even if they weren't Hungarian or if they weren't Serbian? Were there any other minorities that you recall? [Rácz: You mean because of their nationality?] Yes, or otherwise as well.

RÁCZ: The Roma kids were treated differently. Children picked on them. And even though the Roma kids always either went to the Serbian class or the Hungarian class, it was always clear that they were not Serbian or not Hungarian. They were treated differently at school. Poor kids were also treated differently. Often, not always, they were not so good students, and again they were excluded or mocked. The teachers definitely didn't give them as much attention as they needed.

INTERVIEWER: Do you remember any state-sponsored Yugoslav activities that you participated in during your childhood?

RÁCZ: Well, the Pioneers—I was in the [group] before the last generation everywhere in Yugoslavia or at least in Serbia. The 1982 was the last generation. I was the one before the last, which means that somewhere, maybe in the middle of the first grade, when I was seven, there was this celebration, this ceremony. I have some photos of it, even. And then everybody who was a first grader [was inaugurated]. We had this Pioneer uniform, and there were some recitations. I don't really remember. These things were always bilingual, but often Serbian-dominant bilingual. I don't remember [if] I recited anything. And then we had to say this *pionirska zakletva* [Pioneer pledge] in unison. I remember there was a Hungarian version of it. I guess all the kids did it in Serbian, and then we did it in Hungarian as well. I remember we learned it by heart in Hungarian, so we had to do it.

When you are a Pioneer, you have these kids who are four years older than you, who are fifth graders when you are first graders. I don't know what they were called in Serbian. In Hungarian they were something like Pioneer leaders. They were usually good students, well behaving. We had three girls who would come to us for one class every week or every other week. And then it was called a Pioneer class, *pionirski čas*, but it wasn't really anything Pioneer related or Yugoslavia related or Tito related. We played some ball games, or it was a class when you had free time, basically. So that's the only official Yugoslavia-related thing that I can recall.

INTERVIEWER: Who constituted your family when you were growing up? Who did you live with? Was there any extended family close by?

RÁCZ: I lived with my mom and my dad and my sister, who moved away when she was seventeen and when I was four. I mostly remember her coming home for the weekends. Then when I was eight, my parents divorced, and my father remarried. They [Rácz's father and her stepfamily] lived first in Novi Sad, and then they actually lived in this village where I live now. So I have a stepmother and a half-brother. I was mostly at my mom's place, but I would come [to my dad's] sometimes for weekends and for holidays. My family is not very close with our extended family. I had a grandmother and a grandfather in a nearby village and a grandfather in a close-by small town, but I wouldn't say that they were formative in any way. We visited them occasionally, but nothing major.

INTERVIEWER: How present was your identity as Hungarian at home? How aware were you of being Hungarian?

RÁCZ: It was just a given. We spoke Hungarian at home. We had some neighbors who were Hungarians, and we spoke to them in Hungarian. My parents socialized mostly with Hungarians in the town. At that time, I wasn't aware of that, but now I realize it. My father worked as a reporter on the television of Vojvodina, which was divided by ethnicity. He worked in the Hungarian editorial office, and he socialized quite a lot with his colleagues. It was a fact of life.

I remember, there was a neighborhood girl one year older than me, and we played together outside sometimes. She was Serbian, and I remember that she was trying to argue with me that I am half Hungarian and half Serbian. She was like, "Yeah, you have to be like half this, half that because you are Hungarian, but you live in Serbia." I was like, "Yeah, it's true, but it just makes no sense. I'm Hungarian."

Figure 2.1. Krisztina Rácz with brother and grandparents in her father's birth village of Mihajlovo/Szentmihály, near Zrenjanin. *Courtesy of Krisztina Rácz.*

And I also remember that for quite a long time, I wasn't aware that I lived in Serbia. I knew I lived in Yugoslavia. Maybe it was third grade or second; I was probably eight or nine when we learned that Yugoslavia consisted of six republics and that one of those republics was Serbia. [We also learned that] Serbia consisted of two autonomous provinces. I think I knew I lived in Vojvodina but not that Vojvodina was part of Serbia. I knew Yugoslavia, and I knew Vojvodina, but I really couldn't connect them to Serbia. Serbia was always something like *bljak* [yuck]. I had really had bad associations [with it], like it was something backwards. [When I realized the connection,] I was like, "Jesus! I live in this shithole?!"

INTERVIEWER: Why do you think you had a negative association with Serbia?

RÁCZ: I think that I heard my parents and their friends talking about the stereotype of Serbs who were not from Vojvodina, like *Srbijanci*. We had a neighbor who was from central Serbia, or from Šumadija, and we really didn't get along with him. He was quite an awful old man. I heard this a lot, *Srbijanci* or *tamo u Srbiji*, meaning not in Vojvodina but in Serbia proper. It was always something negative. And I never traveled further south than Belgrade.

INTERVIEWER: Do you remember how your family engaged with Yugoslavia? Do you remember any associations that you had as a child with the federal state?

RÁCZ: With my mom, not so much. It was all the clichés. She's from quite a poor family from a small town, Novi Bečej, and for her, it was a big thing to go to the seaside when she was a school kid. I remember she told me [her school class] went to Split [now Croatia] and traveled for a long time by train. It was a "wow" thing [for her].

For my father, it was again another cliché: the army. He was [stationed] in what was then called Titov Veles, which is now Veles in North Macedonia. It was always a place [for him] which was dirty and backward. As most men, it was also this nostalgic thing about being in the army. My father was quite old when he was in the army. He already had my sister, so I think he was a bit more conscientious. It was later, when I was reading about things, that I remembered the absurdity of the situation. My father was trained as a schoolteacher. He never worked as one, but I guess they wanted to use his skills in the army, so he was teaching illiterate people in the army to read and write. But the funny thing was that he was teaching them to read and write in Serbian, and the illiterate people were 90 percent Albanians. So this was a Hungarian teacher teaching Albanians to read and write in Serbian. My father passed away, so I could never ask whether he was teaching them Cyrillic or Latin script. That was quite "wow."

INTERVIEWER: That feels like such a uniquely Yugoslav story.

RÁCZ: Yeah, it was, exactly. Later, I was just like, "wow."

INTERVIEWER: Do you remember if your mom or dad identified as Yugoslav?

RÁCZ: They didn't. I mean, I don't know; I never asked them. I never heard them say this, but I'm 99 percent sure they would say they were Hungarians from Vojvodina. It's also a big difference whether you identify as Hungarian or Hungarian from Vojvodina because, at least in our community, when you say Hungarian, it just means ethnic Hungarian from Hungary. Very few people would identify simply as Hungarian, and it would be mostly nationalists, what we'd call them. So if you say Hungarian from Vojvodina, that used to be, and I think still is, more like an accepted identity.[3] You're still part of the society, and you don't want out. I think it's also a statement.

---

3. Rácz's evaluation of the Vojvodina Hungarian community is consistent with the findings of scholars Lajos Göncz and Ottó Vörös. Based on a survey conducted in 2000, Göncz and Vörös conclude that most Hungarians from Vojvodina had a ranked sense of attachment: Vojvodina, pre-1991 Yugoslavia, Europe, Hungary, and post-1991 Yugoslavia or a successor state (Göncz and Vörös, "Hungarian in the Former Yugoslavia (Vojvodina and Prekmurje)," 199).

Figure 2.2. Krisztina Rácz and her best friend receiving awards for their essays at a ceremony at the Hungarian Cultural Association in Zrenjanin. *Courtesy of Krisztina Rácz.*

INTERVIEWER: Do you remember how your parents reacted when the Yugoslav wars started?

RÁCZ: For my mom, I don't really remember. I guess it was mostly these typical gender things, like you start hoarding flour and sugar. With my father, I remember because, as I said, he worked as a journalist. His job was not so much politics, but he had colleagues and friends who were economists or studied political science. He said his colleagues were sure this was coming; they talked about it coming. I remember myself being like, "Who could have predicted this? This is stupid; they are just saying this now." At that very moment, when the whole thing started, I don't remember their reaction.

INTERVIEWER: What do you remember about the wars?

RÁCZ: In 1991, if we count that as the beginning, I was ten. By then, my parents were already divorced, and my father lived here in this village. He quit his job, and it's not really clear if it was because there were some huge political things in the television [station where he worked]. Some people from the side of [Slobodan] Milošević were installed as editors in chief, so a lot of his colleagues left willingly, and most of them went to Hungary. My father left later, not in 1991, but I don't remember when. I don't know if he got fired or if he left willingly. I don't remember.

I remember poverty, but I also remember that we were a bit more well off. I mean, we weren't well off, but we had some access to some things that other kids didn't, at least the kids around me. Because my father was then working as a freelancer for a television [station] in Budapest, he would go there once every two months to pick up his salary; there was no online banking then. He would go by train, or sometimes he would drive, and then he would do some big shopping and basically spend all of that money on food. I remember having cheese. It was cheap cheese, but then it was something. In general, every morning I would eat bread with margarine and cheese. I remember I hated it, and then of course my mom being like, "A lot of kids don't even have cheese." Now I think [that] most of my classmates were really poor. I think nobody was really well connected. In my generation, a lot of kids had divorced parents like myself, and a lot of people in my class were living with single moms, so I guess that contributed also.

And I remember of course standing in lines for stuff. I remember that we had one teacher, a history teacher, who was very strict, and we were afraid of him. We had history class in the morning, and he came to school late one day, and he was like, "Sorry kids, I had to stand in line for bread." And even though this was a normal thing, I was just like, "Fuck, even teachers have to do this." It was like his authority crumbled down with this, like, "Oh, teachers are humans; they stand in lines." And I also heard that some teachers were selling stuff in the market. My relatives are from a village, and they used to sell in the market. But they're farmers. For a teacher to sell stuff at the market was horrible. So that was really sort of connected with [my understanding that] this was not a normal state. This was something exceptional.

INTERVIEWER: Do you remember if there were any other changes to your everyday life as the wars continued and as Yugoslavia disintegrated? Was there anything else that you noticed that was changing at home, at school, or around Zrenjanin?

RÁCZ: Most of the things were financial, like we had less and less money. We had less money, sometimes a bit less, sometimes a bit more, but generally little. And then the big changes only happened in 1999 with the NATO bombing, when I went to Hungary. That's another story. But until then, from 1991 until 1999, I think it was more or less the same. You go to school; you have your friends. Everybody has little money. When I was in high school, I would go out on Fridays and Saturdays. I remember we had money for one drink, sometimes two, and it was completely normal. I remember seeing some people in military uniform in the street, and I remember my parents telling me, like, "Oh, be careful, these people might be drunk or something; they might have come home from the war." And I think I remember I was afraid of them. Sometimes if I saw somebody in a military uniform, I would go to the other side of the street. But other than that, I don't remember any changes other than the poverty.

INTERVIEWER: Did you notice any administrative or political changes as the boundaries of the state changed from Yugoslavia, then to a smaller version of Yugoslavia, and then to Serbia?

RÁCZ: At one period, we always had to take out new IDs, but it was a minor inconvenience, nothing "wow." Everybody was doing this. When you are a teenager, you have so much time, and it's actually one day you don't have to go to school because you have to go to change your ID. It wasn't a big thing.

INTERVIEWER: How long did you continue to live in the former Yugoslavia or in the region? You mentioned that you went to Hungary in 1999.

RÁCZ: I went there, but only for the period of the bombing. The bombing started in March, so I was there until the summer. Then I went back. That was only for four or five months. I remember when I went to Szeged. My sister lived in a village next to Szeged at that time, and she was super afraid. She wanted to come home [to Zrenjanin]. Instead of telling her to come home, which would have been completely stupid, of course, my parents sent me there. I was there, and it was interesting, but I didn't really want to go. I remember, my father was like, "Oh, you should enroll in school there." I was just like, "No, I didn't want to come here, so the only way I stay here is that I don't go to school." My generation not so much, but a lot of [younger] Hungarian kids who were in first or second grade of high school left [Yugoslavia] and stayed [abroad].

Then I left [Zrenjanin] when I finished high school, so one year after all this. I went to do this prep year in Budapest. Then I studied English language and literature in Szeged, which is in the south of Hungary. Then I came back, and left again, and came back, and left again. Since then, I'm basically in and out of Yugoslavia, Serbia, or whatever the name was.

INTERVIEWER: Which of those places feels like home, if any?

RÁCZ: None, really. I think it's only Zrenjanin and this village where I live—even not so much this village, but this house. Home is mostly Zrenjanin for me. I can imagine myself living in other places like Novi Sad [now Serbia].

Figure 2.3. Krisztina Rácz with friends in Budapest during her preparatory year. *Courtesy of Krisztina Rácz.*

Even though I don't really like that city, I could easily get by. I lived briefly in Belgrade [now Serbia], and that was fine even though it wasn't as homey as what I was used to. I lived three times for one year each in Budapest. At that time, it did feel like home, but I wouldn't say it does anymore because most of the people I was socializing with in those periods are not there anymore. I don't go back that often. I would say that still, outside Vojvodina, not even Belgrade is home.

INTERVIEWER: When you are elsewhere, how do you introduce yourself? Where do you say you come from? How do you present yourself, either nationally or culturally or ethnically?

RÁCZ: Well, it depends on the question. If the question is "Where are you from?" I just say I'm from Serbia. People never ask me, "What's your ethnicity?" But if somehow that's the implied question, then I say Hungarian. Nine out of ten times, I add that I'm from Serbia. If they ask me in Hungary, then it's clear if we're speaking Hungarian that I am a Hungarian from Serbia. If they ask me in the US, I just say I'm from Serbia. Sometimes in some places like Austria or Germany, if I have this feeling that they have enough cultural knowledge that my name doesn't look Serbian, I say [that I'm Hungarian from Serbia]. So it depends on who asked the question.

INTERVIEWER: How would you identify yourself ethnically, culturally, or nationally?

RÁCZ: Hungarian from Serbia.

INTERVIEWER: Did you ever identify as Yugoslav? Or present yourself as a Yugoslav?

RÁCZ: No, no, I don't think I ever have. At the time when it was actually Yugoslavia, I was too small to think about these things. This wasn't an option in my family either. It wasn't like a horrible thing, but as I said, my parents didn't identify as [Yugoslav]. I know a lot of people who are my generation and who insist on this Yugoslav thing. In a way, I can relate to that. I do have some Yugonostalgic things, of course, but I'm not one of those hardcore Yugonostalgic people. I don't think I will ever be. I don't see it as a valid identity anymore. You can say of course that you would like to live in a different time, in a different state that is now nonexistent, but I think it simply makes no sense to claim an identity of a country that doesn't exist. Of course I understand what it means. It's an ideological statement and in a way a grievance for lost privileges, but it's just not my thing, probably partly because I never had some of those privileges.

INTERVIEWER: What are you nostalgic for when it comes to Yugoslavia? You mentioned you have some nostalgia.

RÁCZ: Well, mostly popular culture things like music, movies, and stuff like that. And also the fact that you live in a big country, like relatively big, which has the sea and the mountains and everything. You can travel from one end of the country to the other, and it takes a lot of time. It is different, I think, if the seaside is in your country than if you have to go abroad for holidays. I don't know why I feel that. Now Croatia is something in between because it is familiar and you know the language, but you're still abroad.

But, what else? Maybe just because I was a kid, but I think people were a little bit more open minded, which comes from not having all these experiences that came with the war and nationalism. Maybe [it also comes from] traveling more, living in a bigger country, and seeing more things. From today's perspective, it looks like people were a bit more open to different people and new experiences and doing things in different ways.

INTERVIEWER: When you say that people are nostalgic for Yugoslavia as an ideological statement, what kind of statement do you think they're trying to make?

RÁCZ: Good question. It's not that simple! Well, ideologically, they are [trying to suggest that they are] socialist. Not socialist in general, but one particular type of socialism which was the Yugoslav self-governing socialism. They see that as superior to other types of socialism, and of course they see socialism as superior to capitalism. And [they are also trying to suggest] this very vague thing of believing in brotherhood and unity and some sort of solidarity with people from the other former Yugoslav republics. Yeah, I think these two things.

INTERVIEWER: What does the idea of Yugoslavia or the manifestation of Yugoslavia mean to you now?

RÁCZ: Well, it is basically these two things that I mentioned that these people who identify as such believe in. For me, [it is] this belief in the possibility of socialism as a self-government. And it's a very unique set of social practices that come with that, like taking part in all these meetings, even at a smaller level, like at the workplace, and voting for things, which were often very formalist in nature. I think that was one of the ideas. The other was this brotherhood and unity thing, [with] solidarity and equality between nations and nationalities. Again, it's disputable how much of it was real or not, or formal or not only. I really feel that a lot in these leftist circles, so to say, even today, in the former Yugoslavia, especially in Serbia, [hold] some sense of superiority over other countries of the Eastern bloc. I don't think people were aware of that at that time when they were living it, but from today's perspective and especially from people who would identify as Yugoslav from my generation, plus or minus ten years, it's present.

INTERVIEWER: Do you think that growing up in Yugoslavia shaped your childhood and who you are today in any particular way?

RÁCZ: Yeah, definitely. Especially in those first ten years, the language thing was a huge, huge thing. That you simply lived in a country where your language is not the most spoken one, that's a big thing. In Hungary, it would have been a whole different experience. That teaches you a lot, like that you are maybe a bit different, that you have another community of people like you. And it also teaches you that you have to fight a bit more for things which are given, like to have your name entered on your ID as it is officially written, things that a lot of people don't even think about. I'm not saying it is a bad thing; I think it's good that you have to be aware of your rights and that you have to be able to articulate them. So it teaches you a more straightforward approach to things, at least in my case. You simply have to ask for certain things or demand some things.

This popular culture—the music and the movies and everything—I think it does have quite a huge effect on what you become. I grew up on Serbian popular culture, or Yugoslav, I mean. I was always reading in Hungarian, but music and TV were in Serbian. This is a total cliché, but the kids might speak a different language and everything, but at the end of the day, it's all the same.

INTERVIEWER: When you are abroad, are you interested in making connections with other people who are from Serbia or Yugoslavia? Or do you gravitate towards folks who are Hungarian?

RÁCZ: It really plays out well at conferences, which are now online. But when they used to be in person, I was thinking a lot about it. And again, I can only attribute it to this cultural knowledge thing, but it's always somehow this Yugo crowd that I end up with, which is surprising to me. It is just what I said, that it's very important, at least in my case, what you grew up with. And of course, in these semiprofessional settings, you don't talk exclusively about films and cartoons and stuff like that, but somehow things like the jokes and the humor [become part of the conversation]. After a conference, it would never occur to me to go and have a drink with Hungarians, like never. I guess it could happen if we really click on a professional thing, but I always end up with the Serbs or Croats or whatever. So yeah, the answer is pretty clear.

INTERVIEWER: When you are connecting with folks who are from the former Yugoslav region, what do you call the language that you speak with them?

RÁCZ: At conferences and with semiacademic or academic friends, people who are ideologically similar to me, they would all call it *naš* ["our"] in order to avoid naming it. I speak Serbian really well, but it's not my first language, so I would never call it *naš*. I was actually joking with a friend, like, "Shall I call it *vaš* ['yours']?" Usually in a crowd [of] leftist Serbs, let's put it that way, highly educated, left-leaning Serbian people, I would be the only one who calls the language *srpski* [Serbian] because everybody would just call it *naš*. Actually, one thing I learned from the former director of the institute where I work [is that] he calls it *ovaj jezik* ["this language"]. For instance, we were having a discussion in Serbian about the language in which a conference would be held, and he said "*hoćemo imati konferenciju na ovom jeziku ili na engleskom?*" ["should we hold the conference in this language or in English?"]. So it's like, "In this language, the language that I am speaking at the moment." So actually, this came to me as a good solution. I don't need to name it. I don't have a problem with naming it, but sometimes I've thought that people around me feel the difference that I am the only one who is naming it. If I really want to neutralize it, then I just say *na ovom jeziku*.

INTERVIEWER: In a way, you're saying that this is not necessarily my language, this is your language.

RÁCZ: Yeah, yeah, yeah, yeah. Often it's only if I make this joke—"Shall I call it *vaš?*"—that these otherwise very smart people become aware of these language hegemonies. I think that's why they sometimes feel uneasy when they declare the elephant in the room—that this language is not ours, it's theirs. Several years ago, there was this big initiative to have this declaration of the common language. So these academics—not just linguists, but a lot of linguists—from the former Yugoslavia had this declaration to say this is one language from the perspective of language, but they were also implying other things as well. A lot of people were signing it among my acquaintances as well, and I felt a bit uneasy to sign it because it's not my language. If I was a linguist, maybe I would be able to sign it, but even in terms of linguistics, there are pro and con arguments. I felt a bit like, "OK, it's their thing." And also, in the declaration, there is some vague sentence, I can't remember it now, which says something like, "We are all speakers of the same common South-Slavic language." But I'm not a Slav. It's fine, you can call it a common language, you can call it *naš*, whatever. But I'm not the one to decide. For me, the language I speak is Serbian.

INTERVIEWER: Do you think that there is a similarity in your relationship toward language and the idea of Yugoslavia?

RÁCZ: I have the cultural knowledge, but it's, like, your thing. I can relate to it, but you play Yugoslavs. I can observe, I can understand, but I don't have a right to be part of it. But also, I don't want to be part of it. It's a bit of both. I never felt excluded from it. I think in certain leftist circles in Belgrade, actually, it's a super cool thing to be a Yugonostalgic Hungarian. It actually even adds to your legitimacy. It's not because I didn't feel welcome. I don't want to be part of this. I don't feel I am.

INTERVIEWER: Do you feel welcome in the current Serbian state?

RÁCZ: Good question. No, but also I'm not sure it has to do with me being Hungarian. The current party—the Vojvodina Hungarian Alliance, that's the official name—which is officially representing Hungarians is in a super good coalition with the Serbian government [and] the governing party, so no problems there. Hungarians are accepted as a legitimate part of this country and have certain collective rights. Also, it's important that I speak the Serbian language well. I know the cultural stuff. I get by. I have friends who are Serbian. I'm really not a person the state can point at. I do my duties. I know my rights. I'm integrated to the level they want me to be integrated. I don't cause problems. But I think all citizens here are second-rate citizens except a few very rich people. I don't think that I do super critical stuff as an academic, and I don't think the Serbian state is very interested in what I do. But if we add that element of ideology, I'm definitely not on the right side.

INTERVIEWER: Thank you, Krisztina, for joining me.

RÁCZ: Thank you.

3

INTERVIEW WITH
Artan Sadiku

Artan Sadiku was born and raised in Tetovo (now North Macedonia) in 1983. He studied in other European countries and the United States, then traveled extensively through the former Yugoslav region as the founder of the Culture Club Syndicate and an activist with the leftist group Solidarnost. When we spoke over a video call in early 2023, he was working as a contemporary art curator and living in Skopje (now North Macedonia). In our conversation, he reflected on his experiences in Yugoslavia and the transition to post-socialism as a member of Macedonia's ethnic Albanian community. Sadiku spoke about the opportunities the Yugoslav state extended to his family and how he continued to benefit from them. The most important inheritances Sadiku took from Yugoslavia, however, were ideological. He explained that he found meaning in the former state's "drive toward experimentation" and its pillars of solidarity and social justice. He imagined Yugoslavia as a valuable blueprint for the region's development.

    Sadiku remembered his earliest years in unified Yugoslavia fondly. His parents were gainfully employed, his family frequently traveled abroad, and he was well integrated into local society. Ethnic Albanians were often socially, economically, and spatially segregated in postwar Yugoslavia, and this was the case in Tetovo, a city with a proportionally large Albanian community. Sadiku attended a parallel stream Albanian-language school, but because his parents were highly educated, he lived in a neighborhood that was predominantly ethnically Macedonian. As a result, he grew up as a bilingual member of both Albanian and Macedonian communities. Thinking back on his childhood friends, Sadiku said that "differences were not present... even many years later when we were all grown up and in high school, even during and after the war in Macedonia in 2001. Those friendships remain even up to now. Locally, the neighborhoods developed their own sense of cultural understanding, solidarity, and tolerance." He described neighbors sharing holiday meals and rituals without much concern over one another's ethnicity.

Macedonia's independence and post-socialist transition bisected Sadiku's childhood. His recollections of the 1990s were grim due to widespread poverty and ripple effects of war and unrest in other regions of the former state. Like many Macedonians, Sadiku's parents lost their jobs as companies privatized. "This was a very tough period because we were very poor," he explained. "[It was the same for] some other families and kids that I knew from school. This economic depletion was one significant thing that left a lot of impact on me. I remember that I grew up [worrying whether] my parents would have other jobs, how we would live, how we would feed ourselves." In addition, Sadiku recalled that hundreds of thousands of refugees from the Bosnian War came to Macedonia in the first part of the decade; several years later, another massive wave of refugees arrived from the Kosovo War. Although there was no armed conflict in Macedonia during the Yugoslav wars, nationalism was on the rise across the region. Serbia curtailed the rights of Albanians in Kosovo in the late 1980s and continued to impose restrictions in the 1990s, which mounted tensions among Albanian communities across the former Yugoslavia. "These were times of uncertainty," Sadiku said. "At this age, we knew there was no more Yugoslavia but also that there was still tension in the air.... There were refugees, a lot of police and special units in Kosovo, international soldiers and peacekeepers. I grew up with this gloomy presence in the 1990s. And then there was the Kosovo War." The uncertainty continued further for Sadiku, until the conflict in Macedonia in 2001.

Even with the detrimental impacts of its dissolution, Yugoslavia had a formative effect on Sadiku. Most importantly, he underlined that the opportunities his parents received from the state shaped the course of his life. Sadiku's father, who was from a rural family, was able to earn a university education and, from there, receive placement in an administrative job at a factory. Sadiku's mother, who was from an urban family, was also educated and employed. The family lived in a state-owned apartment in Tetovo, which Sadiku understood as a social benefit that, in addition to other benefits like health care, enabled them to live comfortably. Although few Macedonians are nostalgic for the time of Yugoslavia, many nevertheless recognize that socialism gave them a high standard of life. Sadiku told me that his father, for instance, spoke positively about Yugoslavia. "He usually praised it [because] he benefited a lot from it," he said. "He got free schooling. He got an apartment. He got a job. He could start a family without the hassles of trying to find housing." Sadiku shared a similar appreciation for the former state; he understood that his family's social mobility enabled him to study, work, and live at a higher social standard today.

As we spoke, Sadiku reflected critically on Yugoslavia. On the one hand, he celebrated it as "a noble process of experimentation," particularly in the realm of economics. "I think the biggest value of Yugoslavia was experimenting with different models, even though most of them failed," he said. Sadiku also discussed the state's support of housing, health care, and well-being as major social goods that improved citizens' lived experience. On the other hand, he pointed out many flaws, such as nationalism and authoritarianism, that marred Yugoslavia. Overall, he found meaning in the vision of the future the state offered its citizens. "Yugoslavia to me today is a vision which was not realized," Sadiku explained. "Yugoslavia was a very good vision, and not only for me. It was globally respected, valued, and adored. I experienced it like that. Now if I close my eyes and imagine that Yugoslavia is back there and they are still experimenting and doing new things and trying out new things, I can imagine my life is better than this muck we are still in." The Yugoslav ideals he found appealing were socialist ones like antifascism and solidarity. Moreover, Sadiku was drawn to the framework of a large state in the Balkans that was not as "claustrophobic" as successor states felt to him. "When we had the whole Yugoslavia as one political and territorial entity, we could travel freely and exchange cultural values and products," Sadiku recalled. "These small countries also have failing social and health care systems. If there was a huge country with much more capacity [to provide for its citizens], our lives would be much better. A united space would be tremendously advantageous, which is a thing that I really lack and miss." According to a survey conducted by a Croatian poll agency in 2011, 43.3 percent of Macedonian citizens regret the breakup of Yugoslavia, compared to 70.9 percent of Serbians and only 5 percent of Kosovars.[1] Like Sadiku, most Macedonians did not want to return to the time of Yugoslavia but did see the potential in what it once offered. For Sadiku, those Yugoslav ideals continue to offer valuable models for the future of the region.

INTERVIEWER: What are your earliest childhood memories?

SADIKU: Both of my parents worked for state-owned factories. My father worked at metal industry factory, and my mother worked at a factory that produced plastic medical equipment for hospitals. Both were [typical] working parents in Yugoslavia who had received an apartment from the state.

---

1. Milekic, "Rise of Yugo-Nostalgia 'Reflects Contemporary Problems.'"

Most of the kids in my kindergarten were Macedonian, [maybe] 98 percent of them. In the Albanian community, [it was common for] grandparents to take care of kids [instead of] sending them to kindergarten. It was also very rare for Albanian families to live in apartments given by the state in this particular city. They inherited houses from their parents and lived in those houses. I lived in an apartment block which was about 90 percent Macedonian.[2] When I went to primary school, the students were predominantly Albanian.[3] I learned both languages—Albanian and Macedonian—in parallel, and I was bilingual from birth.[4]

---

2. Socialism disproportionately served Macedonians during the postwar period, privileging them in upward mobility. This disparity reinforced social, economic, and spatial segregation between Macedonians and Albanians. Albanians were also not as eager to integrate into Yugoslav society due to mistrust of the state and its reforms. Scholar Robert Pichler suggests that fewer Albanians migrated from rural to urban spaces and that those who did tended to live in ethnically segregated neighborhoods (Pichler, "In the Shadow of Kosovo," 299).

3. According to the 1981 Yugoslav census, Macedonia had a population of just under two million. Macedonians constituted 67 percent of the population, Albanians 19.8 percent, Turks 6.6 percent, Serbs 2.8 percent, Roma 1.5 percent, and other groups like Aromanians, Bulgarians, Croats, Montenegrins, and Muslims constituted the remainder. Tetovo had a relatively larger Albanian community. In 1981, Albanians constituted 46.7 percent, Macedonians 38.3 percent, Turks 5.9 percent, Roma 3.7 percent, Serbs 1.9 percent, and other small groups made up the remainder of Tetovo's population of 46,523 residents. Macedonia's constitution recognized Turkish and Albanian, in addition to those recognized by the Yugoslav state, thus stipulating that citizens must have access to education in these languages. In 1981, there were seventy-four thousand students enrolled in Albanian language primary schools and eighty-two thousand students enrolled in Albanian language secondary schools in Macedonia, which largely met the needs of the community. However, Serbian retaliation against Albanians in Kosovo in the late 1980s had serious repercussions for Albanians in Macedonia: the state restricted access to Albanian-language instruction across Yugoslavia when it mandated that classes only be offered in communities with thirty or more enrolled students (Tanevski, "The Problem between the Macedonian and Albanian Ethnic Groups in the Republic of Macedonia and Its Future").

4. After the 2001 Ohrid Agreement between Macedonia and representatives of the Albanian minority, languages spoken by more than 20% of the population in any given municipality were designated as co-official languages at the municipal level. Since 2019, Albanian has been made a co-official language of the entire state rather than just of certain municipalities. While Albanians are now guaranteed access to education in Albanian, including university education, the state still employs a double standard for language education. Namely, students attend parallel Macedonian-language and Albanian-language schools where Albanians study Macedonian but Macedonians rarely study Albanian. Scholar Aryn Bloodworth suggests that this perpetuates ethnic divisions in society and discusses recent proposals for integrated interethnic education (Bloodworth, "Educational (De)Segregation in North Macedonia," 311). Moreover, because Macedonian has remained the official administrative language of the state, Albanians have effectively been obligated to be bilingual (Rugova, "The Status of Albanian in Relation to other Balkan Languages," 145).

My earliest memory is of my parents taking me and my brother, who is two years younger, to kindergarten. They had to wake us up early to go to the kindergarten so they could get to work. We did not live close to our grandparents [who could take care of us]. My grandparents from my mother's side lived in a different part of city, and my grandparents from my father's side lived in a village. To reach my father's factory, which was around fifteen kilometers away, outside the city, they had to leave for work around six or six thirty a.m., so they had to wake us up at five thirty a.m. I remember this as a sort of torture when I was small. Sometimes, to spare time in the morning, we used to go to sleep in the clothes that we would wear to kindergarten [the next day]. We would arrive forty-five minutes before the ladies that took care of the kids in kindergarten. There was a wooden bench, and me and my brother and two other poor kids sat there waiting for the kindergarten to officially open. There would only be a guard there, *čicko* Trajfo, and I remember he made Turkish coffee every day. I saw him every day up until I went to primary school.

When our parents picked us up, we went home on foot because we lived very close to the kindergarten. There was a huge supermarket called Tetovchanka on the way back, and our parents would buy us chocolate every day as a reward for another day in the kindergarten.

It was still Yugoslavia when I was in first grade. That was when we got the Pioneer clothes and hat, but then Yugoslavia fell apart. Everybody was disappointed. They said, "Ah, we didn't become Pioneers. It's a pity." Our cousins had pictures of becoming Pioneers that they put in frames and [displayed] at home. We knew that there would have been some sort of inauguration ceremony that [signaled] you were now something other than a kindergarten kid. Everybody was sad. Some teachers tried to stage something like a Pioneer parade, but parents said that they didn't want it anymore. I kept the Pioneer clothes until very recently, but then I lost them.

INTERVIEWER: You mentioned that you went to a predominantly Macedonian kindergarten and a predominantly Albanian primary school. How did you experience those two spaces?

SADIKU: I hung around with Macedonian kids all the time in the neighborhood where I lived. I played football, and I was the captain of the football team in the neighborhood. When we played against the other neighborhood, which was all Albanian, they tried to insult me by calling me *Shkije*, a derogatory term for Slavs. It's used in Kosovo and in Macedonia, like *Šiptar* [is used as a derogatory term] for Albanians.[5]

When I enrolled in primary school, I remember that there was a movement by Albanian parents and teachers to change the school's name from Bratstvo-edinstvo [Brotherhood and Unity] to the name of Millosh Gjergj Nikolla Migjeni, an Albanian poet of Montenegrin descent.[6] There was tension in the school, and there were inspectors and policemen who came to interview parents and kids. After a year of irregular classes, there was a compromise. The school was named Bratstvo-Migjeni, which is utterly stupid. This was in line with the political tensions of the time.

My parents were quite enthusiastic about me becoming some sort of skilled and successful kid. They enrolled me in [supplementary] courses, so I went to private guitar, math, and English language classes after school, which were actually cheap. I was constantly around some sort of educational activity during the day. I remember also being enrolled in this environmental group at school. We cleaned up the school and started to [develop] some initial environmentalist courses.

INTERVIEWER: Do you remember if people were treated differently in any way?

SADIKU: No, at this time there was no difference. I remember that we sometimes ate meals at the houses of other kids. The mother of Dragan and Djordje, for example, would pick me up and say, "Come eat! You haven't eaten in a while." But I remember my mother would also [remind me], "Beware that they don't give you pork and tell them that you don't eat pork." My family didn't practice Islam, but they also didn't eat pork. I wasn't aware of this [nuance] when I was growing up, but it was heritage. So these differences were not present.

---

5. In Albanian, the word *Shqiptar* is an adjective that means "Albanian." In Macedonian (as well as in Bosnian/Croatian/Montenegrin/Serbian), the word *Šiptar* is a pejorative term for Albanians. However, scholar Vasiliski Neofotistos shows that Albanian men in postsocialist Macedonian society have reclaimed and reappropriated the word to signify their own comradery when addressing one another (Neofotistos, "Postsocialism, Social Value, and Identity Politics among Albanians in Macedonia," 882–902). In the early twentieth century, Albanians in and out of Yugoslavia used the word *Šiptar* to signify their own national and linguistic identity. After World War II, the Yugoslav state used *Šiptarski* to denote the Geg-based standard of Albanian language spoken in Yugoslavia from the Tosk-based standard spoken in Albania (referred to as *Albanski*) as well as to decouple the Yugoslav Albanian community's identity from the Albanian one. The term acquired a pejorative association following the rise of Albanian agitation for rights in Yugoslavia and the adoption of Albanian Tosk as the language spoken in Yugoslavia.

6. Millosh Gjergj Nikolla (1911–1938), known by his pen name Migjeni, was an Albanian poet and writer. His work was popularized in communist Albania.

Differences were not present even many years later when we were all grown up and in high school, even during and after the war in Macedonia in 2001. Those friendships remain even up to now. Locally, the neighborhoods developed their own sense of cultural understanding, solidarity, and tolerance. When there were Christian celebrations like *Veligden*, or Easter, [neighbors who celebrated] would give us red eggs.[7] [There was] an old lady who would extend a stick with a plastic bag filled with red eggs from one balcony to another to give them out. My mother would [similarly] give neighbors baklava for *Bajram*.[8] So difference was not present at this time.

INTERVIEWER: Do you remember learning about Yugoslavia in school?

SADIKU: No, it was all completely wiped out [by the time I started primary school]. I don't remember any content. There were no pictures of Tito on the wall anymore. There was no [Yugoslav] insignia. The teachers taught the courses without any mention of Yugoslavia. In high school, [Yugoslav history] was more present, but not in primary school. We had two teachers who were Macedonian. The teacher of physical education was a Macedonian named Jani. We also had a Macedonian teacher who taught us Macedonian language and didn't mention any content that related to Yugoslavia. I think this was the same for both Albanians and Macedonians. It's weird because later, when I got to know other people from Yugoslavia, [I saw that] Yugoslav heritage was kept more alive in [places like] Serbia and some parts of Croatia.[9] In Macedonia, it was derelict the day Macedonia declared its independence. I remember people threw away tons of books from the universities in Skopje that were [related to] Marxism and stuff like that.

---

7. While socialist Yugoslavia was officially a secular state, some citizens continued to observe religious celebrations privately. Christian Orthodox communities traditionally dyed eggs red on Easter, and Sadiku suggested that some of his neighbors continued to do so during the socialist period. Since the collapse of Yugoslavia, religion has had a more prominent place in society. According to the 2021 census, 60.4 percent of the population of North Macedonia identified as Christian (primarily Christian Orthodox) and 32.2 percent as Muslim.

8. In Macedonia, Eid al-Fitr is known as *Ramazan Bajram*, and it is a national holiday. However, it is important to note that Albanians in the Balkans also practice Catholicism and Orthodoxy. Scholar Aydin Babuna suggests that ethnicity and language were distinct and thus more important vectors of identity than religion for Albanians in Macedonia, Kosovo, and elsewhere. In contrast, religion was the primary differentiation between Bosnian Muslims, or Bosniaks, and their Serb and Croat neighbors (Babuna, "The Albanians of Kosovo and Macedonia," 67–92).

9. Scholar Pål Kolstø conducted a large-scale qualitative survey of citizens of successor states in 2001 that showed that Yugonostalgia manifested most in Serbia and Bosnia. In Croatia, the survey showed a continued attachment to socialist symbols but not the state itself. The survey showed the lowest manifestation of Yugonostalgia in Macedonia (Kolstø, "Identifying with the Old or the New State," 760–81).

INTERVIEWER: You mentioned that both of your parents benefited from some state-sponsored programs and worked for the state. Can you tell me more about their experience in Yugoslavia?

SADIKU: Yeah, it was interesting. The [social] position in which my brother and I are now in is quite different from the position of my cousins, who are the kids of my father's six brothers. This is because my father was from a village where neither of my grandparents were educated and could [afford] for only one of their kids to go to school. Because my father had the best grades in primary and secondary school, they decided they would send him to study in Sarajevo. So my father finished [a degree in] political science in Sarajevo. The region of Tetovo had many factories: a textile factory, a wood processing factory, and a metal industry factory. All of my father's brothers and their kids—my cousins who are older than me—work in these factories. Or they work as sewer workers or miners or stuff like that.

After finishing his degree in Sarajevo, my father went back to Tetovo. It was then the practice to register with the employment office and become a member of the local branch of the [communist] party. The party [assigned him] to a position in the administration of the metal industry factory. He moved from the village to the city because he was given [by the state] this apartment where I was born. He worked in HR in that factory up until his retirement because he received benefits even as an unemployed person when the factory was going through bankruptcy in the 1990s.

The other factory [in Tetovo], the one that produced medical equipment for hospitals, was under [the administration of] his factory. So my father interviewed anyone who wanted to work at that factory too. My father interviewed my mother for a job in the factory, and after the interview, he invited her to coffee, and blah-blah-blah. That's how that happened. My mother came from an urban family. My grandfather, her father, was a teacher in a secondary school, and he was at one point also the director of the secondary school. He sent two of his sons to the law faculty, but my mother was like, "Nah, I'm better off to get a job." She finished the medical high school and then went straight to a job after my father interviewed her.

INTERVIEWER: Do you remember how your parents related to Yugoslavia?

SADIKU: My mother has a nonrelationship to Yugoslavia, but my father spoke about it a lot. He actually loved Yugoslavia. He usually praised it [because] he benefited a lot from it. He got free schooling. He got an apartment. He got a job. He could start a family without the hassles of trying to find housing and stuff. He also traveled through Yugoslavia.

My father studied political science during Yugoslavia, and he was a very strong Marxist. He had very strong attitudes towards Yugoslavia. Up until recently, he would say things like, "These kinds of things would never happen in Yugoslavia! These assholes would be sent to jail if they did this kind of corruption in Yugoslavia. Yugoslavia was very respected. With a Yugoslav passport, I could go to Germany and Russia. And we did not pay for health care. We did not pay for housing." After the bankruptcy of the factories, we had to buy the apartment which was given [to him] by the state.[10] His hatred towards the new government increased then, as did his positive attitudes towards Yugoslavia before everything started to fall apart.

INTERVIEWER: Do you remember how your parents talked about Yugoslavia with you?

SADIKU: My father had a positive attitude towards Yugoslavia, but [he was also a realist]. He'd say, "That's gone now, so you have to focus on this new competitive market. You have to be the best. This is why we are taking you to different courses to explore all the possibilities for your development." Although he had a lot of positive attitudes towards Yugoslavia, he was convinced that Yugoslavia was never going to come back. Later, when I was involved with these leftist movements and Marxist and neo-Marxist theories, he was like, "Why are you doing this? It's gone. It was good, but it's gone. It's never going to come back. Why don't you pursue some MBA or business education? Why neo-Marxism?"

INTERVIEWER: Were you aware of your family being mixed in any way?

SADIKU: No, but there was a class [difference] because the family of my father came from the village, and my mother's family was from the city. They always had this distance with my father's family. They would not invite them

---

10. After the collapse of socialism and the breakup of Yugoslavia, the newly independent Macedonia transitioned to a market economy. Apartments that had once been socially owned were privatized, and residents were offered the opportunity to buy them. According to scholars Jasna Mariotti and Daniel Baldwin Hess, 95 percent of Macedonia's housing stock was privatized in the 1990s (Mariotti and Hess, "Enlargement of Apartments in Socialist Housing Estates in Skopje under Transition," 45).

to dinners, and they would not go to dinners when they were invited to the village. They maintained this class difference. Other than that, there was no heterogeneousness in my family. Actually, there were not many mixed families in Tetovo. It was quite ethnically and religiously [segregated]. There were no mixed marriages like there were in Bosnia.[11]

Another thing that I actually remember now [is that] there was a box with pictures that I was always very curious about. We kept that box in the basement. Then maybe twenty years later, I was home texting with an ex-girlfriend from Belgrade, and she asked me, "Is Izair Sadiki somehow related to you?" I said, "Yeah, he's my father." And she was like, "Wow, I'm here with my sociology teacher Ilinka in Sarajevo, and she just told me that she was with your father for six years." So this box [of photos] contained pictures of Ilinka. She was the big love of my father. He wanted to bring her to Tetovo to live there, but the environment was not supportive of this, so they had to break up. He went on to marry my mother. Ilinka sent a long Facebook message for my father [at one point], and I gave it to him to read on the night before my brother's wedding.

INTERVIEWER: Did religion play a role in your life when you were growing up?

SADIKU: No, not even in the families on my father's or mother's side. They celebrated the two religious holidays: *Bajram*, and some of them fasted [for

---

11. As Sadiku suggested, the rate of intermarriage among groups reflected the degree of social distance between them. In Macedonia, where Albanians were often segregated socially and economically—neighborhoods were ethnically divided, and students attended separate stream Albanian-language schools—there were few opportunities for interaction among ethnic Albanians and ethnic Macedonians. According to the 1981 Yugoslav census, 13.1 percent of all registered marriages in the federal state were ethnically mixed. However, only 1.8 percent of Albanians who married that year had a partner of another ethnic background, and that rate gradually decreased during the postwar decades. Scholar Jeroen Smits suggests that intermarriage promotes social cohesion and deters violent conflict, interpreting the low intermarriage of Albanians as reflective of the community's disenfranchisement and disappointment within Yugoslavia (Smits, "Ethnic Marriage and Social Cohesion," 417–32). Scholar Rozita Dimova argues that the low rates of intermarriage in Macedonia can be understood as resistance to assimilation campaigns. "So far, there have been few marriages between ethnic Macedonians and Albanians, thus demonstrating that Albanians have been largely successful at maintaining the 'purity' of their lineage," Dimova writes. "Nevertheless, the few mixed marriages, along with a small number of mixed liaisons and relationships, especially where they occur between ethnic Albanian women and ethnic Macedonian men, have generated inordinate fear among ethnic Albanians. The official goal of ethnic Albanians in Macedonia has begun to turn from 'integration' in Macedonian society to 'protection' of their 'Albanian-ness'" (Dimova, "'Modern' Masculinities," 317–18).

Ramadan]. But none of them went to mosque, prayed, or followed religious procedures. None of my family members wore a headscarf or anything like that. I think religion played probably a bigger role in some other regions. In this area around Tetovo, it was kind of insignificant. It had a traditional presence, but people didn't practice it. I know that later, when I was in high school, some of the students started to become more religious, and we were suspicious of them. They started to wear longer beards and to form small groups. [There were some] foreign influences, and some teachers recruited kids. Apart from this, there was no strong religious presence in my upbringing.

I never attended or participated in any strong religious ceremony. Of course, my brother and I underwent *syneti*, a circumcision ceremony.[12] This was probably the most religious thing that I participated in. My brother and I watched through a peephole while an imam said the prayers. We knew that when he stopped the prayer, they would do the circumcision. It was not painful at all, but it was traumatizing [anticipating] what they were going to do.

INTERVIEWER: Were you aware of the Yugoslav wars starting in other parts of the country?

SADIKU: It was a tragic period. We were worried. We started to receive refugees from Bosnia after one and a half years.[13] My parents housed some refugees in the house of my grandmother in Tetovo. There was war, but I didn't quite understand the dynamics as a seven-year-old. I know that there was talk in the city.

Then this whole process of disintegration of Yugoslavia took place in Bosnia, in Croatia, and a little bit in Slovenia with the war. I remember that me and my brother would stand on the balcony of our apartment

---

12. In the Balkans, Muslim communities mark the circumcision of boys, *syneti*, with lavish celebrations that denote a rite of passage into adulthood. Because there is no prescribed age for circumcision in Islam—unlike in Judaism, where it is performed on the eighth day of a baby's life—boys are usually circumcised between the ages of five and fourteen.

13. During the Bosnian War, 360,000 refugees, most of them Bosnian Muslims, fled to Macedonia. This amounted to about 20 percent of the population of Macedonia at the time. The state opened fourteen refugee camps that sheltered about half of the refugees, and Macedonian citizens accommodated the other half in private houses. According to scholar Maja Muhić, Albanians were at the forefront of assisting Bosnian Muslim refugees despite being ethnically and linguistically different from them (Muhić, "Spiritual Assistance during Two Refugee Crises in the Republic of Macedonia," 75–92).

for hours and watch military trucks leaving. Our apartment building was right next to the military compound of Tetovo. The Yugoslav army took everything from the Macedonian army, and I remember watching from our balcony as these trucks carried out grenade launchers and other military things for days in a row. In Macedonia, there were constantly tensions about the possibly of war breaking out between Albanians and Macedonians as a spill-out effect of Bosnia and then Kosovo. We had this peacekeeping mission, UNPROFOR. They were located at the military compound next to where we lived, so we used to hang around a lot with international soldiers and started speaking English a little bit with them. They were all, "Oh, we're here to keep you safe. The war will not break out here."

And then there was this period when both of my parents lost their jobs because the factories were privatized and then closed.[14] They were bankrupt. We are not religious, but I remember that I was constantly praying to whomever before going to bed that my parents would have jobs. This was a very tough period because we were very poor. [It was the same for] some other families and kids that I knew from school. This economic depletion was one significant thing that left a lot of impact on me. I remember that I grew up [worrying if] my parents would have other jobs, how we would live, how we would feed ourselves. I remember my grandfather was helping us with money all the time. After some time, my parents started to work in other jobs, which were low paid. This continued up until recently, when they wanted to retire.

I remember dreaming that I [could have] a BMX bike, but my parents couldn't [afford] it. I also dreamed that we had a VCR to watch movies. We also couldn't even afford that. Those were two of my small commercial wishes growing up—to have a BMX bike and a video player. [Laughs] During the time of Yugoslavia, we used to go for summer holidays in Greece every year, and we used to come back with our Zastava car full of chocolate

---

14. Macedonia was the poorest republic in Yugoslavia. After it declared independence, it adopted a constitution that abolished Yugoslavia's model of social ownership and embarked on a process of privatization. The first years of transition were slowed by loss of access to the Yugoslav market, Western embargos on the Yugoslav common market, and a Greek embargo due to a dispute over Macedonia's name. They were also accompanied by low economic growth and high unemployment. As Sadiku discussed later in the interview, the unemployment rate was 30 percent in 1995, and it continued to increase in the 1990s and 2000s before dropping off in the 2010s. See Micevska, Eftimoski, and Petrovska Mirčevska, "Macedonia's Transition Experience and Potential for Sustainable Economic Growth," 309–34.

and things from Greece.[15] [After the Yugoslav wars] started, we didn't go for holidays in Greece for almost a decade, probably until 1997 or 1999. We started to go to Albania because it was cheap.

INTERVIEWER: What changed in your everyday life as the Yugoslav wars were starting?

SADIKU: These were times of uncertainty. Basically nothing changed, and it was just extended uncertainty. At this age, I knew there was no more Yugoslavia but also that there was still tension in the air. There was tension in Kosovo constantly. I remember we went once or twice to Kosovo with my parents to buy carpets or something like this. I remember seeing a lot of police everywhere, and I was scared because this was a time when Kosovo was militarized. I asked my father, "Why are there so many police officers?" And he said, "Because this is Kosovo. We are not in Macedonia." This was a gloomy situation. It was clear to me that it was the fallout of Yugoslavia. There were refugees, a lot of police and special units in Kosovo, international soldiers and peacekeepers. I grew up with this gloomy presence in the 1990s. And then there was the Kosovo War. I was in high school then, and we had kids from Kosovo who came to the high school.[16] We were quite grown up by then, so it was obvious what was going on.

---

15. Zastava Automobiles was an international car manufacturer based in Kragujevac (now Serbia). It was founded in 1851 as a cannon foundry and arms producer and evolved into a factory for car repair, parts manufacture, and assembly in the twentieth century. By the postwar years, Zastava was working closely with the Italian auto manufacturer Fiat to assemble Fiat vehicles in Yugoslavia as well as to produce its own models based on Fiat's licensed versions. Zastava produced several iconic Yugoslav cars starting in the 1950s, including the Fića, several Zastava models, and the Yugo. In the *Lexicon of Yu Mythology*, a living archive of Yugoslav popular culture crowdsourced from former citizens, the entry about the Fića frames it as a specific and quintessential Yugoslav product for many postwar families. Scholar Aleksandar Bošković elaborates: "Already established as a familiar symbol of Yugoslav identity in the 1960s and 1970s and as a recognizable national product, the Fića still resonates with cultural, historic, economic, and political meanings.... As the first Yugoslav car, the Fića was not only proof of the Yugoslav potency for material production but also a 'socialist state symbol' of a passionate faith that each new day would bring a better future" (Bošković, "Yugonostalgia and Yugoslav Cultural Memory," 67–68).

16. In addition to internally displaced people, the Kosovo War created 800,000 refugees, 344,500 of whom fled to Macedonia over the course of nine weeks. Scholar Maja Muhić suggests that Albanians who assisted Bosnian Muslim refugees in the early 1990s also helped Kosovar refugees in the late 1990s. Because these refugees were ethnically and linguistically similar to Macedonian Albanians, they were offered material as well as "spiritual" assistance that touted Islam and national awareness (Muhić, "Spiritual Assistance during Two Refugee Crises in the Republic of Macedonia," 75–92). However, scholars John Williams and Lester Zeager suggest that the Macedonian state closed its borders to asylum seekers on several occasions as a way to leverage humanitarian aid from the international community (Williams and Zeager, "Macedonian Border Closings in the Kosovo Refugee Crisis," 233–54).

I remember that we were quite poor at this time, but there was a guy who was coming every month and collecting money from my parents. I remember asking them, "What are you giving him money for?" [They explained that] there was this initiative to open an Albanian university in Tetovo in 1994, which would teach courses in Albanian. At Skopje University, there was a quota, and only 2 percent of enrolled students could be Albanians.[17] Some municipalities agreed to open an unofficial university, but the state didn't recognize it.[18] The state sent bulldozers and tanks, and it just crushed the whole thing and killed one person. Students continued to meet with teachers at their homes. They read books and took exams there. Only Albania recognized this university, but no other countries did. It was only after the war in 2001 that this became a legal university funded by the state, same as other universities in the country. Like every Albanian family, my parents wished they could [contribute] a small amount to fund this university, to buy books for students and pay salaries for teachers. I remember that sometimes my parents made calculations like, "This month, we'll have to give less for the university because we don't have anything." This also contributed to this gloomy 1990s period.

---

17. Very few Albanians enrolled at the University of Skopje because instruction was primarily in Macedonian and most Albanian students had attended primary and secondary school in Albanian. In 1995, likely in response to the development of the State University of Tetova, Macedonia passed a law that guaranteed that 10 percent of seats at the University of Skopje would be held for minority students. In 1997, the state also introduced Albanian-language instruction for future primary and secondary school teachers. Macedonian nationalists pushed back against these changes and criticized the government for accommodating Albanian students. In 2001, the militant group Albanian National Liberation Army led an insurgency that culminated in the Ohrid Agreement that pledged a range of political, cultural, and economic rights to Albanians, including higher education instruction in Albanian.

18. During the time of Yugoslavia, students from across the state could enroll in Albanian-language higher education at the University of Pristina in Kosovo, founded in 1969. By the fall of 1981, more students were enrolled there than at any other university in Yugoslavia (Pichler, "In the Shadow of Kosovo," 300). When Serbian leader Slobodan Milošević revoked Kosovo's rights as an autonomous province, he fired Albanian faculty members and mandated that all instruction be delivered in Serbian. In 1999, University of Priština/University of Kosovska Mitrovica splintered from the university and moved to North Mitrovica (now Kosovo) to offer Serbian-language instruction only. After Macedonia became independent, Macedonian Albanians lost access to the Albanian-language higher education they had had in Yugoslavia. Albanian leaders, including former faculty from the University of Pristina, founded the State University of Tetova in 1994 to provide higher education in Albanian in Macedonia. Because Macedonia did not recognize Albanian as an official language at the time, the State University of Tetova was considered illegal. Protestors attacked the university as a separatist institution, and Macedonian police raided it and shut it down. Macedonia recognized the State University of Tetova only in 2004. See Koneska, "Vetoes, Ethnic Bidding, Decentralisation."

There was a saying in Macedonia for the generation that went through this traumatic period. They're called *deca na tranzicija*, or kids of the transition. It was a presence in your childhood. The kids that were born earlier knew this, but it was not as traumatic for them. The kids that were born later just passed [over] this. [The experience] was traumatic in different ways.

INTERVIEWER: Do you identify with that generational experience?

SADIKU: Yeah, absolutely. I work now with youngsters who are nineteen, twenty, and twenty-five, and people in my circle of friends are sometimes fifty or sixty. But the generation that I hang out with the most and the people at places where I play music are [members of] this transition generation. Whenever you talk about something, they have an immediate reference to that thing that other generations have no clue about. We mention *tranziciski tost* [transition toast], and everybody knows that this was the toast with the vegetable cheese and the worst ham. It was probably better not to eat it than to eat it. Then we would say, "Ha! *Friteza sendvič*" [Friteza sandwich]. There was this fetish about the Friteza, the deep-frying machine that every house had. We started to cook everything in the Friteza.

When [members of] this generation were teens, a lot of their parents lost their jobs. When factories closed down in 1992, unemployment in Macedonia rose to 35 percent. A lot of people lost their jobs. These were the kids of working parents who had flats, who lived in the same kind of neighborhoods [as me], and who had the same access to everything [during Yugoslavia]. But then their parents lost their jobs, and these kids could not afford a lot of things. I grew up near the Šar Mountains, which had one of the most famous ski resorts in Yugoslavia, called Popova Šapka. I still do not know how to ski because my parents did not have money to buy me skis, but I have friends [from other generations] who are professional skiers because they had some family in Germany or Switzerland that sent them money for skis. Now there is this generational split: my generation that has no clue about skiing and other generations that are like professional skiers. The children of the transition could not afford to go skiing because it was an expensive sport even though [the resort] was right here.

INTERVIEWER: What do you remember from your high school years in the late 1990s?

SADIKU: After [we finished] primary school, my parents and my friends' parents were discussing which school to enroll their kids in. There was high competition for the medical school. The business sector was not yet that developed in the 1990s, so doctors had the biggest social privilege. They owned more money than others, so everybody wanted their children to become doctors. I hated medicine, and I had a fight with my parents and said, "I'm going to gymnasium [a secondary school that offered a 'classical' education rooted in the humanities]. No way am I going to medicine." Some other friends of mine [did the same], and we convinced each other that we weren't going to tell our parents that we were going to gymnasium.

During high school, it was just this period when you want to make up your own life. I started to smoke and drink at this time. It was also when I became very active in school. I organized our school's amateur theater. I was the editor of a youth magazine called *Multi idei*, which was [published] both in Macedonia and in Albanian. It had very radical content for the time. Every issue of this monthly magazine was dedicated to a topic like music, theater, literature, science, and sexuality. This provoked a protest [from] some parents, and they said, "This group of guys and girls are ruining our kids." I also started to run a bar/club with seven other friends. One of them had a cousin in Germany who gave us some money to rent a place and to run it. So we developed a small world of our own, a high school kids' world out of a [generally] gloomy situation. This was actually a happy period [for me] because we were hanging with each other twenty-four hours per day. This was a self-made carefree period where there was a lot of solidarity among us until the war broke out in Macedonia. And then I moved to the States.

During the period when I was in high school in the late 1990s, everybody wanted to get rid of whatever was left from the gloomy Yugoslav period. Everybody wanted to change their home appliances, to replace the old Yugoslav ones. When I was in high school, I started earning money because I worked for some NGO projects and at a bar. I would buy some things on my own. For example, we had a very old cassette and vinyl player, but we didn't have a CD player. This was the time when CDs appeared, so I worked hard and bought a CD player. Then we finally threw out the old Yugoslav thing that wasn't working. We still had the Ei Niš [Elektronska industrija Niš] television, which was also not functioning well. Slowly we started to change appliances at home from those that we inherited from Yugoslavia, which were twenty years old, to new ones like Sony, Aiwa, and cheaper versions.

People were also doing their own renovations of their apartment buildings, which completely transformed how their neighborhoods looked. Everybody wanted to forget that bad period of transition. New companies were opening up. New jobs were created. People started to generate some more money and then immediately invested this money into erasing the history and visual identity of the city from the gloomy 1990s. [The results] were actually horrible. Even now, when I go to Tetovo, everything actually still reminds me of this gloomy period. The building where my parents lived has the same entrance door, but [residents] made a monster out of it. Everybody closed their balconies, extended their rooms, and built some floors above.[19] It looks like a monster, but it is still the same on the inside. Some graffiti we wrote as kids, like "Punk's not dead," still remains there.

INTERVIEWER: How did the shifting of state borders impact you?

SADIKU: You could still travel to Serbia and Croatia, but there was war, so we avoided it. Up until 1991, we went to Greece very often on holidays, but when they introduced visas for Macedonia we couldn't go anymore. Greece became an inaccessible territory for us. Albania opened up, and we would go there, but we didn't like it because it was too poor and too backward at this time for us coming from Yugoslavia.[20]

INTERVIEWER: Tell me about your move to the United States after high school.

SADIKU: I went to the United States on a study program when I was actually in the fourth year of high school. I was enrolled in this program, which was at Towson University in Baltimore. I was there during the war in Macedonia. I was constantly refreshing the news on my laptop and seeing what was going on in my city because we lived next to a military compound in Tetovo. I remember that I was not enjoying being in the United States because I was constantly reading the news and trying to get in contact with my family while they were in the village without phone lines. It was a period of uncertainty.

---

19. In a study of a neighborhood in post-socialist Skopje, the capital of North Macedonia, scholars Jasna Mariotti and Daniel Baldwin Hess show that residents significantly transformed postwar prefabricated buildings by illegally expanding or enclosing balconies, converting garages into living spaces or shops, and installing amenities such as additional air conditioners and bathrooms. Residents were emboldened to modify their apartments because many had purchased them from the state after privatization. They were also driven to make accommodations because of a shortage of new and affordable housing in Macedonia in the early years of transition (Mariotti and Hess, "Enlargement of Apartments in Socialist Housing Estates in Skopje under Transition," 39–59).

20. During the postwar years, the People's Socialist Republic of Albania was a one-party communist state primarily ruled by the dictator Enver Hoxha (1908–1985). Albania had strict travel and visa restrictions, which made it difficult to leave as well as enter the state. After the fall of communism, hundreds of thousands of Albanians left the country; many settled abroad permanently.

When I went back, my father arranged for me to come from Skopje to Tetovo by OSCE car.[21] [I saw then that] the actual place where my family lived had been destroyed. It was crushed by grenades. We had to rebuild it after the war. My parents still live there.

INTERVIEWER: Do you remember how you introduced yourself to Americans when you were abroad?

SADIKU: I said I was an Albanian from Macedonia.

INTERVIEWER: And did that make sense to people at the time?

SADIKU: It depended. I was in a program with a lot of international students from Europe, especially the Balkans, so it made sense to them. We didn't move much outside the university campus.

I remember that my identification was stronger at that point because of what was going on in Macedonia. I had antiwar sentiments, but, you know, there were things going on, and you would take a side at a certain point in time. Military bombs killed a girl that went to high school with me along with eleven other members of her family. It was a very sad moment when I read in the news that she was murdered. This preoccupied me a lot, but nobody else [in America] gave a damn about what was going on in this small country far away. Because I was so preoccupied, I couldn't engage much with other events that were going on at the university.

I was completely consumed by what was going on every day while others didn't give a damn. There was no solidarity around this. Around this time, after the US, I developed an affinity for all sorts of revolutionary movements. I was very into reading about the Irish Republican Army and the Palestinian Liberation Organization. These movements were also armed movements. This was my early revolutionary identification. It [evolved into] Marxism, and then post-Marxism, and then postmodernity. Nowadays I work as a curator at a museum of contemporary art. [Lightly laughs]

INTERVIEWER: To what degree do you think growing up in Yugoslavia shaped the trajectory of who you are now?

---

21. During the 2001 conflict in Macedonia, the Organization for Security and Cooperation in Europe (OSCE) was tasked with conflict prevention and negotiation of peace. The organization managed passage from conflict zones and brokered ceasefires to provide civilians with food, water, and medicine.

SADIKU: It shaped a lot, actually. My father and my mother had decent wages. We could afford holidays every year in Greece. We never had issues with food. I know for a fact that if there was no state-subsidized housing, I would not be what I am. I would have grown up in the village, and I would be the same as my cousins. Many of them didn't even go to university. I would probably work in bars. I would not have this education. I would not have gotten a PhD in political philosophy. I recently bought an apartment in Skopje. When you get a loan that you have to pay out for fifteen years, you realize that the major concern of young people in their thirties now—how to find housing away from their parents—was not an issue in Yugoslavia.

It definitely also shaped my ideological identification today as strongly antinationalist and antifascist. I lived through this trauma of ethnic fervors. I lived through the breakup of Yugoslavia. I see nothing that can legitimize a war other than defense against a fascist invasion. Very strong ethnic identifications are troublesome for me. My mother tongue is Albanian, but I identify as an anarchist, if I have to [identify at all]. I have had issues with my parents when I've said publicly, "I don't identify as Albanian." I also had issues with my girlfriend's family, who is Macedonian. Not knowing who I was, they were like, "Oh, he'll probably turn you into a Muslim girl." And I was like, "A Muslim girl? I'm the most antichrist and anti-Muslim [person]." [Laughs]

A lot of the strategies, tactics, and discourses [we had] up until 2018 with the movement Solidarnost, or solidarity, were based on some heritage of Yugoslavia. I've written a lot about this. We were not Yugonostalgics, but today's values are quite regressive and reactionary as opposed to the values that were present in Yugoslavia, which were values of solidarity and social justice. The system now forces competition and leaves a lot of people behind. It's hard for the younger generations. They have different references of rebellion, but they can't believe housing can be universally guaranteed. It's just incomprehensible to them. Because the state provided my house when I was growing up, that actually impacted me a lot when I was developing intellectually.

INTERVIEWER: How do you identify nationally, ethnically, or culturally today?

SADIKU: I identify as an anarchist. I don't feel any emotional attachment anymore to ethnic things. I also often identify as a Balkanophile because I love Balkan music. I'm a big fan of traditional Greek and Turkish music, although I play punk and postpunk music. These things can go hand in hand. My friends in Serbia are sometimes shocked when I'm the only one who knows a [traditional] song playing at a bar. I'm like, "Yeah, of course, this is a Serbian song played with *gusle.*"[22]

INTERVIEWER: Do you identify as Yugoslav in any capacity?

SADIKU: No. I know some people who are from the older generations, like my friend Dragomir Olujić Oluja from Belgrade, who identify as Yugoslav. I was too young to have lived Yugoslav culture [enough to] identify as Yugoslav. I was born too late. It [might have] more to do with region because there are almost no people in Macedonia, even older generations, who identify as Yugoslav.[23] It's more present in Serbia and Croatia, from what I know from friends. In Macedonia, this has to do with the political persecution of Macedonians and Albanians because they were not buying into the new Yugoslav identity at first.[24]

INTERVIEWER: What is the difference for you between valuing the political pillars of the Yugoslav past, such as solidarity and social justice, and mere nostalgia?

SADIKU: I am not a Yugonostalgic. I think that Yugoslavia was a noble process of experimentation, but it failed not because it was too socialist but

---

22. *Gusle* is a one-string instrument that often accompanies the recitation of folklore or epic poetry. While the *gusle* is a traditional instrument across the Balkans, it is particularly inscribed in Serbian and Montenegrin national history.

23. Socialist Yugoslavia recognized Macedonia as a distinct nation in the federation and granted it considerable autonomous rights. However, scholar Hugh Poulton argues that Macedonians as an ethnic category did not develop a high affinity for Yugoslavia: "It is possible that in time, if the Yugoslav state had survived, greater numbers of Macedonians, more secure with their own identity would have declared themselves as 'Yugoslavs' but this remains conjuncture. In the event, the approaching end of the Yugoslav state saw an increase in Macedonian nationalism and a sharpening of the desire for an independent state for the first time in modern history" (Poulton, "Macedonians and Albanians as Yugoslavs," 125).

24. Tetovo, the city where Sadiku was born and raised, has a particularly turbulent history within Yugoslavia because its proportionally large Albanian population experienced systematic repression at the hands of the state. In some instances, Yugoslav authorities appeased demands for greater rights, such as when the state established the Albanian-language University of Pristina in Kosovo in 1969. More frequently, the Yugoslav state rejected the demands of Tetovo's Albanian residents or met them with violence. When Albanians demanded that Albanian-populated areas of Macedonia join Kosovo and become a constituent republic of Yugoslavia, for instance, state leaders framed it as an Albanian separatist plot and stringently punished protesters.

because it was not socialist enough. Many things remained [from the period before socialism], such as nationalist tendencies. The strong centralization of Yugoslavia was positive because there were these tendencies of disintegration. [At the same time,] it was very often an authoritarian state. It was a culturally conservative state as well. The first serious criticisms of socialism from the inside came from the left, from students in 1968.[25] There was the initial oppression. [They] beat up students who had demanded more socialism and who were more socialist than the system. The level of bureaucratization of Yugoslavia was hugely problematic.

I think it is positive to keep alive the drive toward experimentation. Some things were my lived experience, such as housing, health care, and wellbeing. There were state-owned factories that experimented with worker self-management. But the factories also competed against one other, which was not beyond capitalist market operations. So there were setbacks in Yugoslavia. This is why I'm not nostalgic. [I don't] accept that everything in Yugoslavia was good. I think the biggest value of Yugoslavia was experimenting with different models, even though most of them failed. The tendency toward experimentation was, I think, the biggest value. This is why Yugoslavia didn't end up as Stalinism. It was an open model of trying out new and different practices, mainly in the economy.

INTERVIEWER: Is there anything about Yugoslavia that you miss?

SADIKU: Ah, of course! I miss when Yugoslavia was one territory. I would also like to include Albania and Bulgaria [in that territory] because these small countries like Montenegro, Kosovo, Macedonia, and Slovenia feel claustrophobic.[26] When you leave Skopje, you reach the [north] border with Kosovo in fifteen minutes. If you go south, you reach the border with Greece in an hour and a half. It's the same [if you travel] west and east. Wherever you drive, you reach a border in roughly an hour. This causes claustrophobia, and it also develops, for me, a very localized *polemička kultura* [polemical culture]. When we had the whole Yugoslavia as one political and territorial entity, we could travel freely and exchange cultural values and products. These

---

25. For an additional discussion of student protests in Kosovo in 1968, see Hetemi, *Student Movements of the Republic of Kosovo*.

26. There have been proposals for the creation of an enlarged southeastern European state since the early twentieth century. Some proposals imagined an integral South Slavic state, while others were inclusive of non-Slavic groups as well. Proposals imagined the inclusion of some combination of the territories of Yugoslavia, Albania, Bulgaria, and parts of Greece and Italy.

small countries also have failing social and health care systems. If there was a huge country with much more capacity [to provide for its citizens], our lives would be much better. A united space would be tremendously advantageous, which is a thing that I really lack and miss.

INTERVIEWER: What does Yugoslavia mean to you today?

SADIKU: Yugoslavia to me today is a vision which was not realized. It was a very noble vision which failed tragically. There are still consequences of this. The fact that we have a shitty health care system in Macedonia is a direct result of the breakup of Yugoslavia. Yugoslavia was a very good vision, and not only for me. It was globally respected, valued, and adored. I experienced it like that. Now if I close my eyes and imagine that Yugoslavia is back there and they are still experimenting and doing new things and trying out new things, I can imagine my life is better than this muck we are still in.

INTERVIEWER: How do you relate to people from the former Yugoslav region who might not live in Macedonia today?

SADIKU: I have hundreds of friends in the ex-Yugoslav countries because of the political activity that we did. I think that what made it possible for us to become so close was the shared experience from Yugoslavia and the values that we kept from Yugoslavia. It's not that we got together and then said, "Oh, let's all start liking and loving Yugoslav values." It is because these values brought us together. I was just writing a piece about post-Yugoslav practices in public art spaces as a way to keep alive some of the values of solidarity and antifascism, which are being now attacked. Especially in Croatia, they're trying to erase everything that was positive from Yugoslavia and input new Croatian values.[27]

INTERVIEWER: How do you feel when you are in the other regions of former Yugoslavia now? Do you feel at home in a place like Croatia, Bosnia, Serbia, Slovenia, Montenegro, and Kosovo?

SADIKU: To a certain degree. You know why? Because some things are familiar. I went to the Croatian coast last summer, one year ago, and I was like, "Yeah, this is kind of very familiar to me." I was also a little bit angry that some things have developed [in Croatia] more than in Macedonia or Serbia. There were new buses that were [part of] a transportation system that had "Donated by the EU" signage. These new advantages in Croatia are because

---

27. See Sadiku, "Public Art as Class Struggle in Post-Socialist Yugoslavia."

of the EU, which [Macedonia] has not yet joined. The split of [a country] that used to be one thing and is now developing differently in different parts kind of saddens me.

INTERVIEWER: Is there anything that I didn't ask about that you'd like to talk about?

SADIKU: No, actually, I talked more than I thought I would. Things kept popping into my mind.

INTERVIEWER: I appreciated you sharing your reflections and memories. So, thank you so much for that.

4

INTERVIEW WITH
Iva Radivojević

Iva Radivojević was born in Belgrade (now Serbia) in 1980 and grew up in Novi Sad (now Serbia). Her family emigrated at the beginning of the Yugoslav wars and resettled in Cyprus. Since her late teens, she has lived in the United States and Greece. Today, Radivojević is a filmmaker and artist based in Greece. When we spoke in spring 2022 over a video call, she was working in Fairbanks, Alaska. In the interview, she discussed her family's decision to leave Yugoslavia after the wars started. Radivojević recounted memories of growing up in an ethnically mixed family and navigating her identity over time. Having a sense of self as a Yugoslav, Radivojević explained, remained important to her; she nurtured this identity through creative work, language use, and travel.

The Yugoslav wars displaced millions of people. Most refugees were fleeing violence, but some migrated in response to worsening political and economic conditions in the region. Radivojević's family was part of this latter group of skilled migrants, often referred to as a brain drain, who left because they saw no viable future in the country after the onset of the 1990s crisis. As scholar Drenka Vuković writes, "this represents a new trend in comparison with the situation in the early migration years, characterized as it was by the movement abroad of a largely unskilled labour force."[1] Whereas Yugoslavs had participated in temporary guest worker programs for unskilled labor during the postwar decades, the collapse of the country drove out many trained citizens. Radivojević remembered that safety was one of the most important factors that motivated her family's move to Cyprus. "Mafia [activity] was starting to rise in Serbia,"

---

1. Vuković, "Migrations of the Labour Force from Yugoslavia," 142.

she explained. "My mom and dad had made some money with [their cleaning] company. One day, my dad received a call from the mafia, the infamous criminal called Lajavi. He wanted extortion money. On the call he specified, 'You have two daughters. These are their names. This is the way they walk to school.'" Organized crime thrived in the wartime years, permeating everyday life and intertwining with state institutions. Moreover, Radivojević's family was driven to leave Yugoslavia because quality of life decreased markedly after the international community imposed sanctions on the rump of Yugoslavia during the Croatian War of Independence and the Bosnian War. "Suddenly there was also a shortage of everything," Radivojević remembered. "There was no gas, no clothes. There was an embargo. If you walked in the street with new sneakers, someone would literally have you at knifepoint for those sneakers. It was generally starting to become unsafe." Because her family had the means to emigrate, they relocated to Cyprus. Although some migrants later repatriated, Radivojević herself never returned to live in the region, and in our interview, she explained that she did not aspire to.

Many of Radivojević's childhood experiences were shaped by dual belonging to her mother's ethnically Croatian family and her father's ethnically Serbian one. According to the 1981 Yugoslav census, about 12 percent of marriages in Yugoslavia were mixed. This number fluctuated from region to region. In Vojvodina, the ethnically heterogenous region of Yugoslavia where Radivojević grew up, 28 percent of marriages were ethnically mixed.[2] The mixedness of her family was part and parcel of everyday life. Radivojević recalled noticing regional differences such as language use when she visited family in Croatia, but she did not think of them as markers of difference. "By these little linguistic differences, you would know that this sentence or person comes from somewhere else. It was almost like, 'Oh, what a cute thing you do.' It wasn't an othering," she said. Only in the aftermath of the Yugoslav wars did Radivojević notice that successor states mobilized regional differences as national signifiers. She was aware that language policies delineated phonology, grammar, and basic vocabulary, but she was surprised that others from the former Yugoslavia policed her belonging based on how she spoke. She narrated one such experience in New York City: a Croatian friend introduced her as "ours" (*naša*) to an acquaintance, and the person replied that she was "not ours" based on her Serbian accent.

When she moved to Cyprus—and, later, lived in the United States and Greece—Radivojević maintained a strong affinity for her identity as a Yugoslav.

---

2. Botev, "Where East Meets West," 468. Also see Smits, "Ethnic Intermarriage and Social Cohesion," 417–32.

"As time has progressed," she reflected, "I think I have a need to reconnect to what it means to be from that region, what it means to have grown up with multiple identities and multiple nationalities, and what it means to have gone to and lived in other places as well." Radivojević acknowledged that every place she lived added layers to her sense of self. For instance, she studied and worked for two decades in the United States and had a sense of belonging there. She currently resides in Greece, a country where she speaks the language fluently and feels at home. "I also really love the idea of a fluid identity that moves in between spaces and that is not so constrained by any one thing," she said. Radivojević hesitated to align herself with one ethnic group or successor state of Yugoslavia because she believed doing so would oversimplify her identity. "Even though I grew up with my mother who is Croatian, I cannot identify as Croatian," she explained. "[It's only that] the passport I use the most is Croatian. I am closer to the Serbian experience, but it just feels weird to identify as Serbian. This is why I keep saying Yugoslav." Like many others in the youngest Yugoslav generation, Radivojević held on to Yugoslavia as an inclusive category that reflected her identity.

Radivojević engaged with her Yugoslav past in multiple ways. As a filmmaker, she recently started interrogating her relationship to the former state in her work. She also discussed the importance of language for her sense of identity. "When I hear that particularly Bosnian accent, my heart feels warm, like 'Yes!' It's such a beautiful distinction. . . . I think it's the language that provides the home," she said. Most importantly, she visited the region often as a way to reinforce her connection to her childhood. "I love visiting now," Radivojević told me. "I love it. I love going to Bosnia. I love going to Croatia. I love going to Serbia. For me, there's a kind of understanding and a [feeling of] familiarity and kinship. Obviously, I am generalizing because there is a lot of hurt there as well, which again is why I can't live in that area of the Balkans." While she recognized that no place in the former Yugoslavia was her home anymore, Radivojević imagined how it might once have been a community where people could "live together in celebration of those differences, not despite those differences." Instead, her life was irreversibly marked by war and state collapse. For instance, the war in Ukraine was just starting when we met for the interview, and Radivojević noted that it triggered feelings from the Yugoslav wars for her family. "My mom started having vertigo the moment the war [in Ukraine] started because she had unprocessed feelings about leaving. Everything was coming back," she said. In this way, Yugoslavia served as a reference point for understanding the world as much for her mother as for Radivojević herself.

INTERVIEWER: Where did you spend your childhood?

RADIVOJEVIĆ: I was born in Belgrade [now Serbia]. I grew up in Novi Sad [now Serbia], and I lived there until the age of almost twelve.[3] That's the place that I remember most. The reason I was born in Belgrade was that there was an outbreak of meningitis in Novi Sad [at the time of my birth], and my mom had to go to Belgrade.

INTERVIEWER: What do you remember about Novi Sad?

RADIVOJEVIĆ: It's almost like snippets. I remember our neighborhood, Detelinara, very well. I remember the buildings we lived in—Pariske komune—and the dynamics within my building, all the friends and neighbors, and things like that. We had a joint yard that was a shared by a block of seven buildings. I remember my [elementary] school, Ivo Lola Ribar, very vividly. And that small town feel of Novi Sad, the coziness. I remember of course the Danube River.

INTERVIEWER: How would you characterize your childhood?

RADIVOJEVIĆ: I remember a lot of sisterhood and brotherhood within our block of buildings. We would watch the neighborhood from our apartment on the fifth floor. I would see Jova and Tamara from the adjacent building, who were on the third floor. [There was] Tijana, whose window was right next to mine, and we would lean out of the window and chat. Then [there was] my next-door neighbor Snežana. It was such a beautiful little community of people. [There was] this neighborliness and taking care of each other. My mother and father would go on a trip and leave us [Radivojević and her sister] with the neighbor. So that was really special. There was less of that in school, but the neighborhood community was very alive and potent.

Because my mom is Croatian and my dad is Serbian, we spent the summers in Croatia. We were on the island of Pag [now Croatia] and in Zagreb [now Croatia]. I didn't necessarily feel strong distinctions, but there was a small difference because we would use language in a way that's different. In Croatia, they inject a specific thing in a sentence. For example, instead of "*kupila sam sladoled*" ["I bought ice cream"], people say, "*kupila sam sih sladoled*"

---

3. Novi Sad was located in the Socialist Autonomous Province of Vojvodina, a northern region of the People's Republic of Serbia.

["I bought myself ice cream"]. It's always pointed at yourself. By these little linguistic differences, you would know that this sentence or person comes from somewhere else. It was almost like, "Oh, what a cute thing you do." It wasn't an othering.

INTERVIEWER: Were you aware of your family being different? Was that something you were aware of at the time, or is that something you are reflecting on now?

RADIVOJEVIĆ: No, I remember that because it was quite a different reality being in Croatia and being in Serbia. [There were] the accents. [There was] being by the sea. It was quite a distinction. It's kind of like when you go to your mom's mom and go to your dad's mom. It's a different world, regardless of if they're from Croatia or Serbia. But then, as the problems were brewing and we were going back from Croatia to Serbia, I started hearing nationalist discussions and talks. That's when I started to feel a divergence between each place.

INTERVIEWER: Do remember if anybody else around you was similarly different or differently different?

RADIVOJEVIĆ: Yeah, in school there were six of us who were hanging out in a group. One of the girls was Mirela, and she was half-Czech. It was never a thing. It was like, "Oh, Mirela speaks Czech." But it was never weird; she wasn't different or differentiated from anyone else. I remember also in our neighborhood, there were a lot of Hungarians. There was a boy in the neighborhood, and we knew that he was Hungarian. It was a particular characteristic, but it wasn't a thing, really, for me as a child. Except [this] kid was cute, and so we would ride bikes by his house to see him and stuff. [Laughs] If anything, it made him more special [that he was Hungarian].

INTERVIEWER: Do you remember if anyone was treated differently during your childhood, by teachers or by neighbors?

RADIVOJEVIĆ: Yeah, the Roma kids and Roma people in general. There was a Roma girl in our school called Violeta. She was unruly, let's say. Of course, if you spent some of your life not being in school and stuff like that, then it's just a new experience you have to adapt to. But I remember that my friend Olja was really close to Violeta. She was the only one Violeta would listen to because they lived in the same neighborhood and hung out in the street. Violeta had a lot of respect for Olja. I suspect that Olja herself had some Roma roots, but it was never talked about. She was a really strong sort of character in this group of six people. She started karate, and she was very capable, beautiful, and strong. There was another boy, Dejan, whose parents struggled because they were working class people. He gave the teachers a hard time and would tease and provoke everyone for attention. These were the two kids, and I remember they were labeled as "problematic."

INTERVIEWER: Do you remember participating in any Yugoslav activities at school?

RADIVOJEVIĆ: That's an odd thing. Of course, I have so many pictures wearing the red Pioneer scarf. Of course, I remember all the songs. But I don't remember the actual experience of doing [any activities]. I have the pictures to prove it, but I don't remember doing those things.

INTERVIEWER: Why do you think that is?

RADIVOJEVIĆ: Maybe because they weren't emotionally engaging. Maybe it was just a technicality. You're made to repeat those things so many times, and of course they stay in your head. Not only do they make you repeat them, but they are on all the TV channels and in all the celebrations and blah-blah-blah. I remember emotional things, emotional experiences and situations and events that happened.

INTERVIEWER: Is there anything that stands out to you about school?

RADIVOJEVIĆ: I mean, I remember things very well. There was a history teacher who was a very small lady, and her hair was receding. She was losing her hair. There was a terrible nickname that we had for her, which was Ćelava, or "Baldy." She was always smoking, and she had a ... actually, now [my memory is] splitting into two. Okay, the one that was smoking was the art teacher, and Ćelava was not smoking. [Laughs] The art teacher was very nervous and skinny and walking and smoking in class all the time. Ćelava was more strict but quiet.

I remember my [homeroom] teacher because each class had a specific teacher assigned to it. I don't remember her name, but I remember she had a big mole on her face, and she was very kind [and] compassionate. I remember the structure of the school very well. I remember everybody was smoking during breaks in the back of the school. I remember the PE [physical education] area. There are a lot of snippets of images that are coming back. I remember the toilets, which were a hole in the ground. It's just like those things you used to step on and pee. And I remember specific characters because they stick out. It's the nuances or exaggerated things of someone's personality that stick out, so those are the things that I remember.

INTERVIEWER: Were the toilets interesting because they were squatting toilets? I was meeting with a professor at the University of Belgrade when I was doing research in Belgrade about ten years ago, and I was surprised to see that the women's restroom also had squatting toilets in the faculty.

RADIVOJEVIĆ: They were the squatting toilets. Recently I was somewhere and I had to use that kind of toilet and was like, "Oh, this brings back memories." It was normal then.

INTERVIEWER: Can you tell me a little bit about the family you grew up with in Yugoslavia?

RADIVOJEVIĆ: I grew up with a mother and a father up until a point. My dad is Serbian from Kragujevac [now Serbia], and most of his family was in Belgrade at the time. My mom is from Zagreb. They got married pretty young. And of course, the Croatian family wasn't so happy about that [because my parents] quit their studies to get married and have children. Then they decided to live in Novi Sad, which is not where their family was. I have a sister, Vanja, who is two years older.

My mom and dad came from working class families, especially my mom. They [my parents] worked in a bank, but then they quit their jobs and started a cleaning business, cleaning carpets and stuff like that. We had to help them out with all these different things, and the business grew and grew. They actually made some money, which is why we were able to leave [Yugoslavia when the war started].

My granddad was a general in the army [Yugoslav National Army], so he was a respected character. He divorced from his first wife. His second wife was Macedonian. He had two children from the first marriage, and his third [child], my uncle, [was] a child from the second marriage. It started to get really mixed in terms of like Macedonian, Croatian, Bosnian, and so on.

But I think this kind of womanizing—not that having a second marriage is womanizing—was the history of my grandfather. My dad sort of inherited that as well. What I remember, for example, is my dad secretly bringing people to the house and things like this. So technically, yeah, I had a mother and a father, but it was problematic, let's say. Your first experience with trust is with your parents. A lot of the memories that still come back to me all the time are those, unfortunately, of my dad.

INTERVIEWER: How often did you travel from Novi Sad? Do you remember traveling to visit family in Croatia or in Belgrade or elsewhere?

Figure 4.1. A gathering of Serbs, Macedonians, and Croatians at a family celebration. *Courtesy of Iva Radivojević.*

RADIVOJEVIĆ: We were in Croatia every summer. I can't tell you when that started, but those summers are very strong memories for me: on Pag, the beach and the water, the smells and jumping off the diving boards. In Belgrade, we would go to visit family there too. I remember my granddad's apartment, and I remember my uncle's room, his guitar, his dinosaur drawings. I can't say how often [we went]. I know we went to Croatia every summer, but I can't say how often we would go to Belgrade.

INTERVIEWER: You mentioned that one of your grandparents was in the military. Did any of your other family members work for the state?

RADIVOJEVIĆ: My grandfather's second wife was also a secretary, or something like that, in the military as well. My aunt [the daughter of the same grandfather] worked for the government. She's now retired. I can't remember what her position was, but she did work for the government.

INTERVIEWER: Do you remember how your family talked about Yugoslavia?

RADIVOJEVIĆ: Back then when it was Yugoslavia, nobody questioned it. When we think about our granddad, the general, what we remember is him being sent on a mission to Kuwait as part of the Yugoslav army that was deployed to the UN, not as part of the Yugoslav wars or anything like that.[4] By that time, he was very much retired. He died in 1999. So yeah, it was more like, "Granddad is part of the United Nations." It wasn't a country specific, nationalistic thing.

INTERVIEWER: Did anybody in your family have, for example, a portrait of Tito hanging up at home? Did anybody actively engage with any state activities?

RADIVOJEVIĆ: I wouldn't know this, but I heard this from my uncle. My uncle and my father—they're half-brothers—have very opposing opinions on politics. This is something I grew to learn later. My dad has become a bit of a nationalist. My uncle is the complete opposite. Even when [Slobodan] Milošević was just getting into power, he [my uncle] was already opposing him as a sort of dubious character, whereas my dad wasn't. I knew there was a disconnect in that sense, and [it continues] still today. When I talk to my uncle, for example, he tells me that his father, the general, would get angry when he [my uncle] would want to find American books at the American embassy. His father [the father of my uncle] learned Russian when he was young, and he was a communist.

We weren't baptized because my granddad was in the communist party and my father was in the communist party. They eventually both left. After the war, my father became more religious and, sadly, more nationalist.

INTERVIEWER: Do you remember when you learned about war starting in Yugoslavia? Was that something you were aware of when you were a child?

RADIVOJEVIĆ: The first memory I have [of war] is being in Croatia for the last time. I suppose it was the end of summer, and I was in my granddad's and grandma's house. We were gathered at the gate, and he was talking with his neighbors. It was a bunch of men and me, and they were talking about

---

4. Socialist Yugoslavia was an original member of the United Nations from 1945. The Yugoslav National Army contributed soldiers to United Nations Emergency Forces (UNEF) peacekeeping operations during the Cold War. When UNEF was formed in 1956 to secure an end to the Suez Crisis, Yugoslavs participated in its mission to establish international peacekeepers on the border of Egypt and Israel from 1956 to 1967. Like other units, members of the Yugoslav National Army were specifically trained to work in desert conditions. They primarily offered medical and hygiene services (Životić, "Sanitetsko obezbedjenje odreda Jugoslovenske Narodne Armije na Sinaju 1956–1967," 130–38). The Yugoslav National Army contributed to UNEF peacekeeping missions through the start of the Yugoslav wars; Radivojević's grandfather likely took part in them.

the current political situations and saying pro-[Franjo] Tudjman stuff. Being from where I was from, I threw in some opposing views because all this that they were saying was very new to me. Maybe the little me felt an attack. I can't remember. But I said something, and they all sort of jumped on me. These old men jumped on a ten-year-old child. That was a very intense experience, and that's when I realized, "Oh, something is happening."

After that, back in Serbia—and this is a bit about what my next film is about—I received a call from Croatia.[5] Back then it was very hard to get calls through because it was already wartime. So for a long-distance call to come in was already a sort of achievement. They really quickly asked me, "Is anybody home?" I said, "No, it's just me." They said, "Okay, tell your mom that your granddad is dead." He died from natural causes, though a heart attack is not necessarily a natural cause. In my mind, it was that [event] that created the whole disconnect because soon after that, we were packing up to leave. There were other things. Small things were accumulating and creating a feeling of unease. [It was a] feeling of tension. Almost like an intense presence because it was heightened by this feeling that something was about to happen.

Everything that happened is sort of meshed together as a single thing. It wasn't, obviously. It happened over time. That is what I'm trying to concentrate on in this film. Exactly how are memories formed, and why do we remember some things as opposed to other things? How fragmented is [memory]? How powerful is [memory] to actually build a narrative for yourself?

INTERVIEWER: Do you remember your parents discussing a departure or planning for a departure?

RADIVOJEVIĆ: There was talk of leaving, but I can't remember those discussions. There were a lot of things that built up to [the decision to leave]. My mom is Croatian. Nothing violent happened, but she remembers divisive comments starting to come up. It was mostly that it was not safe. Mafia [activity] was starting to rise in Serbia.[6] My mom and dad had made some

---

5. Radivojević's film *When the Phone Rang* was released in 2024.
6. War and international sanctions during the 1990s left Serbia economically isolated. A nexus of militaries, state security services, and organized crime groups facilitated arms, drug, and oil trafficking in cooperation with international crime networks. Organized crime groups were also responsible for wartime and political violence. In 2003, members of organized crime groups planned and executed the assassination of Serbia's prime minister, Zoran Djindjić (1952–2003), who had begun instituting democratic reforms. See Nielsen, "The Symbiosis of War Crimes and Organized Crime in the Former Yugoslavia," 6–17, and Nikolić and Petrović, "Organized Crime in Serbian Politics during the Yugoslav Wars," 101–22.

money with [their cleaning] company. One day, my dad received a call from the mafia, the infamous criminal called Lajavi.[7] He wanted extortion money. On the call, he specified, "You have two daughters. These are their names. This is the way they walk to school." [My parents] quickly took us out of school and drove us to Belgrade.

Suddenly there was a shortage of everything. There was no gas, no clothes. There was an embargo. If you walked in the street with new sneakers, someone would literally have you at knifepoint for those sneakers. It was generally starting to become unsafe. All this was happening around the same time. In my young mind, it was almost as if my granddad's death sparked everything.

INTERVIEWER: How did your family decide to go to Cyprus?

RADIVOJEVIĆ: Because a lot of countries weren't receptive to people coming from Serbia, [we had to consider where] we would go. Do we go to Greece? Do we go to Cyprus? Do we go to Russia? My parents knew somebody in Cyprus, and their idea was to open a business in Cyprus. It was a small island and safe [for them] at the time with two kids. I think that Greece was on the table as well, but I think this connection with somebody in Cyprus solidified it. I think my mom went early to see it and came back and picked us up. The idea was that my dad would still work from [Yugoslavia] and somehow make it work and that he would come eventually. My dad was obviously having other affairs and relationships, so for him it was almost a convenience [that my mom and sister and I left] because he didn't come with us.

INTERVIEWER: Do you remember leaving Yugoslavia?

RADIVOJEVIĆ: We had to travel to Bulgaria because the borders were closed. I mean, the airports were closed. So we had to drive to Bulgaria and then catch a charter flight to Cyprus. And again, there was this person that we knew in Bulgaria. I remember throwing up all the way in the car. We eventually reached it, and I remember Sofia as this very gray city. That's all I remember. And then we got on the plane, and the plane was a little, small, rackety plane. Again, I threw up seven times on this two-hour flight, and then we arrived in Cyprus. The first thing I felt was this wave of hot air, and everything was yellow. And then of course, the jarring difference, like all the houses were very small and white, I guess to reflect the sun. It was such a drastic difference of place, of location, and . . . I mean, everything. Yeah, that is what I remember.

---

7. Branislav Lainović (1955–2000), known as Lajavi, Krakati, or Dugi, was active in organized crime and the paramilitary group Serbian Guard.

INTERVIEWER: When you arrived, how do you remember settling into Cyprus?

RADIVOJEVIĆ: There are things I remember, and [there are] things I don't remember but that were told to me afterward. I remember when we first arrived. We stayed in this hotel and tried to figure out where to live, where to go to school, and stuff [like that]. I was almost twelve, and my sister was fourteen. We couldn't go to Greek school because we were too old—we didn't speak Greek, so we had to go to private school. Of course, private school cost money, and it was in English. We had to take placement exams for English and math. I passed because I was entering the first year, but my sister didn't pass. She didn't speak English. She had to go to a different school in a different town. So what ended up happening was that my mom was working twenty-four seven. I went to this one school in Larnaca. My sister went to a different school in Nicosia. Essentially, we were isolated from each other, and that was very hard. We were not only isolated from each other, but [we were] isolated from the community, the neighborhood, and [our] family. My grandma, my mom's mom, told me that she asked me once if it was a hard time for me. She said, "You told me that you cried, but not for anyone to see." I have no recollection of crying. I have no recollection of telling her this.

INTERVIEWER: Do you remember how you introduced yourself in Cyprus?

RADIVOJEVIĆ: No, but I still say that I am from Yugoslavia, so I imagine it would have been the same.

INTERVIEWER: What did you miss about Yugoslavia when you moved to Cyprus?

RADIVOJEVIĆ: One [thing] was that sense of community and support. When somebody is stripped of that, it is probably the hardest. I was missing my friends a lot. I was missing my family.

In terms of identity, it was very hard to hold onto anything that you are. You have to adjust and recalibrate and become something new.

I look at refugee movements today. The first time you leave your place and settle somewhere else, it's the first instance when you feel like an other. The idea that this new situation and these new people are treating you as that other becomes a very interesting and intense experience. I've worked with a lot of refugees from Palestine and Iraq and Syria, and they have a very strong reaction to the first place where they land because they are treated differently for the first time. They were not treated like they used to be treated. It was similar for me going to Cyprus. I still cannot live there anymore. Even visiting sometimes doesn't make me feel good.

INTERVIEWER: How long did you end up living in Cyprus?

RADIVOJEVIĆ: Seven years. I literally waited to finish high school to get out. I couldn't wait to get out. And I did. My mom is still there. My sister is still there. She also went to the United States for a little bit to study, and then she went back and is married with kids. I find it impossible to live there.

INTERVIEWER: How did you decide to leave Cyprus after high school?

RADIVOJEVIĆ: My mom was huge on educating us, and her number one thing was to get us through school and make us international citizens. So the idea was always that we would go to study. I wanted to go to Spain, but we didn't have much money. We heard that you could work under the table in the US, and we had a lot of Cypriot friends and Greek friends who did that. They worked at restaurants and bars and made enough money to survive, pay rent, and pay for school. That's why we came to New York. In Europe, we couldn't do that at that time as Yugoslavs or Serbians.

INTERVIEWER: How did your later move to the US compare to the one to Cyprus?

RADIVOJEVIĆ: There was so much diversity in New York, and it was a more relaxing feeling. Still, it was a very different culture. The culture in the US in general is extremely different from anything in Cyprus or Serbia or Europe. I spoke English with a British accent because our school [in Cyprus] was mostly British-educated teachers. I had to transform into something else to be understood. But at the same time, I think there was this idea of possibility. Everybody is from everywhere. It was definitely very lonely at the beginning, but I don't think it was the same [as the move to Cyprus]. Maybe because I was older, it wasn't as drastic.

INTERVIEWER: Did your feelings about Yugoslavia change when you moved to New York? You would have been moving to New York in the early 2000s [Radivojević: 1999], and a lot was happening in the region at the time.

RADIVOJEVIĆ: I think that's tricky. At that time, communication went dead, and it sort of started to dwindle over the next ten years. That was when Serbia was getting bombed. I was watching stuff on TV where Novi Sad was being bombed.[8] I actually remember those images. I just remember fire and stuff. I think what was most affecting me was the fact that my granddad's second wife, my grandma, died from cancer. She was very young. Then the bombing started, and six months later, he died from nothing at all, just in his sleep. He died from sorrow, basically. I remember talking to him on the phone and telling him, "Granddad, I'm going to the US to study." He was just not there. Usually he was this very strong and present figure in the family, but he wasn't there in that moment. It was like my whole life was disappearing.

INTERVIEWER: Do you remember if you found a community of folks from the former Yugoslavia in New York?

RADIVOJEVIĆ: When I came to New York, I was in a predominantly Greek neighborhood. There were a lot of Greeks and a lot of Cypriots, who now felt closer to me. But [there were] a lot of ex-Yugos as well. There were Bosnians. There were Croatians. We met a friend who was from Serbia, and he became our roommate. I worked in this bar, and everybody would come in. The Bosnians and the this and the that, so it was a really nice mix of things that felt somehow connected to home. And [I made] a friend that I still have today, a Bosnian friend. [There was] just so much warmth because we all found ourselves in this situation. The war was not talked about, but we felt an affiliation with one another.

But also there was this one guy who was Croatian, and we would always chat. He would come to the bar, and it was always kind of happy and light. One day, he brought a friend. He went to introduce me, and he said, "This is Iva, she is ours," or *"ona je naša."* When I said hello, the guy swiftly said, "She is not ours" because I had a Serbian accent. That was the first "punch"... because I'm Croatian too. So both worlds existed.

INTERVIEWER: How do you identify today, whether its nationally, culturally, ethnically? What would you say are the pillars of your identity?

---

8. After Belgrade, Novi Sad was the second largest city in the iteration of Yugoslavia that existed in 1999. NATO bombing targeted oil refineries, roads, bridges, and other infrastructural sites. The bombing of refineries and storage facilities in Novi Sad caused oil spills that led to fires, toxins and carcinogens in the air, and contamination of rivers and groundwater. The environmental impact of the NATO bombing of Yugoslavia spread to the broader Balkan region. For instance, polluted waterways flowed into the Aegean, the Adriatic, and the Mediterranean seas and impacted the health of the region's human, animal, and plant life. See Nježić and Ačanski, "Da se ne zaboravi," 75–78.

RADIVOJEVIĆ: That's a very hard one. As time has progressed, I think I have a need to reconnect to what it means to be from that region, what it means to have grown up with multiple identities and multiple nationalities, and what it means to have gone to and lived in other places as well. But then, of course, at the root of it, there is something very Balkan about me. Even the way I talk, the way things come out.

Even though I grew up with my mother who is Croatian, I cannot identify as Croatian. [It's only that] the passport I use the most is Croatian. I am closer to the Serbian experience, but it just feels weird to identify as Serbian. This is why I keep saying "Yugoslav." As we move in time, people are like, "What are you talking about?" Maybe at the beginning it made sense, but now it is so far. I am fluent in Greek. I've spent most of my time now in Greece. And I spent twenty years in the US. It's tricky. But I also really love the idea of a fluid identity that moves in between spaces and that is not so constrained by any one thing. I think what feels most comfortable is to say that I am from the Balkans.

INTERVIEWER: Is there any part of your identity that's not just Balkan but particularly Yugoslav?

RADIVOJEVIĆ: When I think about things particularly Yugoslav, it is the ingrained dogma we've been taught. I think of *bratstvo i jedinstvo*, or brotherhood and unity, if there's any ideal to take out of it. For me, it was a very happy time between my family in Croatia, my Macedonian family, my Serbian family. It was a togetherness. Even after we'd gone to ex-Yugoslavia for the first time and traveled all around Bosnia and Croatia and so on, I suddenly felt this incredible community when I was speaking the language. [I felt like the people were] my brothers and sisters just by language alone. The language felt like a home.

INTERVIEWER: What do you call the language that you speak?

RADIVOJEVIĆ: That is contested. [Laughs] Today I call it Serbian because it is a very particular dialect. Even in Yugoslavia, we completely excluded Bosnian from the Serbo-Croatian equation. Of course, languages change over time. Croatians are doing their job to make Croatian distinct, changing *aerodrom* to *zračna luka* [both words for "airport"]. I would say that I speak Serbian.

INTERVIEWER: With whom do you speak Serbian or, in general, your mother tongue?

RADIVOJEVIĆ: With my dad. With my grandma, I speak Serbian, and she speaks Croatian. [I speak Serbian with] all of my family because all of my family is still there except my mom and my sister. With my mom and my sister, we go back and forth. When I read books, [I read in Serbian].

INTERVIEWER: How would describe the impact that growing up in Yugoslavia had on you?

RADIVOJEVIĆ: I would go back to the idea of community and the idea of unity, which did seem real to me at that time. In Novi Sad, we had Hungarians and Czechs and Croatians and Serbians and so on. It just felt effortlessly functional and beautifully intertwined. I have not experienced that community that I described through that neighborhood and the buildings and the children coming in and out of apartments and so on. Maybe in Greece a little bit, but it's a very particular way to be. The US is extremely individualistic and particularly trained for the capitalistic system, whereas Yugoslavia was not. It was socialist. Growing up with this distinction was crucial.

INTERVIEWER: What does Yugoslavia mean to you today?

RADIVOJEVIĆ: It is kind of an ideal of being able to live together in celebration of those differences, not despite those differences. We lived together without thinking of ourselves as Serbian or Croatian. We knew that there was something there that made us distinct from each other, but it was a beautiful thing. It was a celebration of those things. I think those are less Yugonostalgic [memories]. Maybe it's [because I'm part of] this generation that was too young to know the problems but old enough to feel some kind of a magic in [Yugoslavia]. And I think coming from a multiethnic family was also a contributor [to my feelings].

INTERVIEWER: Is there anything that you are nostalgic for?

RADIVOJEVIĆ: I think I am nostalgic for some family members who I lost too early. [I miss] not knowing more [about them], not having experienced them more, not having a more solid idea of who they were. I can talk to you about my general grandfather, but they are such small snippets that I can remember. I can't tell you what his politics were, aside from what was told to me from my father and from my uncle. People who grew up there until they were twenty or twenty-five and who left later, they have a very specific identity that's rooted in that reality. I don't. That [makes me feel] a bit like I live in this in-between land, in no man's land. There are a lot of positives about that too. I am also nostalgic for what it could have been.

INTERVIEWER: Tell me more about that. When you think about the things that could have been, what are the things you feel you never got to experience, never got to have, never got to live through?

RADIVOJEVIĆ: One is to exist in the language more. It's such a beautiful language, and it's a beautiful way to be in a world because each language has its own universe. I'm also feeling my gaps now in knowledge and in history. When the war happened and when our emigration happened, I think we started to disassociate and to figure out new ways of being in the world. That's when the gaps started to appear. I think those are the things that I miss.

I go to these old bookstores. There's one particular store that sells used books in Belgrade which I love. It's this guy's own library. Every time I go there, it's such a treat. And when I speak to him, he has a similar sort of disappointment in that nobody's reading. [He says that] nobody knows the value of the poets and of the writers. And how the hell did we get to this place where we have a right wing, pro-Russian government?[9] I'm really nostalgic for an intelligentsia and things that could make this place [better]. I don't know. I think that history [in the region] was never addressed. For me, there's a sort of longing [for the region] to move on to a different point. Yugoslavia, as an idea, was a good one.

INTERVIEWER: What other experiences do you have when you visit the region, whether it's Serbia or Croatia or elsewhere?

RADIVOJEVIĆ: I love visiting now. I love it. I love going to Bosnia. I love going to Croatia. I love going to Serbia. For me, there's a kind of understanding and a [feeling of] familiarity and kinship. Obviously I am generalizing because there is a lot of hurt there as well, which again is why I can't live in that area of the Balkans. Greece is the Balkans too. I go to Kosovo, for example, for a film festival, and I meet Croatians and Bosnians and Serbs and Kosovars there. This is what it could have been like, and should have been like, and can be like! And when I hear that particularly Bosnian accent, my heart feels warm, like "yes!" It's such a beautiful distinction. But I think it's the language that provides the home.

---

9. At the time of Radivojević's interview, the president of Serbia was Aleksandar Vučić (1970–), a long-time politician who had served as minister of information under Slobodan Milošević. Vučić was a member of the Serbian Progressive Party, a party characterized as right of center with conservative, populist, and economically neoliberal policies. Vučić was initially a Euroskeptic, but he has since supported Serbia's bid to EU accession and shifted to a platform of EU cooperation. However, Vučić has also actively maintained relations with Russia. For instance, he has resisted pressure to impose sanctions on Russia during the war in Ukraine and continued to expand economic ties with Russia.

INTERVIEWER: Has anything come to mind that I haven't asked you about or anything that you haven't had an opportunity to share?

RADIVOJEVIĆ: I'm just thinking about how complicated it all is. What I described is the reality of millions of people at the moment who are migrating and running away from war and famine. This idea of roots becomes really interesting. I don't even know how to think or talk about it because the fluidity is beautiful. But there is also something very beautiful about having a connection to a place and the trees that grow there. More and more people are going to be feeling like us [in the future]. How to even prepare for that?

INTERVIEWER: In my recent conversations for this project, as the war in Ukraine has been going on, a lot of people have shared a similar experience. The war is bringing back a lot, whether it's a traumatic experience, a painful one, or a confusing one. Watching those images on the news and hearing peoples' stories feels so familiar to them.

RADIVOJEVIĆ: My mom started having vertigo the moment the war [in Ukraine] started because she had unprocessed feelings about leaving. Everything was coming back. For the moment, everyone is opening their doors. At some point, they are going to close them as they did with refugees from Yugoslavia. And of course, refugees from other countries are not even talked about. I get very angry. I live on Lesbos most of the time and just seeing the differences in the experience of Ukrainians [compared to other refugees] makes me angry.[10] Of course, Ukrainians should be welcomed, but so should everyone else.

INTERVIEWER: Thank you for your time and for sharing your thoughts and memories with me. I enjoyed our conversation.

RADIVOJEVIĆ: I hope it was useful.

---

10. Asylum seekers often enter Greece by way of the Aegean Sea or the land border with Turkey. For many from Africa or Asia, Greece is the byway to Europe and other Western states. International observers have long criticized Greece's asylum and migration reception system. There are too few asylum centers; many refugees lack access to housing, health care, and work opportunities; and most face discrimination, inhumane treatment, or even violence. However, when refugees from Ukraine started arriving in Greece in 2022, they were treated differently. Greece's migration minister, Notis Mitarachi, described Ukrainians as "real refugees" (compared to those from Syria or Afghanistan, whom he described as "irregular migrants") and accommodated them with a significantly easier asylum process: they did not need visas to enter, were able to easily apply for protection status, and received access to essential support services (Pawson, "Hot and Cold").

5

INTERVIEW WITH
Gordan Pejić

Gordan Pejić was born in Sarajevo (now Bosnia) in 1978 and lived there until the start of the Bosnian War. He has since lived in Belgrade (now Serbia), Canada, and the Czech Republic. When we spoke in the winter of 2022, he was working as an infrastructure businessman based in Prague. We conducted the interview over a video call as he was traveling for work and visiting family in Makaraska-Zaostrog (now Croatia). In our conversation, Pejić spoke at length about how growing up as the child of an ethnically mixed couple in Bosnia, the most diverse of the former republics, shaped his understanding of Yugoslavia's "unconditional inclusiveness." He shared why he held tightly to his identity as a Yugoslav and continued to believe in the Yugoslav project. Based on his experiences living in Europe and North America, Pejić also discussed his impressions of differences among Yugoslav diasporic communities.

Many of Pejić's childhood memories were marked by an unquestioning embrace of Bosnia's diversity. According to the 1981 Yugoslav census, conducted a few years after Pejić was born, Bosnia's population was 39.5 percent Muslim (Bosniak), 32 percent Serb, 18.4 percent Croat, and 7.9 percent Yugoslav, with small communities of Montenegrins, Roma, Ukrainians, Albanians, Slovenes, and Macedonians (all under 1 percent). Bosnia was the only Yugoslav republic that did not have an ethnic majority or a corresponding constitutive people. By contrast, 75.1 percent of residents in Croatia identified as Croat on the 1981 census. For Pejić, growing up in Bosnia meant that his childhood friends had different types of names that he accepted as a matter of fact and only later learned to decode by ethnicity. Similarly, he did not make much of his family's mixedness—his mother was Serbian, his father Croatian and Montenegrin—until the Yugoslav wars were underway.[1] Pejić remembered that his mother spoke in a dialect more common in Serbia, but as a child, he did not understand it to be a marker of her difference in Bosnia. "She sounded different, but there was never any frame in my mind to say she spoke like this because she's of a different ethnicity," he told me. "No, she spoke like that because that's how they spoke in the city where she came from, which happened to be in another republic—no significance to that difference, no consequence, no misunderstanding based on that. Nothing." Historian Fedja Burić argues that intermarriage in Yugoslavia, like ethnicity itself, was relational; it took on the stature of social concern only at times of political fragmentation in the late 1960s and late 1990s.[2] During Pejić's childhood, intermarriage was part and parcel of Bosnia's implicit heterogeneity, which defined his childhood experience of Yugoslavia.

Pejić viewed many early memories through the lens of Yugoslavia's ideal of brotherhood and unity, which prescribed peaceful coexistence of nations, nationalities, and national minorities. Early in the interview, he described the clothes he wore to his induction into the Pioneers and explained that the clothes had worked as a leveling tool among classmates. "We wore the uniform so we would all be the same. We didn't have the concept of this guy is rich, this guy is poor, this guy is this, this guy is that. No, all we are equal, not forcefully but in a positive sense of the word." He returned to the metaphor to underline an instance when he and his classmates accepted a newcomer to the school ("He still wore the uniform. He still pledged like all of us") and explain his engagement with difference today ("We are all walking this world in the same uniform, in my eyes. Until you prove me otherwise, we all wear the same uniform"). When he considered how growing up in Yugoslavia had shaped him, Pejić explained that the state's ideals had imprinted tolerance and inclusiveness on him. "The main point of that is absolute tolerance of different opinion, views, religion, skin color," he said. "If I like you as a person, you can be whatever you want in any sense—political, religious, even gender roles today. I don't care. Call yourself whatever you want. I don't mind at all. This inclusiveness is almost unconditional inclusiveness toward everybody. Everybody gets a chance, everybody—just like in Yugoslavia." While Pejić's experiences and memories are certainly not universal, they correspond with the findings of

---

1. On the eve of the Yugoslav wars, 13 percent of all marriages in Bosnia were considered ethnically mixed, while 34 percent of all marriages in Sarajevo were considered mixed (Crosby, "Mixed Marriages as Another Casualty of Bosnia's War").

2. Burić, "Sporadically Mixed," 83–109.

scholar Pål Kolstø that show higher manifestations of Yugonostalgia among former residents of the Bosnian republic.[3]

Pejić continued to passionately embrace the Yugoslav identity, insisting that he was "born as a Yugoslav, lived as a Yugoslav, will die a Yugoslav." In part, this identity summed up the complexity of his family background and kept him from having to align with a single successor state. He narrated a recurring conversation: "People tell me, 'You cannot be Yugoslav. You have to be [an identity out of these] one, two, three, four, or five [options].' This happened with the taxi driver, the bartender, my work colleague, a new friend, an old friend, a lady, everywhere. Then I would say, 'Okay, let me explain to you. My father is half Croatian, half Montenegrin. My mother is Serbian, and I was born in Bosnia. So what am I?'" Moreover, Pejić has lived in several other countries since the Yugoslav wars and appended additional layers to his sense of self. While he culturally, socially, and even legally became a member of several other national groups, he continued to identify primarily as Yugoslav because he believed this identity best reflected who he was.

Moving through different diasporic communities reinforced Pejić's conviction in his identity as a Yugoslav. When he lived in Canada, he noted that Yugoslav émigrés from the World War II era tended to divide into "clubs" aligned with ethno-national identities. He struggled to navigate these spaces because he did not fit neatly into categories such as "Serb" or "Croat." In addition, he was not legible to members of communities who had not lived in socialist Yugoslavia. In the Czech Republic, where large numbers of Yugoslavs began emigrating in the 1990s, Pejić found a community of people who grew up with similar ideals and experiences of displacement. He remarked that the Yugoslav diaspora unified in the face of Czech xenophobia as well as the nationalism that had instigated wars in Yugoslavia. As he spoke about the diasporic community in Prague, Pejić pointed out that that there was one "club" that brought together citizens of the former Yugoslavia: the organization Lastavica. "You can just be a Yugoslav here, and nobody's going to challenge you. It's just brilliant," he told me. "And to this day, there is no Serbian club or Muslim club or Croatian club. It's just Lastavica, and everybody's there. That's it. That's why I still manage to be the Yugoslav I am today." The ideals of inclusion Pejić grew up with lent him a blueprint for navigating the world and seeking out community after Yugoslavia ceased to exist.

INTERVIEWER: What are some of your earliest memories of life in Yugoslavia? What do you remember about your hometown of Sarajevo?

---

3. Kolstø, "Identifying with the Old or the New State: Nation-Building vs. Yugonostalgia in the Yugoslav Successor States," 760–81.

PEJIĆ: [My earliest memory] is the first day of school, when I was seven years old. My mother walked me to school for the first time, and I received a beautiful uniform. It was a blue coat and a *pionirska kapica*, a Pioneer hat, which was technically derived from the [League of] Young Communists [known as the League of Socialist Youth after 1948]. That is my first memory because they gave us a little speech about Yugoslavia, about the importance of education, about brotherhood and unity, or *bratstvo i jedinstvo*, and of course about Tito, who was always politely mentioned, especially in Bosnia. So on the first day of school, I started to understand the society that I lived in.

We took a [class] picture every year with the map of Yugoslavia in the background. When I finished the first grade, I knew that that was the country that I lived in. I was already aware that it was comprised of six republics, that we had a big war against the Germans, and how Tito came to [power]. The reason why I knew that right away at that age was because my grandfather was a war hero. He was a decorated soldier, and he was a colonel in the Yugoslav army. He was wounded during World War II. I remember that because he showed me the scars he had on his chest. I remember some of the stories he told about the war and how they were fighting the good fight for everybody's well-being. He was a big communist, a big Yugoslav, ethnic Croat, but that did not matter. I did not know about ethnicity until 1989 or 1990, but already after I finished the first year [of school] in Sarajevo, I was fully aware of the society that I lived in.

INTERVIEWER: Do you remember if there were other activities that you participated in that were state-sponsored?

PEJIĆ: There were a couple of trips that were organized by school. One was a historical trip when we went to a museum. There was also the Pioneer induction. I almost remember the pledge, the *pioniska zakletva*. When we did the pledge, we again had the uniforms, and they gave us the *šal crveni mali*, a little red scarf. When we were inducted, there were speeches by teachers and directors, and parents were there. It was a really nice ceremony, and I remember that pledge the most because we were pledging to be good people. For me, that was *pomagat starijima* [helping elders], *čuvati tekovine* [caring for the homeland], *bratstvo i jedinstvo* [brotherhood and unity], *sloboda* [freedom], *antifašizam* [antifascism]. It gives me goose bumps, I swear to God, right now when I remember that.

That was probably one of the most innocently dear moments for me in the sense that every child feels the need to belong somewhere. I think it's a natural, human need, and I really like that [Yugoslav] idea because it was based on good behavior, on helping people, on helping the old lady across the street. Don't lie, don't cheat, be a good person, help your fellow man. We wore the uniform so we would all be the same. We didn't have the concept of this guy is rich, this guy is poor, this guy is this, this guy is that. No, we were all equal, not forcefully but in a positive sense of the word.

INTERVIEWER: Do you remember much about your classmates?

PEJIĆ: I remember many people from my school because I interacted with a lot of people. I guess I'm an outgoing person. In the later grades, we got some new kids that we didn't start with. I remember one guy because he just moved to Sarajevo from a small, small town with a specific name, Medjedja [now Bosnia], and his last name was Gazivoda, which is funny because it means "stepping in water" [in Bosnian/Croatian/Montenegrin/Serbian]. His first name was Elvir or Ermin. I remember him specifically because he came in the second or third grade and we sat together, two by two, on the benches. I remember welcoming him and trying to be his friend and sharing my lunch with him. He came from a very disadvantaged family. I knew that for a fact. He just looked very sad. It's not that I felt sorry for him, but I always cared for him. He was one of us. He still wore the uniform. He still pledged like all of us. We had fun, played soccer outside, and just [did] normal stuff.

But there are many others. I had friends like Srdjan Todorović, with whom I immigrated, almost together, to Belgrade. [I remember] Maša Kulenović, my first love when I was eight. She lives in Rome now. I remember Brano Jakubović, my classmate who is the founder and active member of the band Dubioza Kolektiv.[4] I remember Vedrana Maslić and Marina Leder. I remember a lot of other people, like Mensur Aljukić and his brother Mirza Aljukić, Samira, Elvir. I remember a lot of names from my class, especially from my elementary school. Some of them I'm still in touch with, believe it or not.

INTERVIEWER: You mentioned earlier that you were not necessarily aware of ethnicity before 1989. When you were growing up, was there any kind of

---

4. Dubioza Kolektiv is a Bosnian band founded in 2003. Since its inception, it has released eleven studio albums that feature vocals in both Bosnian/Croatian/Montenegrin/Serbian and English. On its website, the band describes its sound as a mixture of ska, punk, reggae, electronic, and hip-hop. Band members support civic movements that oppose right wing nationalism and xenophobia across former Yugoslavia, advocating for freedom of information and making their music freely accessible. The band's self-description echoes Pejić's sentiments about the Yugoslav diaspora: "If you're looking for macho, money-and-ego driven posturing, you won't find it here; no MTV 'rude boy' gangs, no strippers or bling, no corporate endorsements from the international fashion industry. Rather, they take on traditional musical forms with their unique perspective, shaped by war that changed their lives forever, and delivered with a level of positivity that hits you like a blast of fresh air. If you are open to the experience, it could change your life too" ("About Us").

indicator among classmates or neighborhood friends that there might be differences among you?

PEJIĆ: In Yugoslavia and in Bosnia, we differentiate ethnicities only by names, which is wrong. We assume if somebody's named Mirza that he is probably Muslim. If somebody's name is Danko, maybe he's a Croatian guy. If there's a Nikola, he is a Serb guy. But it was such a nonissue because when [Muslims] had *Bajram*, they invited me sometimes to share some food. When others celebrated Christmas quietly, they also invited me. [The differences] were cultural only. "Oh, these people have these customs, these people have those customs." Nobody ever said in the classroom, "This guy's Bosnian; this guy's Serbian." I never heard that in the classroom until the war started. I did not hear it at *all*. From anybody. Even my parents.

My mother is a 100 percent Serbian woman who spoke with a Serbian accent, or *ekavica—mleko, belo*. She still spoke the way she spoke in Serbia with her friends [in Bosnia] who said *mlijeko* [in *ijekavica*]. I never even asked her, "Why do you say *mleko* and not *mlijeko*?" She sounded different, but there was never any frame in my mind to say she spoke like this because she's of a different ethnicity. No, she spoke like that because that's how they spoke in the city where she came from, which happened to be in another republic. No significance to that difference, no consequence, no misunderstanding based on that. Nothing.

INTERVIEWER: Did you notice anybody being treated differently by teachers or neighbors?

PEJIĆ: Not at all. If somebody was being treated differently, it was because he or she was a troublemaker. I was one of those people. Some of the teachers [came] from different republics. We had a homeroom teacher who was named Miloslav, and later, when the whole shit happened, I went, "Oh, that guy was from Serbia actually." I didn't connect that until the war. And it dawned on me later that's why he was one of the first teachers who stopped appearing in school when the war started. At the time, I was completely unaware of it. We made fun of him because we all thought he was sleeping with one of the school administrators. That was the only topic regarding that person, which is 100 percent individual and has nothing to do with the color of his skin, the way he spoke, his religion, or where he was from. I was really lucky to grow up in that environment, you know?

INTERVIEWER: I wanted to ask you more about the family you grew up with in Yugoslavia. Did you live with parents? Did you have siblings? Was there an extended network of family in Sarajevo or otherwise?

PEJIĆ: I didn't have extended family in Sarajevo because both my father and my mother came from Belgrade when they finished university. I think that's where they met. My father was born in Bosnia, and he's half Montenegrin. My mother was a Serbian person. She was born and schooled in Serbia. It was circumstance that they came to Sarajevo. They managed to get jobs [there]. My father was a journalist, and he got a job at TV Sarajevo. Mother was a chemical engineer. She worked for a clothing company.

My parents are divorced. I lived with my mother my whole life. She was a single mother for a while. She stayed in Sarajevo even after the divorce. She loved Sarajevo. She loved, loved, loved Bosnia. So even though my father moved away, she stayed there. I spent my childhood mostly with my mother and my sister. She's a year or two older. She's also a journalist. She lives in Belgrade and works for a major news agency in Serbia, which she hates because of the way the media is set up in Serbia. I'm very close to her. She has three kids in Belgrade with a Belgrade guy. I visit them often. I'm a funny uncle now; that's my role.

It was almost a rule in our country that you go to your grandparents' [place] during the summer, wherever it is—in the village, by the sea, in the mountain, in a city, in this republic, in that republic. I spent my summer and part of my winter vacations [with different grandparents]. I had family members in Serbia, whom I visited often during the summer or winter. [I had] a little bit of family in Croatia. When I was in Croatia, I would be with my father's mother, who was Montenegrin, and his father, who was a war hero. From my father's side, from Bosnia, his sister has two kids. They lived in Tuzla [now Bosnia], so I would spend some time with them as well. And to me, the cousins from my mother's side were equal to those on my father's side. They were equal because we were family. That's all.

It was a very normal upbringing, typical for Yugoslavia, [that spanned] across multiple republics. We traveled on the night train from Sarajevo to Ploče [now Croatia] or Kardeljevo [now Croatia]. Also, we could take a train from Belgrade to Sarajevo via Podlugovi [now Bosnia]. No issues in any republic. Even with my accent, I never had an issue. I was just traveling to the different republics seeing family as a *Bosanac* [Bosnian]. When I went there, that would be my identity. At my mom's village in south Serbia, all my village friends there were like, "Oh, *Bosanac, Boske, Bosanac.*" Our people like to give nicknames, so that was the territorial nickname I got.

INTERVIEWER: Were you aware of any mixedness in your family when you were growing up in Yugoslavia?

PEJIĆ: I was aware more [of] territory. My mother is from here, and my father's father is from here, and my father's mother is from there. And I have family here, here, here, here. I have cousins there, there, there. It was more territorial, not ethnic. That was the only paradigm of difference and division. Nothing else, honestly, until the war. After the war, it was a different story.

INTERVIEWER: Did religion play any role in your family life when you were growing up?

PEJIĆ: Religion was not part of my life, my family's life, or many of my friends' lives. Nobody ever said, "I have to do this because of religion" or "I'm not eating that [because of religion]." I never heard that. All my Muslim friends would eat ham.[5] There was no difference. My grandfather and his wife in Serbia [celebrated] *slava*, and they went to church here and there.[6] That's it. Nothing really worth discussing. Nobody ever talked to me like, "You know, you should choose this religion." It was not a dinner table conversation at all. We didn't even celebrate Christmas really because it wasn't a holiday in Serbia or Bosnia. My only connection to Christmas was when I was on the winter vacation with my grandparents in the village, and they did do the whole Christmas thing with the Christmas *badnjak* [oak branch] and putting the *slama* [straw] in the house and making a special cake and special food.[7] But that was more culture for me. I understood it as the custom of my mother's side of the family.

My father's side of the family had different customs because they were a bit communist. My grandfather was a Partisan, [so he did not ascribe to] religion, just peace and love. [But he was] not anti-religion in the sense you cannot go to church. Nobody ever told me what to think or what to feel

---

5. While there were some opportunities for Muslim children in Bosnia to attend religious school, most of Pejić's friends in Sarajevo likely attended state school and were socialized in secular society. Socialist Yugoslavia generally curbed the influence of religious communities by removing religious officials, closing religious institutions, and discouraging religious practices.

6. *Slava* is a Serbian Christian Orthodox tradition that celebrates a family's patron saint. During the socialist period, families that continued to observe the celebration did so more privately and less strictly. The celebration involved the preparation of ritual foods, including bread (*slavski kolač*) and minced boiled wheat (*žito*), and the blessing of the home by a priest, as Pejić mentioned later.

7. The Serbian Orthodox Church follows the Julian calendar. As part of the Christmas ritual, families bring a *badnjak*, an oak branch, into the home and place it in a fire on Christmas Eve, similar to a yule log. As they bring in the oak branch, they also spread straw on the floor. Christmas Eve is a fast day; ritual foods may include a loaf of bread (*badnji kolač*), fish, beans, and nuts. Meats are included in ritual foods on Christmas Day in addition to a bread loaf (*česnica*) the family breaks together.

about this, at all! Ever! Even from my mother's side, nobody cared if I was baptized or not. The priest didn't care who came to the house, who cut the *kolač* [bread] for *slava*. He would spread the *tamjan* [frankincense], that thing that burns nicely. We didn't even have that stuff in our house in Sarajevo. We didn't even have a picture of Jesus or a cross. We had nothing. We had photos, art, and sculptures on the wall.

INTERVIEWER: What was the role of Yugoslavia in your family's life?

PEJIĆ: From my mother's side, her father couldn't [join] the Partisans because he had a bad heart, but his brother went to war as a Partisan. My father's father was also a big Partisan, a colonel in the army. When I spoke to them, it was always [about] Yugoslavia, positivity, peace and love, brotherhood and unity—nothing negative. But it was in the Yugoslav context. Especially my father's father, he would tell me war stories. He was in the air force. As a young boy, of course I was interested in my grandfather's stories and his gun. He had a luger he took from the Germans. My father lost it during the war, unfortunately. But I remember that gun. I remember the uniforms and some of the pictures my grandpa showed me with other Partisans. That was important in these interactions with these two family members. Outside of that, nothing really.

INTERVIEWER: How did your parents speak about Yugoslavia?

PEJIĆ: At the end of the day, their memories were positive. They were young in Yugoslavia. They married in the 1970s. They went to Opatija [now Croatia] for concerts, music festivals, theater shows, exhibitions, monologues, dialogues, open stages, that kind of stuff. [They had] unlimited travel. They both went to Russia. My mother ran a marathon there. My father went for some cultural exchange. I heard from them that it was the best time to be young—in Yugoslavia in the 1970s and early 1980s.

My father actually had a small issue in Yugoslavia. In the late 1960s, he was a prominent student leader in Serbia. When there were student protests, or *studentske demonstracije*, he led the protest from Serbia, and he spoke to me about how he organized marches with the Croatian representative of the students in Bosnia. He told me that when he was organizing those marches, his father came to visit him in Belgrade in a uniform to convince him *not* to engage in these protests because the students wanted something from Tito. But Tito gave them that, at the end of the day. They won. People say that it was a very hard-ruled country, but we, as the students, managed to incite change, even from a dictator. We got what we wanted. So even in that political sense, there was a process, and my father was the right political person. [He] still spoke very highly of that system and the possibilities. They could complain. They could protest. I don't want to say [they had] freedom of speech, but it was freedom of expression.

[He also had] a lot of positivity about *lokalna samouprava* [local self-management] and *samoupravljanje* [self-management], which my father constantly keeps reminding me about. I say, "Why do you keep mentioning this?" He says, "Because, my dear son, in 1988 or 1989, I was the first elected editor-in-chief of TV Sarajevo, elected by the workers and confirmed by the government." So my father speaks very highly of that process and of that experience from these two instances.

My mother was less politically involved. She had only one small complaint about communist Yugoslavia. She said that part of the grading system in schools back in the day was the subject *dobro vladanje*, or good behavior. You got graded on behavior, which influenced your overall GPA if you skipped class, if you were difficult for the teachers, or if you did shenanigans like me. [I remember] climbing on the first floor of the school after hours while they were having private English lessons and, you know, just mooning them. I would have gotten a zero in behavior class. When my mother was finishing her elementary school in the village in south Serbia, she got a low grade in this behavior class because she fasted and went to church. She told me that *dobila je keca iz vladanja jer je otišla na pričešće* [she received a 1, equivalent to an F in behavior class, because she went to communion]. She didn't moan about it. She said, "Yeah, it was like that, but I still went. It was my choice. I didn't fail. I was still top of my class." So, there was no *real* punishment. It was more symbolic.

INTERVIEWER: Would you say that your parents are nostalgic for Yugoslavia now?

PEJIĆ: Many people of that generation are, and I know that because I travel in this region and meet people my age and much older. Ninety percent of the people that I talk to in Serbian villages, in Bosnian villages, in Croatian villages, in Montenegrin villages, in Kosovo, in all those places, anybody of that generation [is nostalgic]: "Oh, yeah. That was something else. That was special. We had this. We had that. We were strong; we were union organized." I don't know, maybe I didn't speak to enough political prisoners, but I am yet to meet a person who would have half of negative intensity that other people have of positive intensity when they speak about this country and that period.

Many people that I talk to of that generation are nostalgic for Yugoslavia because they were young in the 1970s and early 1980s, which was the *best* time to be young in Yugoslavia. Even my current girlfriend's parents—they are 100 percent Croatian, go to church—who were a little bit younger than my parents reminisce in the same way as my parents. They went to the same festivals as my parents. They went to the same cultural events. They read the same books. They went to the same libraries. And they reminisce in the same way: "We were young. We could do whatever we wanted. We had food on the table. We could travel."

I will give you an example. My colleague from Belgrade who is now sixty-five said, "Man, I had a guitar on my shoulder, and I was just having fun for two summers. I was in Croatia. I was in Montenegro. I was in Serbia. I was playing in Bosnia. I was organizing concerts." It was amazing to them. They were young people who felt free, who could do whatever their hearts wanted. I mean, who can survive two or three summers just by playing guitar and organizing parties and concerts? They also had the [Yugoslav] passport, and they could travel anywhere in the world with that passport. They would go to Trst [Trieste] for shopping to buy Levi's or whatever was trendy, new coffee, drinks, or whatever.[8] They could go to Berlin and London. They could do all that with almost no job, no money, no concept of a credit card, no concept of "Oh my god, how much is it going to cost?" I wish I was born earlier when I hear those stories.

INTERVIEWER: That generation was very much the beneficiary of a system at its height.

PEJIĆ: Yeah, they collected the crème de la crème of that time. We got the scraps.

[That generation also has] lots of memories of *radna akcija* [work actions]. It was unique to Yugoslavia because it was voluntary, and it was considered a privilege. Not just anybody had the privilege to go to *radna akcija*. You had to be good student. You had to be honorable. You had to be the best of the

---

8. Yugoslavia's political nonalignment facilitated bilateral cultural fluidity—foreign influences were allowed in just as Yugoslavs were allowed out. Armed with the Yugoslav passport, many citizens crossed the border, often just for a day, to shop for Western goods. Historian Patrick Patterson explains that "Croats around Zagreb and Slovenes near Maribor, for example, could easily travel to Graz in Austria for household items, groceries, and appliances that were unavailable or more expensive in Yugoslavia. Slovenes living in or around Ljubljana could be over the Alps and in the shopping centers of Klagenfurt in an hour or so. People in Macedonia and southern Serbia had fairly easy access to the markets and shops of Thessaloniki. And Yugoslavs of every variety poured into Trieste to buy all sorts of Western items. In particular, shoppers in Trieste were keen to bring back more fashionable clothes than they believed could be had back home" (Patterson, *Bought and Sold*, 5).

best. My business partner, he's an Albanian guy, he goes, "Oh man, I was in Zagreb building the *Bratstvo i jedinstvo* Highway [Brotherhood and Unity Highway].[9] I built this with Serbs. It was the best time because we were all the same. Nobody cared if I'm Albanian. They didn't even make fun of my accent. It was the best time." You had different religions and different ethnic groups making a bridge in Macedonia, building something here. If that's not about brotherhood and unity, I don't know what is.

INTERVIEWER: Then there was war, though, and that generation's world collapsed. Do you remember the Yugoslav wars starting? Were you aware of something changing?

PEJIĆ: My father was a prominent journalist for TV Sarajevo for many years, so I was aware of [the war] at the early stage. I think in 1988 or 1989, I was already beginning to be aware of it. I would watch my father on TV, and in the rare moments he would visit, I would ask him [about the war]. He would tell me, "Things are not looking good, my son." He said that a thousand times. He didn't explain why, but he just said that things were not looking good for our country.

I have a specific memory. I watched Gazimestan 1989, the famous speech of Slobodan Milošević, on TV.[10] That was the first time I heard a mass of thousands of people chanting not "Yugoslavia" but "Serbia." I was confused, but I put it in the context that something was happening. I went to my grandparents' house in 1989, and I heard older people talking. I realized that people in Serbia had one story. My grandfather who was communist had a story that was a little bit different. Then I would talk to my father's sister and her husband, who is a Bosnian Serb—they were both in the police—and they had their stories. And then I came back from that summer vacation in 1989, I heard more from my classmates.

---

9. The Brotherhood and Unity Highway stretched across the territory of the former Yugoslavia and connected four republics (Slovenia, Croatia, Serbia, and Macedonia) and some major cities. Recruits of the Yugoslav National Army and participants in the Youth Work Actions built the highway in several sections between 1950 and the mid-1960s.

10. Slobodan Milošević, then president of the Republic of Serbia, delivered the Gazimestan speech in Kosovo on June 28, 1989. The speech was part of an event marking the six hundredth anniversary of the Battle of Kosovo, a battle won by the invading Ottoman army and enshrined in Serbian national mythology as a moment of oppression needing to be avenged. Milošević's speech came after years of tension in Kosovo. In the speech, delivered to a crowd of about one million Serbs, he likened the battle Serbian leaders fought against the Ottomans in 1389 to the present-day relationship between Serbs and Albanians. Milošević stressed the need to redress Serbian victimhood and protect the history of Serbs in Kosovo. Although the speech referred to some socialist ideals, it encapsulated the mounting Serbian nationalism in Yugoslavia. National and international critics feared the speech was a call to arms for Serbian interests.

Some teachers would come to me and make comments about what my father said on TV.[11] The mom of my best friend, who was a Serb—I found out later on—told me, "I like you, but the things your father is saying are not right." I was like, "What?" But I still didn't fully grasp it. We had to change our phone number because people were calling us so many times and asking for my father, cursing, and threatening. Me and my sister had fun [with it though]. When these people called, we would turn on the hairdryer and be like, "This is the airport! This is the airport! There's no Nenad Pejić! This is the airport!" [Laughs]

INTERVIEWER: Did anything change in your everyday life as the war was gearing up?

PEJIĆ: Everything was the same, except people were disappearing. People were leaving. Whoever had the opportunity and knowledge that this was not going to end soon left. This guy had a cousin in Germany. This guy had somebody in Slovenia. We had a lot of Serbs living [in our building], and they just left. There was paramilitary entering the building. They were looking for apartments that were owned by JNA [Yugoslav National Army], or *vojni stanovi*, where there may have been Yugoslav army personnel of known Muslim persuasion. They broke into these apartments. I even saw Juka Prazina doing something in our building.[12] He was one of the known figures during the civil war in Bosnia who [was making], let's say, "ethnic visits" to these apartments. Things started to go down from 1990 very, very, very quickly.

As a child, I was running a radio TV program, believe it or not, on Radio Sarajevo. We went to Šibenik [now Croatia] for a radio conference right in 1990. I was in the van, and then I saw the flags and [heard chants of] "*Hrvatska, Hrvatska*" [Croatia, Croatia]. I asked the editor, Zlata, "What is this?" She told me, "Shh, don't talk about that. Let's focus on the radio." I realized I needed to be quiet. I would deflect or ignore or assume it was

---

11. Pejić's father, Nenad Pejić, worked for TV Sarajevo until 1992. After he left Yugoslavia, he started working for Radio Free Europe/Radio Liberty, where he founded and directed the South Slavic and Albanian Language Broadcast Service. He is a media expert, university lecturer, and author of several books, including one that chronicles his recollections of the early 1990s media climate in Sarajevo, *Isključi TV i otvoriti oči* (*Switch Off the TV and Open Your Eyes*), that was published in 2013.

12. Josuf "Juka" Prazina (1962–1993) was involved in organized crime in the 1980s and led a paramilitary group called Juka's Wolves in the early years of the Bosnian War. Prazina was at times affiliated with the Army of the Republic of Bosnia and Herzegovina and the Croatian Defense Council, and he has been accused of various war crimes.

"grown up stuff." That's how I was processing it at least until 1992, when I was thirteen or fourteen. But when the guns started shooting and the barricades [went up], it was clear to me that we were entering a civil war. When the shit started in Croatia, I was starting to [understand that] this was the end of brotherhood and unity.

[For a long time] we lived under the illusion, my mother included, that this would not come to Bosnia. We are strong. We are united. We are not divided along ethnic lines. "*Jebeš Bosnu koja zemlje nema*" [fuck a Bosnia without a country] was a saying. So "*jebeš zemlju koja Bosnu nema*" [fuck a country without a Bosnia] became [a saying] for Yugoslavia.[13] Bosnia was the heart because everything was mixed there. If we fell apart, then the whole country would fall apart. In Bosnia, we had this naivete that [the war] would end soon. Why do I say naivete? Because when we left Sarajevo, we were running. My mother didn't bring family pictures, a pathetic collection of her jewelry, or documents. She made us carry books, so we didn't miss school. This was going to end soon. We were going to come back. What a mistake that was. We don't have a single family photo. I have a few family photos that were made by other family members when I was in Serbia or in Montenegro, but I don't even have any of my classroom photos. There was a lot of naivete that our unity was so strong, that absolutely this would not happen in our little Bosnia. But it did.

INTERVIEWER: Do you remember your departure from Sarajevo?

PEJIĆ: Oh, vividly. One of [my father's] drivers drove us through Sarajevo and dropped us off at the airport. [There was] a lot of waiting at the airport and lots of military checks. I remember all these stupid checkpoints and questions and barricades. Serbs were checking us. Muslims were checking us. I remember very vividly people getting pushed off the plane. I remember gunshots at the airport. I remember sitting at the airport for *hours* on end. I don't even know how my mom managed to organize the thing. I think we took the last flight.

INTERVIEWER: Was it a cargo plane?

PEJIĆ: Yeah, of course, [it was an] ATR-72 or whatever you call those early, small airplanes. A lot of bags were thrown away. We were all sitting inside, and the pilot made us move in front or else we wouldn't take off. I remember that.

---

13. The first phrase, "*jebeš Bosnu koja zemlje nema*," implies a nationalist argument for Bosnian independence. By contrast, "*jebeš zemlju koja Bosnu nema*" implies that Bosnia was an important part of Yugoslavia. The popular Yugoslav singer Lepa Brena (1960–) released a song titled "Mani zemlju koja Bosnu nama" in 1984, which extols sentiments similar to the latter phrase.

INTERVIEWER: From Sarajevo, you all briefly resettled in Belgrade, right?

PEJIĆ: Yes, correct. I lived in Belgrade as a refugee from 1992 to 1995. Even though my mother was a Serbian citizen, she still did not have Serbian papers. We lived with refugee IDs for multiple years and received the UNHRC help, or the *HRC pomoć*: powdered milk, biscuits, some vegetable oil, some *really* shitty ass toothpaste![14] That refugee toothpaste was *horrible*! You had worse breath after you brushed, but apparently it would clean your mouth.

I remember being a refugee in Belgrade, which was not easy. I heard people always blaming refugees for not having this, for not having that. I vividly remember the refugee days in Serbia: changing schools, getting in a couple of fights, and things like that. Being in Belgrade in the 1990s as a refugee was better off than being in Sarajevo under the bombs and the grenades, but it was not a pleasant experience for a fourteen-year-old boy with a single mother.

I brought all my stupid old books, but they were all thrown away, and I started fresh. They didn't put me back one grade back because my mother brought the *knižica*, like a transcript in a book, so I didn't lose a year or even a semester. I just went straight and continued. It was the same curriculum. Everything was the same. Just history was different. That part of the transition was seamless. I spoke the language. The school system was pretty much the same. I wasn't stupid. I was hardworking. I had pretty decent grades too, to be honest, despite all that stuff.

INTERVIEWER: How did you introduce yourself to folks in Belgrade?

PEJIĆ: *Bosanac* [Bosnian]! They gave me the nickname right away: *Boske, Bosanac*. They labeled me right away. Every classroom that had a *Bosanac* [gave them the nickname] *Boske*. Unless they had a few of them, then they would change. But I was the only one, at least in the beginning, when I first transferred to the Belgrade school in Novi Beograd.

INTERVIEWER: And then you spent some time going between Belgrade and Prague, right?

PEJIĆ: Yes. I was in cooking school in Belgrade—*gostinska škola*, or hospitality school. It's called *treći stepen*, which means third degree, which is the

---

14. United Nations Human Rights Council (UNHRC) is the United Nations refugee agency designed to provide emergency aid, protect human rights, and develop long-term solutions for refugees, displaced communities, and stateless people.

lowest form of specialized high school in Serbia you can enroll in. It's like all the rejects go there. If you don't get into the gymnasium, they dump you to be a cook, a chef, a waiter, a bartender, or whatever. And the main reason why I chose that was in spite of my father. My sister was going on his path: gymnasium [a secondary school that offered a "classical" education rooted in the humanities], then journalism. I'm like, "Well, I'm not. I don't want to ever get married. I don't want this. I don't want that. I'm going to be a cook." So I went to the *lowest* form of education you can possibly get in Serbia.

Towards the beginning of 1995, it was already clear that the Dayton Agreement would be signed and that the war in Bosnia was going to end. Everybody knew that there wouldn't be any more territorial exchange or ethnic cleansing [after that]. There was a big push from the Bosnian Serb army to gain as much territory and defend as much territory as possible. There were mobilizations in Belgrade, even with underage kids. I did not have a Serbian ID. I just had the refugee card. There were stories that [military agents] would stop the train in the middle of Belgrade, make everybody show their ID, and send men of fighting age with refugee IDs on a chopper to Pale to defend those Serbian lands in Bosnia.[15] My father knew that. At that time, he was already the director of Radio Free Europe/Radio Liberty. He said, "This is too dangerous. Let's bring him to Prague."

I didn't even want to go because I had just got my friends in Belgrade. We were going to school to be cooks. We were having fun during the practice cooking [sessions] in Hotel Palas. I didn't want to go, but I had to. So I went. I finished high school at ISP, the International School of Prague, and then I decided to go back to Belgrade. I enrolled into the higher school of hotel management because I wanted to continue on the hospitality path. I thought it was good business. I wanted to be a hotel manager.

By that time, I was grown up, and I was reading the news. I knew what was happening in Kosovo. I smelled another war. I told my mom and my girlfriend at the time, "I got to go." I packed my bags, and I fought hard to get a visa because I had a Serbian passport, finally. After many, many, many months of waiting, I managed to get a visa. I escaped Serbia a little bit before the bombing started. Maybe one week before Slobodan Milošević closed the borders. I took a bus to Budapest, caught a train to Bratislava,

---

15. Pale (now Bosnia) is located just southeast of Sarajevo. As the Bosnian War started, Pale became a hub of Bosnian Serb forces and the administrative center of the nascent Republika Srpska government. It is currently a municipality of Eastern Sarajevo and the de jure capital of Republika Srpska (Banja Luka is the de facto capital).

and got a train to Prague. And then I started my second run at Prague in 1998. They did draft me. I got the envelope. There was a red and a blue one. I think the blue was to get recruited, and the red was to already go to active [service]. I got a red envelope. My mom told me [later]. I didn't even know. I didn't want to go to any war for any army, especially in Yugoslavia.

INTERVIEWER: How did your sense of self change when you left and came back?

PEJIĆ: My identity did not change. I was always a *Jugosloven* [Yugoslav]. Even in the taxi, [when the driver would ask me,] "Where are you from?" I would say, "I'm from Yugoslavia." [If they replied] that the country doesn't exist, [I would say that] it does to me. I did not want to let go of this identity. And to this day, [when] people ask me where I'm from, I say, *"Ja sam Jugosloven"* [I'm a Yugoslav]. I will never let go of that identity.

Here's a funny anecdote. My girlfriend is from Zagreb. She [is] a little bit younger. She was born in 1989, and I was born in 1978. We were in a taxi in the Czech Republic and speaking our own language, and the Czech [driver] asked, "Where are you guys from?"—[expecting] to hear Serbia, Bosnia, or Croatia. I was like, "I'm from Yugoslavia. She's from Croatia." And that's how, to this day, I identify myself.

Prague is a *unique* place for Yugoslav refugees. There was slang that Czech people used for us from Sarajevo or anywhere from Yugoslavia. Czech people are a little xenophobic—every country is—and they [called] us *"jogurti, jogurt, jugoši, jogurt."*[16] So we had printed T-shirts, hundreds of them, [that said] *"jogurt, jogurt, jogurt."* It was easy for me to maintain that [Yugoslav] identity in Prague because I lived in an environment in Prague where it was reinforced. [It was] much harder in Belgrade. I also didn't emigrate to Frankfurt, Munich, or Vienna, where you have a Serbian club, a Croatian club, a Bosnian cultural center, a Muslim cultural center. [Émigrés there] go to their little clubs, little restaurants, and little bars. We did not have that in Prague. We were just Yugoslavs, and they called us that. It reinforced my identity.

I have a Canadian passport now. I love Canada. That country gave me a lot. When I go to Canada, people ask me where I'm from. I say, "I'm from Yugoslavia. I'm a Yugoslav. That's it." And people tell me, "You cannot be Yugoslav. You have to be [an identity out of these] one, two, three, four, or five [options]." This happened with the taxi driver, the bartender, my work

---

16. In Czech, "Yugoslavia" is *Jugoslávie*, but it is sometimes referred to by the shortened term *Jugoška*. The words Pejić recalled some Czechs using to refer to Yugoslavs can be interpreted as pejorative both in their reference to yogurt and their essentialization of the community.

colleague, a new friend, an old friend, a lady, everywhere. Then I would say, "Okay, let me explain to you. My father is half Croatian, half Montenegrin. My mother is Serbian, and I was born in Bosnia. So what am I?"

I'm proud of two things: that I didn't let go [of my identity] and that I didn't assimilate. I didn't change my accent. I never became a Serb. I didn't become a Croat. I didn't search out my identity in Montenegro like [some] Americans. They go, "Oh, I'm quarter Irish, so now I'm Irish." No, I wasn't a Montenegrin. I'm a Yugoslav, made out of all those pieces that were one country at the time of my birth up to the unfortunate events of the 1990s.

INTERVIEWER: From talking to other folks who have similar experiences like you, people who have different family members from different regions of Yugoslavia and then who acquired new citizenships, I know it is difficult for them to say, "I'm Croatian, but also Serbian, and also Montenegrin, but also Canadian, and also Czech." "Yugoslav" feels like the most inclusive category for them.

PEJIĆ: That's a very good word. It's a very inclusive category, 100 percent. You want to be in this club? You are welcome. Just by you wanting to be in this club, you tick all the boxes for me.

INTERVIEWER: Have your feelings toward Yugoslavia changed over time?

PEJIĆ: No, my feelings didn't change, but I did learn more history. I read a lot about Goli otok,[17] about the Red Army,[18] and about Hanždar Divizija.[19] I also

---

17. Goli otok was an uninhabited island in the Adriatic Sea used as a political prison and labor camp by the Yugoslav government between 1949 and 1989. It was initially used to incarcerate known Stalinists and Stalinist sympathizers after the Tito-Stalin split in 1948; anticommunists and criminals were also incarcerated there. Until the 1980s, it was taboo to discuss Goli otok, which is likely why Pejić only learned about it later.

18. Scholarship on the Red Army during World War II focuses on its rampages of violence and sexual assault of civilians in enemy countries. Historian Vojin Majstrović suggests that troops were more restrained in friendly countries like Yugoslavia because of sympathetic propaganda about Yugoslavs, stricter disciplinary measures, and a more welcoming local environment. Nevertheless, Majstrović writes, "Soviet soldiers and officers were generally convinced that as warriors they needed and had a right to sex. These impulses were reinforced in Yugoslavia by the fact that they liberated the country from Nazi clutches, and by an accompanying atavistic belief that as victors they were entitled to a tribute from the local population, which for some troops included Yugoslav women" (Majstrović, "The Red Army in Yugoslavia, 1944–1945," 421).

19. Hanždar (Handschar) Divizija was the Thirteenth SS Waffen Mountain Division, an infantry division comprised of Bosnian Muslims, Croats, and some Yugoslavs of German descent. During World War II, Hitler courted Muslims in the Balkans with carefully targeted propaganda that presented the Third Reich as protector of Muslims and patron of Islam. See Motadel, "The 'Muslim Question' in Hitler's Balkans," 1007–39.

read about the first Yugoslavia, where they were shooting each other in the parliament.[20] I learned more and in a bigger context because I had a Western education. But even the extra knowledge that I obtained did not put out a flame of this feeling. I am still positive, and I feel the same about Yugoslavia.

I loved reading about this because there is still so much that we don't know. The government or whoever controlled us didn't allow us to see the full history of what the secret service did and the deals Tito made. It's still a bit of a mystery. Despite all that, despite having this black hole about the whole of the Yugoslav story, my passion, my identity, my feelings toward Yugoslavia did not change. From that first day in elementary school, Yugoslavia was *bratstvo i jedinstvo*. Not in the forced sense, but [to] help your fellow man, be a good person, help the old lady cross the street, don't steal, help your neighbor when he's harvesting.

Nobody locked doors! We never locked doors in Sarajevo! I lived in a twenty-story building. I lived on the nineteenth floor. I think we had six or seven apartments per floor. That's a hundred and twenty apartments, yeah? Times five people per apartment—that's like five hundred people, man, living in one building. That's just an example that speaks for itself. That was Yugoslavia for me, and that feeling is not going to be changed by whatever happens in the world today or a few years ago. And many people of my age have the same feelings. They know what the Serbs did, what the Croats did, what Slobodan [Milošević] did.

INTERVIEWER: To what extent do you think your childhood in Yugoslavia shaped who you are today?

PEJIĆ: Huge. It was my personal experience based on these very few principles that were engraved in me and that really stuck with me. I translated those into my dealings with people, into my dealings towards the city, towards the environment, towards public transportation, towards public services, and towards education. It was simply the only way for me to conduct myself and view the world. The main point of that is absolute tolerance of different opinions, views,

---

20. Pejić is most likely referring to the shooting spree of Puniša Pačić (1886–1944), a member of the People's Radical Party from Montenegro, in the Yugoslav parliament on June 20, 1928, that mortally wounded the Croatian People's Peasant Party founder Stjepan Radić (1871–1928). The incident highlighted tension among interwar politicians and eventually prompted King Alexander I to attempt to force unity by abolishing the constitution, banning political parties, declaring a dictatorship, and renaming the country the Kingdom of Yugoslavia (formally the Kingdom of the Serbs, Croats, and Slovenes). For more on the politics of the first Yugoslavia, see Djokić, *Elusive Compromise*.

religions, skin colors. If I like you as a person, you can be whatever you want in any sense—political, religious, even gender roles today. I don't care. Call yourself whatever you want. I don't mind at all. This inclusiveness is almost unconditional inclusiveness towards everybody. Everybody gets a chance. Everybody. Just like in Yugoslavia. We are all walking this world in the same uniform, in my eyes. Until you prove me otherwise, we all wear the same uniform.

INTERVIEWER: What does Yugoslavia mean to you today?

PEJIĆ: Obviously [it is] the place where I grew up until a certain age. [It is] the place and time of bliss, peace, and joy. That's it: utter peace, utter joy, utter bliss. [It was] pleasantry all around. 100 percent. Put simply. Nothing more, nothing less. Of course, I can say, "Yeah, it was a great time and a great country." Put that aside. The effect that that great time and that great country had on me is how I feel about myself with this identity that I'm not letting go of under any circumstances. Even to spite some people, including my girlfriend. [Laughs lightly]

For example, the 29th of November is *Dan republike* [Day of the Republic], a very important holiday for me. I never forget it. I was going to meet [my girlfriend's] sister on the 29th of November. This was by accident. So we wake up in our hotel in Zagreb, and I immediately go to YouTube and play a couple songs, which I play every year: first, Zabranjeno Pušenje, "Danas je Dan republike" [1987] on repeat, then "Od Vardara pa do Triglava" [from the band Riblja Čorba, 1988], then a classic Miroslav Ilić and Lepa Brena, "Živela Jugoslavija" [1985], and of course, the national anthem, which I find beautiful. I know it by heart to this day. I sang it with my brother-in-law, my sister's husband. I was in Belgrade on the 29th of November, and he played the same three or four songs that I would play. We drank *rakija* [plum brandy], and we were like, "Hey, good times!" This guy, my sister's husband, is a Belgrade guy, a Serbian guy 100 percent, and he was totally on the same wavelength because he's a product of that generation just like me but not poisoned by war, hate, and nationalism. I'm not patting myself on the back. I think we're lucky and privileged. I think that is a product of my personal upbringing and the time when we lived. Escaping the war helped. That's why people like me and my brother-in-law are not letting go easily. We didn't get poisoned by hate and propaganda and all that stuff, like, "Serbs did this; Croats are bad." Nobody's bad. If you're Yugoslav, you're not bad. All the others are bad.

INTERVIEWER: You've mentioned that you are friendly with lots of folks from the former Yugoslavia region across the world. Is this generally how you approach the Yugoslav diaspora?

PEJIĆ: No, I don't seek it out, no. It's very organic for me. If I meet somebody and we click, that's just the potential for the beginning of a nice friendship. But I don't seek out [others], like, "Oh, I'm going to Canada, let me hook up with Yugoslavs." No, not at all. I had some really good friends in Canada. I liked them a lot, but they didn't share the same view on the whole Yugoslav story. I was in many fights with a great friend of mine from Vancouver. [He's an] amazing guy. He identified as a Serb, and he had a tattoo. He would never tell you he was Yugoslav. But I still liked him because I'm inclusive. It doesn't matter. He was a good guy. You're a Serb, and I'm a Yugoslav, but we're still buddies.

The Yugoslavs I met in Vancouver were not the same people I met in Prague. These Yugoslavs were either Serbs, Croats, or Muslims. The people who migrated to Canada in the 1940s were very much the Četniks and the Ustaše who couldn't live in Yugoslavia. They migrated there and raised these kids that were totally brainwashed by their own immigrant parents. They came from a specific ethnic group and maintained that ethnic identity, while I maintained a Yugoslav identity.

INTERVIEWER: What do you call the language that you speak?

PEJIĆ: There is a term for my language, and technically it is *južno-slovenski jezik* [South Slavic language]. I still say *srpsko-hrvatski, hrvatsko-srpski* [Serbian-Croatian, Croatian-Serbian] because to say *jugoslovenski* [Yugoslav] is not the right word. You can say *južno-slovenski* [Slavic language], but somebody might tell you, "Macedonian is also a *slovenski jezik*," and I don't speak that. So I would say *srpsko-hrvatski* or *hrvatsko-srpski*. Usually, I would say both, *srpsko-hrvatski* or *hrvatsko-srpski*, or SHHS. In Sarajevo, we wrote "SHHS" in our notebooks. [We wrote] one week in Cyrillic, one week in Latin. So I would just say, "I speak *srpsko-hrvatski*" without any issues. In Croatia, I would say it. In Bosnia, I would say it. In Serbia, I would say it. They would tell me, "That's not that. That's *srpski* [Serbian]. That's *hrvatski* [Croatian]." I say, "Yeah, whatever. It's what I speak." As simple as that.

I'm still using *ijekavica* in my accent, and my dialect is Bosnian because that's where I lived most of my life. I did not want to let that go. My sister did. She speaks beautiful Serbian. She [worked] on TV in Serbia, so she had to take classes to have a proper accent. When she speaks Serbian, it is more proper than any Serbian person ever because she studied it. She had to adapt. I was younger, a rebel, so I always say *srpsko-hrvatski, hrvatsko-srpski*. I don't care if I'm going to offend somebody. I don't care. My girlfriend's father fought in the Croatian War [of Independence]. To him, I would say that I'm speaking *srpsko-hrvatski* without any issues. He wouldn't comment on it. I would say, *"Evo, na našem je"* [here, it's in our language]. He would say, "Oh yeah, let me read. Yeah, yeah, I see." No issues. Maybe I'm meeting just the good people. I don't know. I don't have a negative memory of this. I would just stick to my guns, my inclusive guns, and that's it. My Yugoslav guns. [Laughs lightly]

INTERVIEWER: How do you feel today when you travel through the former Yugoslavia region?

PEJIĆ: I feel amazing. This was my dream—to live in Prague and work in my region—and it happened by accident. I am so happy that I can live in Prague, which is still the Western world, and I can just visit [the region]. My company thinks I'm crazy, but then I tell them my customers are here, so I need to spend time here. I [follow] politics too much. I hate it. It's poison, but I don't let it faze me. I still feel great when I come here. Every time. And I just love it.

But to tell you, I do absolutely notice the differences between people in Croatia and Serbia and Bosnia now. As the years are passing by, they are drifting away from each other even though it's the same culture. They listen to the same music. They have the same jokes. They watch the same movies. They're doing the same things, but they are saying different things and trying to act differently. It's a bit sad, especially if you watch political commentary and especially if you watch the nationalist television in Bosnia, Serbia, and Croatia. God forbid you start reading online commentaries on *Index*, *B92*, *Klix*, or *Večernje novosti*. It's disgusting. I still read it, and I need to stop. I can see this poison runs deep.

On the surface, the younger generations don't seem to be as poisoned. But their identity is, for example, "I'm Croatian. We won against the Serbs. They wanted to take our country. So they're losers in this war. I don't like them." You go to Serbia, [the rhetoric is] "Them Croats, [they are] Ustaša." They still talk about Jasenovac, NDH, [Ante] Pavelić, [Franjo] Tudjman, this village being burned, these people being slaughtered, yadda-yadda-yadda.[21] If you go to Bosnia, of course, it's still "Četnici, murders, killing us, fuck them,

---

21. Most of these references are related to the Independent State of Croatia (NDH), an Axis puppet state led by the Ustaša during World War II. Pejić likely brought up these references to illustrate that the history of World War II started to be used in nationalist discourse after the Yugoslav wars. Scholar David Bruce MacDonald suggests that Serbs and Croats both called on persecution myths from World War II to justify wartime actions in the 1990s as primarily defensive (MacDonald, *Balkan Holocausts?*).

blah-blah-blah. Nothing good came out of that country, blah-blah-blah." I feel that. I hear that.

I hear that because I interact with a lot of people professionally and personally. I'm in infrastructure business. I understand by drinking with these customers. My primary goal is just to understand their customer needs, issues, and things like that. But they do let their guard down, so I do hear some comments. They know I live in Prague, and they know that I'm a Yugoslav because I'm Bosnian. I do kind of slip in [other parts of my identity]. Like, "oh, I'm going to Serbia because my mother is there." Or, "hey I'm going to Montenegro. My grandmother is there." They do open up, but I see that divergence.

My father said it best about Yugoslavs: it's as if we're all watching the same movie in the same theater, but we changed seats, and we entered the movie to watch it at different times. We did not sit in the same place to watch from the opening scene to the last one. Maybe I came later and switched seats in the meantime. Or I left for a break and came back. There's no real consistency. And that's kind of like a metaphorical feeling that I have. We're all watching the same movie in the same language, but somehow we understand the movie differently because we didn't watch it at the same time, with the same subtitles, in the same place, with the same light. But it's still the same movie, but we don't see it as the same movie.

Given my background and the way my family is oriented toward journalism, it's a bit sad what I've seen. I've talked to my best friends who ended up in the Serb army during the Bosnian War, or in the Croatian army during the Croatian War [of Independence], or in Kosovo even. I grew up with a person who told me later on that he was a sharpshooter for the Republika Srpska military. I would digest that and [talk] to another friend whose father was a civilian killed during the war. I cannot marry those worlds. I can just see them, but it is difficult [to reconcile them]. I [get] emotional about it. I do understand, and I can't judge. It is not the Yugoslav way to judge. They had their experience. They had their poison in their wounds. I had mine, which was maybe different than theirs. I have to respect the scars of the people [I] interact with because the scars make them who they are today. You have to accept that. I can't expect them to have the same view of things. That's why I don't discuss politics with friends, only in general terms.

I managed to escape the war. Nobody close to me died in the war. That was just by accident. I was lucky. I'm lucky that even my uncle, my mother's sister's husband, [survived]. He was in the war on the Serb side. My good friend who is *distrofičar* [a person with muscular dystrophy] was also in the war [and survived]. He hates the war. I understand that. I spoke to him many times. I know the war changed him. The scars changed him, but I still accept him for who he is. I will not debate him: "You're wrong. This was not Serbia." It's also not Yugoslavia. I'm not going to correct [anyone's] opinion, and I don't try to do that. I accept them for who they are with their scars, with their pains, with their mutilations in their mind and in their soul, if I can use that word. I do just accept them for who they are. That's it.

INTERVIEWER: As we've been talking, has anything come to mind about Yugoslavia, your childhood, or experiences before or after Yugoslavia that I haven't asked you about or you haven't had the opportunity to share?

PEJIĆ: I will tell you just one thing. The reason I probably didn't get poisoned too much is because I went to Prague. Nobody was really running to Prague. Most refugees went to Germany, Canada, America, Sweden, Norway, and all those countries. [The Czechs] had their communism, and they were just opening up. There is no traditional Yugoslav or Serb migration to the Czech Republic like there was in Germany, Canada, France, and Italy. There you have Serbian and Croatian clubs from the 1940s and 1950s. Prague didn't have that. There was not a single incident that I was aware of when Serbs were fighting Croats or different ethnic groups. There was none of that.

Prague got this crème de la crème of the true citizens of Yugoslavia, mostly from Sarajevo, who came from very different backgrounds to start their life in Prague. The first wave was the Bosnian diaspora, and the second wave came from Serbia. But in this first wave, it was like mini-Yugoslavia, man. It was like my classroom in Bosnia: Samir, Mirza, Adnan, Ognjen, Lazar. It was so amazing. Doctors, lawyers, engineers, people from commerce, and people from the educational world all came in a short period of time to Prague. All original Yugoslavs. All successful. When I say successful, I don't mean they're all Elon Musk or Bill Gates, but they all found their way under the sun. I literally don't know anybody from my generation who I met in Prague that is a bum in the sense that he failed, lives under a bridge, is a junkie, is going to rehab, is a wife beater, or is in jail. None of that. Zero. And that's amazing.

There is one club in Prague, and it's called Lastavica. In the chapter of the club, it says we are accepting everybody from the former Yugoslavia who speaks this language. They do the first of May, *Prvi maj* [May Day], party. They do the barbeque. They invite the poor villagers from Croatia and Serbia. They bring some cultural folklore groups from Bosnia or Serbia. They organized money for Croatia when there were earthquakes a few years ago. They had these book exchanges. [It is] just an amazing community. I'm in the group chat, and man, when it's the first of May, they send pictures. When it's *Dan republike*, it's all peace, love, and Yugoslavia.

The leader of this organization, Lastavica, is Edo Jaganjac. He also wrote a book called *Sarajevska princeza* [Sarajevo Princess, published in 2015]. He was the main trauma surgeon during the Bosnian War in Sarajevo. He would patch up thousands of people. He amputated hundreds of arms and hundreds of legs. And he is in Prague now, and he is the chief surgeon traumatologist in the entire Czech Republic. He works out of the main hospital in Prague called Motol [University Hospital], which was built by Yugoslav companies that were building infrastructure. By some coincidence, my work colleague Rade, who is now in Belgrade, was in Prague as a Yugoslav engineer building that hospital. And now a Yugoslav guy is the head traumatologist surgeon in that hospital.

Everything that I learned in Sarajevo, especially in that early stage, I managed to somehow live [out] at my later stages today in Prague. All the best restaurants [here] are run by Yugoslavs. All the best waiters are Yugoslav. Some of the best taxi drivers are Yugoslavs. Many doctors are Yugoslavs, and so are nurses, lawyers, real estate people, shop owners, you name it. In Prague, I go to all these places, I speak *srpsko-hrvatski*, and it's amazing. I buy some Yugoslav food from Serbia or Croatia: *kajmak, pršuta, ajvar*, you name it.[22] It's like I never left.

And that's why I came back from Canada, actually. I missed Europe. I missed Prague. You can just be a Yugoslav here, and nobody's going to challenge you. It's just brilliant. And to this day, there is no Serbian club or Muslim club or Croatian club. It's just Lastavica, and everybody's there. That's it. That's why I still manage to be the Yugoslav I am today, and I hope to God I will be that until my dying moment. I'm so happy that I'm Yugoslav.

INTERVIEWER: Thank you so much for your time and sharing your stories.

PEJIĆ: Thank you, it was my pleasure. It was a slam dunk. I told you in the email, I am the biggest Yugoslav you will ever find. Not in the sense of "Oh, everything else sucks." No. What was good for me was the product of that environment at that time, and it stuck with me. I am born as a Yugoslav, lived as a Yugoslav, will die a Yugoslav. That's it.

---

22. *Kajmak* is a thick, creamy dairy food enjoyed as an appetizer spread or a condiment on meat patties and beef shanks. *Pršuta* is a dry-cured ham similar to prosciutto most often eaten as an appetizer. *Ajvar* is made from smoked and minced peppers, eggplant, and other herbs. It is often sweet, but it can be seasoned to be piquant. It is often consumed as a spread on breads or a condiment on meats or other dishes.

6

INTERVIEW WITH
Elena Stavrevska

Elena Stavrevska was born in Pančevo (now Serbia) in 1984 and grew up in what is now North Macedonia. She remained in the region until her early twenties, then studied and worked in other parts of Europe and North America. Today, she is an international relations and feminist peace studies scholar based in the United Kingdom. When we spoke via a video call in spring of 2022, she was visiting family in Kavadarci (now North Macedonia), a town where she spent most of her childhood. As she shared her memories, Stavrevska recognized that her understanding of Yugoslavia has sharpened over time. As she learned more about the region, she realized that there were many aspects of society that she had not been aware of at the time. For instance, she reflected critically on aspects of Yugoslav society not publicly discussed during her childhood, such as the marginalization of Albanians and Roma. At the same time, she spoke at length about the opportunities, particularly educational and vocational, that the socialist state extended some of its citizens, including her own family. Stavrevska's Yugoslav childhood fundamentally grounded her sense of self, and toward the end of the interview, she articulated how her identity has evolved to be post-Yugoslav.

Stavrevska's scholarship shaped her understanding of Yugoslavia's history. She explained that her intellectual curiosity led her to study the nuances of ethnic relations and the pervasiveness of inequality in Yugoslavia. When she thought back on her own childhood in the former state, she recognized its problems all the more. "I'm fully aware that it had its shortcomings," Stavrevska said. "It had its shortcomings in centralization, in terms of oppression of people who even questioned the idea or questioned anything, in terms of people who were not recognized majorities in the different republics and how they were treated. I am fully aware of that." Stavrevska specifically discussed how she came to grasp the systematic discrimination of the ethnic Albanian and Roma communities she grew up with. She recalled that inequality was a topic of conversation her parents introduced at home, but she had no memory of learning about it in school in Yugoslavia or, after 1991, in Macedonia. "Especially if this is a country I self-identify with," she said, "I'm meant to know these things."

At the same time, Stavrevska discussed how the former state had extended valuable opportunities to some of its citizens. Even if not fully actualized, the socialist ideals of equity and progress were foundational for Yugoslav social programs. For Stavrevska, education stood out as a critical social good Yugoslavia provided many citizens, and she spoke at length about the impact her parents' access to education had on her family. Socialist Yugoslavia was invested in the education of its citizens. Sociologist Jana Bacevic shows that the Yugoslav parliament initiated comprehensive educational reforms in the early 1970s, culminating with the Law on Vocational Education.[1] Stavrevska's parents were the beneficiaries of this expanded access to education, and it shaped their personal and professional trajectories. Both of her parents came from poor, rural, working-class families. Stavrevska speculated that without state support, her parents would have never met. Her father might not have been able to move to Skopje to study, and her mother might not have had the opportunity to attend university at all. Not only that, but Stavrevska wondered if either parent would have been able to secure comparable employment or provide for their family had it not been for support from Yugoslavia.

As we talked, Stavrevska directly linked her parents' gainful employment and social mobility to their education. Stavrevska explained that her mother began to work as a dentist immediately after completing her degree. She was placed in Kosovo as part of a federal program that sent essential service providers like dentists across the state. Once political tensions began to flare up in Kosovo, the family again relied on the parents' educational and vocational training to relocate to Macedonia. "The reason why we moved to Kavadarci specifically was [that] my dad got a job," Stavrevska narrated. "We had no strong connections to the town otherwise, although we did have relatives—uncles and aunties—of both of my parents living in Kavadarci at the time. My dad got a job at a factory here, and at that time, with his employment also came the employment of a spouse and an apartment to live in." Stavrevska

---

1. Bacevic, "Education, Conflict, and Class Reproduction in Socialist Yugoslavia," 77–94.

underlined that her parents' access to education ultimately facilitated the family's vertical mobility. "They started out without any kind of financial support from their families because both families were poor, but they were eventually able to afford to buy their own flat and have a decent life," she said, noting that "many things would have been impossible without the support they had from the state." At another instance, she explicitly articulated that Yugoslavia's investment in the education of its citizens showed a degree of welfare that no longer exists in the region. She also keenly recognized that the opportunities her parents received in Yugoslavia directly impacted her upbringing, especially her family's emphasis on education.

Stavrevska's childhood in Yugoslavia and her shifting perception of it unmistakably influenced her. She described how she considered herself Macedonian and post-Yugoslav. Like many members of the youngest Yugoslav generation, Stavrevska found that identifying with only one successor state did not accurately reflect her sense of self; the category Yugoslav, or as Stavrevska framed it, post-Yugoslav, encompassed a wider spectrum of influences that shaped her. "For me, answering where I'm from in one word has always been difficult," she told me. "But in addition to that, your mom is from one place, your dad is from a different place, you were born someplace, you grew up elsewhere, and now you live in a completely different place. It's very difficult to answer that question in a straightforward manner. So because of that, for me, being post-Yugoslav is a way of saying that I have been shaped by different parts of this region that used to be one country. And I think all of them have played a role as well in different ways." Many others interviewed in this collection shared similar sentiments about Yugoslav as an inclusive identity category. It validated the mixedness of their families and allowed their sense of self to evolve over time and space. Stavrevska and others of her generation embraced Yugoslav as a foundational identity component that pushed against the narrowing set of nationalizing options left after the collapse of Yugoslavia.

INTERVIEWER: I know you were born in Pančevo and then later spent some of your childhood in Macedonia when Yugoslavia still existed. [Stavrevska: And in Kosovo.] What are the first memories that you remember of your spatial surroundings?

STAVREVSKA: My whole family spent the period around my birth and then [my mom's] maternity leave in Pančevo and Jabuka [now Serbia] because my father's family was located in Jabuka, so they were able to help with childcare, especially as I have an older brother. But before and after that, we were in Kosovo.

I have snapshots of some things that happened in Kosovo, but my first proper memories were from Kavadarci—what I would call my hometown, which is in Macedonia—where we moved to when I was about three or four. So spatially, I would say that the only place I remember as a child was Kavadarci. The other places—of course we visited Jabuka—I'm not entirely sure whether those are my memories or memories based on my family's retelling of some stories.

INTERVIEWER: Do you remember school? Do you remember home or your neighborhood?

STAVREVSKA: Yeah, I remember all of it. Kavadarci is quite a small town, and at that time, *komšiluk*, or neighborhood and neighborliness, was a strong thing. The reason why we moved to Kavadarci specifically was [that] my dad got a job here; we had no strong connections to the town otherwise, although we did have relatives—uncles and aunties—of both of my parents living in Kavadarci at the time. My dad got a job at a factory here, and at that time, with his employment also came the employment of a spouse and an apartment to live in. Before we were able to move into what was eventually to become our own apartment—after a certain period of time of living in it, tenants were allowed to purchase their flat—we were renting part of a house.

I remember my family building relations quickly with all the neighbors in that part of town, and we still have good relations [with them] even though we lived there for just about a year. Sometimes some of the neighbors would come pick us up from kindergarten—my brother and me—if my mom or my dad had a later shift. I remember the kindergarten was really close to where we lived, and I really loved going to kindergarten. It was really like a community. I remember all of those things.

I also remember things from *stokovna kuća* [department store]. It was like the biggest department store, or rather the only department store in Kavadarci then. I remember it was always joyful to go there, not because I would necessarily get something but because there were always different toys on display. It was always so colorful there. That was a place to also bump into people.

Some of my early childhood memories were also impacted by the Yugoslav wars. For instance, I remember meeting people from Bosnia and Herzegovina, refugees displaced by the war, who were temporarily staying with some of the families in our neighborhood before leaving for different countries in Western Europe and North America. A little boy around my age who I became friends with, for example, moved to Sweden.

Also, Sašo Gešovski, a soldier in JNA [Yugoslav National Army] who is considered the first victim of the Yugoslav wars and who was killed in May 1991 in Split, was from my hometown.[2] I remember [that] vividly because the whole hometown went to the streets when his body was brought back. And I was out on the streets, too, with my family. Some of the memories are of war, unfortunately, although not firsthand necessarily. But those are also spatial memories because I remember the streets were filled with people. Everyone was crying and distressed about what the future [would] bring. I mean, it's bits and bobs of different things.

INTERVIEWER: Tell me a little bit about other kids in your neighborhood or at school. Do you remember any friends or folks you went with to kindergarten or school?

STAVREVSKA: I went to two kindergartens. One was close to where we were renting a flat, and one was when we moved to our flat, close to that neighborhood. I remember the kids, and actually some of the kids who went to the second kindergarten with me lived in the same neighborhood. We would consider it a big neighborhood. It had this massive parking lot around which there were several buildings, with some 105 apartments or so, and all the children would come to the parking lot and play every day. And I'm actually in contact with some of them still, whenever I come back or by social media. [Socially,] I think it was a mix. I would say that it was primarily a working-class and middle-class kind of a neighborhood because many of the flats were given on the basis of employment at that time.

The neighborhood was primarily inhabited by ethnic Macedonians, like most of Kavadarci. In terms of diversity, especially racial or ethnic diversity, I don't think there was much in Kavadarci at the time. And the Roma population, which was small but not insignificant, was largely invisibilized, like in much of Yugoslavia. Many of them lived in a couple of neighborhoods. I do

---

2. Sašo (sometimes written Saško) Gešovski (1971–1991) was a soldier in the Yugoslav National Army. As Stavrevska noted, he was born in Kavadarci. He was killed in Split (now Croatia) on May 6, 1991, while serving mandatory military service and working as a security guard at the naval command post. A masked and still-unidentified person shot and killed Gešovski during a thirty thousand–person protest organized by a Croatian nationalist group, Hrvatske unije sindikata. The protest was aimed at the blockade of a village by Serbian nationalist forces, Republic of Serbian Krajina. Protestors targeted the naval command post because they believed the Yugoslav National Army was supporting the Serbian nationalist group despite its proclaimed neutrality. Gešovski is widely considered the first military victim of the Yugoslav wars. As Stavrevska narrated, the following day, on May 7, Kavadarci residents organized a rally to honor his death, and twenty thousand people attended his funeral.

remember there was a Roma family—I think they were, at the time, the only Roma family in the neighborhood—that moved into the building next to ours. And I remember them because they had a daughter whose name was Rase and who was my friend. She would often come to my house, and I would go to her house. We would play with dolls and pretend to drink tea from tiny plastic cups.

As for religious diversity, I don't know if at the time everyone would declare themselves Christians, but in terms of what was publicly visible, Orthodox Christianity was the dominant religion. There was also one mosque. It was actually near the neighborhood where we first lived in Kavadarci, but I don't know when the mosque was built. Of course, during Yugoslavia, there were also many people who declared themselves as atheists. I don't know what the percentage of atheists in Kavadarci is now, but certainly much smaller, as many former communists "discovered religion" after the breakup of the former federation.

INTERVIEWER: Were you aware of difference around you?

STAVREVSKA: Yeah, well, there were several differences. The reason why I was aware of the religious difference is because my mom's father was a priest, while my dad's father was a communist. I come from a family that's part hard-core religious and part hard-core atheist. I wasn't always aware that this was the case, but I remember when we were with my mom's family, a prayer was said before every meal. My dad and anyone from his family would get up but not necessarily cross [themselves]. It was never tense. It was always a respectful coexistence. But it was just something that I became aware of. I don't remember having conversations about that until later on, but it was something that I noticed.

But I did have a conversation with my dad—we had a lot of conversations—about the gendered division of labor. Well, we didn't call it that, but that's what I would call it now. My mom, who was a dentist, worked in shifts. Some weeks it would be mornings, and some weeks it would be afternoons. My dad worked [regularly] seven to three. There used to be cheap electricity in the middle of the day. So my mom used to set up the laundry machine between, I don't know, twelve and two, whatever the time was, so that my dad could spread the clothes when he came home from work. I remember the children of the neighborhood teasing me and saying, "Oh, why does your dad spread the clothes to dry? Is he a woman?" Of course, this was all very patriarchal. I remember coming home and [telling] my dad this was what the children said. I remember him explaining to me how the two of them were working toward raising a family together and [that] of course there were no such thing as women's and men's [roles]. I remember having those conversations.

Another conversation I remember having with him, although indirectly, was about class differences and social justice in some ways. You know *djevreci*, right?[3] The circular doughy thing? So in my hometown, there were people who sold *djevrek* in these little push carts. They would go into neighborhoods and say, "Warm *djevreci*, come and get them," announcing their arrival. I remember once I was downstairs playing with other kids, and we were mocking that person, who actually happened to be a Roma person. They said, *"Ajde, topli djevreci!"* In response, we repeated the same thing back to them mockingly. My dad apparently heard me, so he asked me to come home. He asked me, "Why are you mocking this person?" And I said, "Well, you know, he is disturbing the peace of the people, blah-blah-blah." And he said, "Do you make fun of me when I go to work?" And I said, "No, but you're an engineer." I don't know where I picked that up. Nobody in my family was like, "Oh, he's this and that." And he said, "Yeah, but that's because I had the opportunity to study, and now I go to work to earn money so you and your brother can study and have a good childhood. And I'm sure that's what he's doing as well. He's supporting his family, so if you mock him, you have to mock me when I work as well if that's the logic you're going by." I remember I became a little fighter, arguing with the other kids when they mocked the street vendors when they came to our neighborhood. These conversations have stuck with me.

INTERVIEWER: Do you remember if other children treated Roma folks differently at school? Or did the teachers approach them differently?

STAVREVSKA: I don't remember. In high school, I don't think there were Romani children in my class. In elementary school—because we studied with one group through fourth grade and then a different group from fifth to eighth—to the best of my recollection, there were no Romani children in my classes. In the neighborhood, I don't remember the details. I remember who I was friends with, but I don't remember other people or who other children were hanging out with. I don't remember, sorry.

INTERVIEWER: Do you recall participating in any Yugoslav-related activities in school or any kind of community space? For example, the Pioneers, a singing group, or excursions.

---

3. *Djevrek* is a circular and sometimes braided bread often covered in sesame, poppy, or other seeds. It was common across the former Ottoman Empire; its size, crust, and chewiness vary from region to region. The Macedonian word *djevrek* comes from the Turkish *gevrek*, which means "crispy" or "crunchy." It is commonly sold by street vendors but can also be found in bakeries.

STAVREVSKA: No, I started school after the *pioneri* [Pioneer] period. My brother, who is three years my senior, was a Tito's *pioner*. I remember I would sometimes wear his little hat around the house. Because I started school in September of 1991—by that time, Macedonia had declared independence, on September 8, 1991—I don't think that we did anything Yugoslav related. I do know that later in life, like in my late teens and early twenties, there were informal gatherings, like when I would go internationally for a conference or whatever. The Yugos would inevitably come together, singing some Yugo song like "Hajde da ludujemo,"[4] "Igra rok' en' rol cela Jugoslavija," or something else of the kind.[5] But in a formal setting, especially in an educational institution, I don't remember if there was anything like that. My memories are quite imperfect. As all memories, they have been affected by things that happened after.

INTERVIEWER: Tell me a little bit about the family that you grew up with. You mentioned your mom and your dad. Did you have a larger family network?

STAVREVSKA: My mom comes from a mountainous region in the southwest of Macedonia, near the border with Albania, and she has three siblings. We grew up having a closer relationship to her family here in Macedonia, including the grandparents and the families of two of her siblings. I should probably mention that with Yugoslavia and Albania breaking off relations in 1948, my grandma on my mom's side had not seen her family for nearly fifty years because with the closing of that border, her family remained on the Albanian side, and they had no way of seeing each other.[6] She actually had a sister who

---

4. "Hajde da ludujemo," translated to "Let's Go Crazy," is the title track of the 1990 record by the performer Tajči. The song won the Yugovision song selection contest in Zadar (now Croatia) in 1990 and became Yugoslavia's entry to the Eurovision Song Contest, held in Zagreb (now Croatia) in 1990. Eurovision was held in Yugoslavia in 1990 because Yugoslavia's entry—Riva's "Rock Me"—had won the competition in 1989.

5. "Igra rok' en' rol cela Jugoslavija," translated to "All of Yugoslavia's Dancing Rock 'n' Roll," is a song by the Belgrade rock band Električni Orgazam. It is a track on their 1988 studio album *Letim, sanjam, dišem*.

6. In 1946, Yugoslavia and Albania signed the Treaty of Friendship and Cooperation, which stipulated the integration of the two states' economies; later discussions proposed the integration of their militaries. In 1948, the Albanian politician Koçi Xoxe (1911–1949) even advocated for bringing Albania into the Yugoslav federation as a seventh republic. However, following the split between Tito and Stalin that year, relations between Yugoslavia and Albania came to an abrupt halt because the Soviet Union supported the establishment of Albania's independence under leader Enver Hoxha (1908–1985). The two countries only established diplomatic relations again in 1971. During most of the years after World War II, the People's Socialist Republic of Albania had strict travel and visa restrictions, which made it difficult to leave or enter the state.

was born after the closing of the border, and she had not seen her until the sister was forty-eight. But anyways, that was this part of the family.

My mom and my dad met at university in Skopje where my dad came to study. His family is originally from a village on a mountain near here, near Kavadarci. In the 1940s, after the Second World War, I think they were moved to Banat, Jabuka [now Serbia].[7] My dad and his sister were born there and grew up there, and then my dad decided to go to university in Macedonia. While Yugoslavia existed, we went to [visit] those grandparents really frequently, [on] national holidays like, for instance, November 29. I spent a couple of summer vacations there as well. I was quite close to those grandparents until the early 1990s, when they remained in Serbia. I know my parents were really trying to get them to come live with us here because they were fearful [for my grandparents] due to the situation in Serbia and in the region. My parents were sending all sorts of things to my grandparents, like flour, sugar, and medications during the early 1990s embargo too. Unfortunately, during those years, we weren't really able to see each other much at all. During the Yugoslav years, I would say that was the family I have more memories of than the Macedonian part of the family. It's a bit complicated.

---

7. After World War II, Yugoslavia's socialist regime made a deliberate attempt at large-scale industrialization. Yugoslavia's proposed method was collectivization, or the consolidation of private land, animals, and labor into state and cooperative farms. The 1945 Law on Agrarian Reform and Resettlement nationalized private farms, denied peasants ownership of pastures, and restricted use of mountain land for transhumance (Vucinich, *Memoirs of My Childhood in Yugoslavia*, 118). This law went hand in hand with forced relocation of people to places where their labor would be "optimized." While Tito was initially prudent in requisitioning land and property, he doubled down on rural collectivization after Stalin critiqued his leniency toward kulaks and redoubled it after he broke with Stalin in 1948. "This decision would turn out to be economically unsound and politically dangerous," historian Jože Pirjevec writes, "destabilizing the alliance between the working masses and the peasants, and alienating from the regime precisely those social classes that had participated most passionately in the struggle for liberation" (Pirjevec, *Tito and His Comrades*, 154). Peasants began resisting collectivization, forcing the state to ease up by the early 1950s. Postwar Yugoslavia also saw an increase in voluntary internal migration. According to scholar Oli Hawrylyshyn, one third of the Yugoslav population had migrated from one locality to another by the time of the 1961 census. Much of this migration was internal to each Yugoslav republic. In Macedonia, for instance, 27.5 percent of the population had moved within the republic, while 4.8 percent had moved from another republic. Stavrevska's father's family, however, moved from Macedonia to Serbia. Hawrylyshyn shows that Serbia (excluding Vojvodina and Kosovo) had the highest rate of intrarepublic migration in Yugoslavia—7.8 percent of the population in 1961 had moved from another republic—and suggests that this rate was driven by its central location, urbanization, industrial opportunities, and ethnic affinity (Hawrylyshyn, "Ethnic Affinity and Migration Flows in Postwar Yugoslavia," 93–116).

INTERVIEWER: That's a Yugoslav story—a complicated story [Stavrevska: It is, yeah. Without Yugoslavia, my parents wouldn't have met.] Were you aware of anything you'd ascribe today as mixedness in your family when you were growing up?

STAVREVSKA: In terms of political views, yes. But in terms of ethnicity, no, not so much. My auntie, my dad's sister, who was an ethnic Macedonian, married a guy who was an ethnic Macedonian too. I think ethnically, there has been not much, to the best of my knowledge—at least, within the immediate family. Of course, the part of my mom's family that is in Albania is quite mixed.

But in terms of political views, there is quite a bit of a difference. Even currently, some of the members of my immediate family probably differ in political views from me. But I remember during the wars, there were big discussions around [Slobodan] Milošević. My uncle—as in, the husband of my auntie, the husband of my dad's sister—worked as a musician in the police band at the time and had a picture of Milošević in his house. I know. [Sighs] And I remember when we visited, my dad threw it in the bin every time he passed by it, and my uncle picked it up and put it [back] up. I remember we kids would be sent to bed, and there were intense discussions around the dinner table late into the night, with my dad trying to reason with my uncle and explain how Milošević was destroying Yugoslavia and overseeing the bloodshed in different parts of the former country—but to no avail, from what I remember. So there was difference in those terms but otherwise not much of a difference, I would say.

INTERVIEWER: Were there political differences present in the communist era? Were there folks who were more socialist-leaning and others who were more religious leaning?

STAVREVSKA: To the best of my knowledge, my entire immediate family believed in the idea of Yugoslavia. Or at least my parents did, but I don't recall ever talking about it with my uncles and aunties. I mean, to be honest, if Yugoslavia hadn't existed, my mom wouldn't have gone to school. Her mom died not knowing how to write, and my mom finished university. That's quite a bit of vertical mobility that would not have been possible without the support that she received from the state. And it's not just that; that's just one example. I remember I asked [my mom's family] at some point—this was way later—how they, a priest's family, lived together with a family of communists. And they [said] that, in their view, they both boiled down to a commitment to social justice and humanity. I remember at some point we had a conversation about whether religion, or Christianity specifically, advocates for the same thing [as communism], and their understanding of it does, but that's a separate discussion. But no, actually, during that time, I don't think there was much of a political difference. In my recollection, my mom's family practiced their religion without many problems, but from speaking with family members in the aftermath and some very recently, I realize that the experiences vary greatly even within Macedonia. It might depend on where they were located—my mom's family was in a mountainous village—so perhaps they were a little more under the radar, so to say.

INTERVIEWER: How much do you remember of religious rituals? Growing up, were you baptized? Did you attend services? Did you celebrate any of the holidays?

STAVREVSKA: Yeah, all of it. I was baptized. I don't remember that because I was a baby, but I was baptized, without my knowledge and consent, of course. [Laughs] Kidding, kidding. Or rather, I'm not kidding, but it's irrelevant in this case. We celebrated all the holidays. We celebrated the Day of the Republic and May Day maybe almost as much as we celebrated Christmas and New Year's. And New Year's was celebrated not with Santa Claus but with *Dedo Mraz*, the communist version of Santa.[8] Of course, Christmas was never about gifts; it was always about family being together. This remains the case in my family to this day. We celebrated Easter. Again, it was always the emphasis on family being together for all these holidays. My parents, I think, were engaged and had the registration [of their] wedding on a state holiday so that the whole family could come together. We celebrated all the holidays in the spirit of everyone coming together. In the 1990s, because I was spending a little more time with my grandparents here, I became a little more familiar with what it meant to fast and what it meant to pray and all these things.

INTERVIEWER: You mentioned that among your family, there was this appreciation that Yugoslavia provided opportunities that might not have existed otherwise. Was that something you were aware of at the time? Were you aware of your mom, your parents, or other relatives engaging with Yugoslavia and being aware of Yugoslavia actively changing their lives?

---

8. *Dedo Mraz*, translated to Grandfather Frost, is a figure similar to Saint Nicholas. During socialism, when religious traditions were discouraged or banned, *Dedo Mraz* was embraced as a character who brought children gifts on New Year's in many East European countries.

STAVREVSKA: Yeah, I mean honestly, we talked about it for as long as I can remember. They [my parents] met in a student dorm, and they would always call it just *dom, studentski dom*, or home. I remember there was always this talk of the centrality the student dorm played in their relationship; it was how they met and how they met some of their friends who I knew. I remember them talking about getting student loans and buying clothes. My mom would buy clothes for her siblings as well. There was a lot of talk around that, especially considering how precariously both of them lived and how little their families were able to help in any way.

After graduation, my mom, a dentist, applied and got a job in Kosovo as what was then called *deficitaren kadar* [insufficient staffing]. This meant that people in professions that were considered essential services, like dentists, got a bonus in addition to their salaries as a way for the state to ensure that all the parts of the country had access to essential health care services. Of course, that was possible because it was a centralized state, but they [my parents] always would acknowledge how they got their jobs and how that related to the functioning of Yugoslavia. Sometimes they would also speak of how they bonded with the people in the village in Kosovo where we lived. Much of that bonding was over food and commonalities to which Yugoslavia contributed one way or another. But I think them moving back to Macedonia was, in some ways, also related to them realizing that this idea, this state that worked—or that worked out for them, rather—was coming to an end. I think that partially informed their decision to move to Macedonia.

INTERVIEWER: Why did they move back to Macedonia?

STAVREVSKA: When we lived in Kosovo—this was probably in 1988 or 1989—it was a time when there was increased police and security-structure violence in Kosovo against ethnic Albanians. There was increased dissatisfaction by the Kosovar Albanians, of course, with that violence as well. My brother was coming to a point where he had to start school, and I don't think there were any schools in his native language—which was Macedonian—in the area where we lived.[9] He spoke Albanian, but Macedonian was his mother tongue. My brother actually fluently spoke Albanian because as child he was out playing with the kids, and he picked it up quite fast.

---

9. According to the 1974 constitution, the Socialist Autonomous Province of Kosovo, located in the Socialist Republic of Serbia, recognized Albanian and Turkish as minority languages. Depending on the region, education would have been available in one of those two languages and Serbo-Croatian, but not in Macedonian.

In addition to this, my parents were, after all, foreigners in Kosovo even though they say that it had been the place where they felt the most welcome and the safest of all the places where they ever lived. And when things started brewing across Yugoslavia, the decision to move to the country that was the home country of at least one of them probably factored in. I don't remember how it was explicitly mentioned, but they mentioned that it factored into their decision to move to Macedonia.

INTERVIEWER: Is it safe to say that both parents viewed Yugoslavia positively while it existed?

STAVREVSKA: Yeah, it's safe to say that they viewed it positively while it existed and after it existed as well. I do think they were aware of the shortcomings, or some of the shortcomings, especially having lived in Kosovo. But I think that they did nevertheless view the country quite positively, drawing on their experiences. I think it is possible to consider and live with that difference as two aspects of the experience of that country. I think also [that] in the aftermath of Yugoslavia, it was quite difficult to not view it positively because Macedonia was quite isolated internationally: there was the Greek embargo, we needed visas for everywhere, and so on. Macedonia was denied all sorts of things for all sorts of reasons. I think that those things were quite difficult, and then transition—well, transformation, I would call it, because I don't know what we were transitioning toward—was quite difficult as well. There was a lot of unemployment in my hometown. There was a lot of societal and social destruction in different ways. There were people who committed suicide. I think it was quite hard not to view Yugoslavia positively both because of the active role it played in their lives and also [because of] what the aftermath looked like.

INTERVIEWER: Would you say that either of your parents is nostalgic for Yugoslavia?

STAVREVSKA: Yeah, well, my dad [was]. He passed away. My mom is. In both of their cases, many things would have been impossible without the support they had from the state. They both came from poor, working-class families. So to have the vertical mobility they had and to have the opportunities to study, I don't think that would have been possible [without Yugoslavia]. In the current state it would not be possible, for instance. And they certainly would not have met. My dad would not have necessarily studied in Skopje; he would have probably studied closer to home. They started out without any kind of financial support from their families because both families were poor, but they were eventually able to afford to buy their own flat and have a decent life. I'm not entirely sure that would have been possible in different circumstances, or at least that's their view, and that's what they passed on to us as well.

INTERVIEWER: You've mentioned a couple times that you were aware of war when it started and that you were aware of visible public demonstrations. Do you remember how you first heard about the start of war? What are your first memories of the Yugoslav wars?

STAVREVSKA: We used to be allowed to watch the evening news with my parents, and that includes of course the commentary from the family as well. I think my first memory is the one of May 1991, which was the funeral. It was the funeral of the soldier and the town honoring the soldier's body coming home, after which there were demonstrations. I don't remember if I remember them or if I'm thinking that I'm remembering them. Anyways, there were demonstrations in the country demanding that Kiro Gligorov, then the president, pull the Macedonian soldiers out of JNA and bring them home, with the demonstrators asking, "Why are our children dying for someone else's wars?"[10]

I remember Sašo Gešovski and the demonstrations. I remember the meeting of the presidency of the communist party, when they walked out.[11] I remember my dad saying that they're going to break up the country. I'm not sure I knew what that meant. And then I remember seeing my dad tear up when the Mostar Bridge was destroyed.

Also, you know how back in the day, everyone was in JNA? We knew about different parts of the country also through [my dad] talking about where he was stationed. I remember them [my family] talking about that, about what JNA used to stand for and about what JNA had become during the wars. Then,

---

10. Kiro Gligorov (1917–2012) served as first president of the Republic of Macedonia from 1991 to 1999. He had been involved in the political leadership of Yugoslavia since World War II as finance minister, president of the assembly, and member of the Yugoslav presidency, among other roles. Gligorov actively participated in discussions that led to the independence of Macedonia; the Assembly of the Republic of Macedonia elected him as its president in 1991.

11. During the Fourteenth Congress of the League of Communists of Yugoslavia, held in Belgrade on January 20–22, 1990, delegates from the Republic of Slovenia walked out after the assembly defeated several of their reform issues. They had been advocating for an amendment mandating that the Communist Party relinquish its monopoly on power and thus grant greater autonomy to the republics. Resistance to the amendment came from people like Slobodan Milošević, then a delegate from Serbia. Although Milošević argued that the session should continue, the congress was dissolved when Croatian and Macedonian representatives pledged support to their Slovenian colleagues. The walkout of the congress is considered a critical juncture on the path to the dissolution of Yugoslavia.

as I said, there were refugees from Bosnia here in the neighborhood where I lived. My dad had Bosnian friends, so we were trying to get in touch with them. I remember there was a lot of stress and anxiety around getting in touch with them, especially because they were a mixed ethnic family living in what is now Republika Srpska, so they were not safe. I remember seeing images from Vukovar and all the destruction on TV too.[12] And [I remember] us talking about what's going to happen in Serbia as well—not us, but my parents were talking, and I was just doing the listening—and what's going to happen to the grandparents, whether Macedonia was safer than the other countries or whether they should come [here]. These are some snippets from the early years.

When we moved toward 1994 and 1995, I was becoming much more aware. I knew about what was happening in Bosnia and in Croatia. That was constantly on the news. That actually triggered my interest in the research that I do. I remember wondering what kind of people would want to kill their neighbors.

INTERVIEWER: What changed in your everyday life as the wars were starting?

STAVREVSKA: I think there were a lot of conversations at school. Different children would hear different things from their parents. They would be like, "Oh, my parents were talking that Macedonia might go into war." And of course, no one knew what that meant. I remember having many, many conversations like that. Because we used to travel freely around Yugoslavia and viewed Yugoslavia as our country, I think that spatially, our imagination of where we were safe, rightly or not, shrank. We used to visit grandparents for the holidays, or we would frequently go to Montenegro. And these things [related to] where you belong changed. This is not a result only of the wars but also a result of transition.

But lot of things in this country changed as a result of this transformation toward liberal capitalist democracy. I think it started becoming dysfunctional really quickly. A lot of things existed only if you could pay for them. Many things that we took for granted were no longer. Like every day, we'd hear about different kids' parents losing their jobs, or a lot of people started doing

---

12. Vukovar, a city in present-day Croatia, was the site of a major conflict during the Croatian War of Independence. After Croatia's declaration of independence from Yugoslavia, violence erupted in ethnically mixed regions bordering Serbia. Vukovar was home to a sizable Serb minority; this group reported incidents of discrimination and violence following independence. The Serb-dominated Yugoslav National Army and Serb paramilitary groups surrounded Vukovar in the fall of 1991 and held it under siege for three months. While the city was only lightly defended, the Serb military and paramilitary forces waged a violent assault that devastated the city, killed around three thousand people, and displaced tens of thousands.

informal economy activities, sometimes illegal economy activities as well. Had Yugoslavia not fallen apart, this might not have happened in that way. I remember a lot of kids would try to sell different things that their parents brought from Bulgaria or somewhere else. I remember a couple of my friends' fathers had committed suicide, and it was said that it was because they were under a lot of pressure as they could no longer provide for their families. They lost their jobs; they ended up in debt. It's not a direct consequence, and of course, my life was in no way impacted as directly as people who were in the areas where there was war. But these were some things that did change for sure.

INTERVIEWER: As you continued to attend school in Macedonia, did you notice a shift toward a different form of education or different ideologies?

STAVREVSKA: I have no comparison from before because I only attended school in independent Macedonia. There was a lot of emphasis on ancient Macedonia in history, so I don't know if that was the case from before. I've never compared notes, but it would be interesting to know. In 2008, when the whole Skopje 2014 started happening and the antiquization of the country, I remember thinking back that in school, [there] was no questioning of the understanding of who might have come out of ancient Macedonia.[13] There

---

13. After the dissolution of Yugoslavia, neighboring states like Greece, Bulgaria, Albania, and Serbia questioned the legitimacy of the Republic of Macedonia. Greece in particular blocked Macedonia's membership in all international forums, claiming that "Macedonia" was the name of a Greek province and could not be used by a sovereign republic without a designator like "North." In 2008, Greece vetoed Macedonia's membership to NATO. Macedonia's government responded with an aggressive nationalization agenda that laid claim to ancient figures like Alexander the Great and Philip II of Macedon as national inheritances. This antiquization suggested that ethnic Macedonians were the descendants not only of the Slavs but also of the ancient Macedonians. Antiquization was a form of domestic nation building, but it was also an attempt to distinguish and legitimize Macedonia's independence vis-à-vis neighboring countries (see Vangeli, "Nation-Building Ancient Macedonia Style," 13–32). Macedonia was officially called the Former Yugoslav Republic of Macedonia (FYROM) from 1995 until 2018, when it was renamed North Macedonia. It joined NATO in 2020. Skopje 2014 was an urban renewal project intended to give the Macedonian capital a more classical appearance. Launched in 2010, it resulted in the construction of 136 structures, including colleges, museums, government buildings, and monuments, over the course of four years. Supporters argued that Skopje was too modern; its national character had been eroded, especially as it was rebuilt after the 1963 earthquake that destroyed 80 percent of the city. Critics argued that the project was a nation-building endeavor that imposed a linear narrative of Macedonian history, from antiquity to the present, onto the built environment. Moreover, they suggested that the project's costs, estimated between 80 and 500 million euros, were an unwarranted use of resources in a country struggling with poverty and unemployment. The project was funded by the Macedonian government, ruled at the time by the nationalist party Internal Macedonian Revolutionary Organization—Democratic Party for Macedonia (VMRO-DPMNE).

was this kind of direct line drawn between who they were and who we are. I think there was a lot of that, of building a historical mix of nationhood. And at the same time, in line with the goal of the project, those in power heavily underplayed the fact that Macedonia had its first statehood basically in 1944 as a result of the Partisan movement in Macedonia, which related to the Yugoslav period.[14]

INTERVIEWER: Do you remember if you began to identify as Macedonian more explicitly or if there was something about your identity that changed in those postindependence years?

STAVREVSKA: No, I don't think so. I've always identified as a Macedonian and as a Yugoslav and then as a post-Yugoslav. I don't think that changed in any way. To this day the way I identify remains the same in my mind. Macedonia is the primary identity that I have, and then post-Yugoslav is my social identity of where I come from. And those have always coexisted. And if anything, during the time of the antiquization, there were moments where I was questioning things even more. I was questioning things before, but then [I was questioning] even more. It was just this madness; it was like nationalism on steroids.

INTERVIEWER: Tell me more about the way you conceive of yourself as post-Yugoslav. What does that mean to you as an identity?

STAVREVSKA: For me, answering where I'm from in one word has always been difficult. I'm sure it is for anyone who is [part of] a diaspora of any form. But in addition to that, your mom is from one place, your dad is from a different place, you were born someplace, you grew up elsewhere, and now you live in a completely different place. It's very difficult to answer that question in a straightforward manner. So because of that, for me, being post-Yugoslav

---

14. After the Axis invasion of Yugoslavia in 1941, Macedonian communists waged political and military resistance against Bulgarian, German, Italian, and Albanian forces. As the Yugoslav Partisans gained momentum several years later, they promised support for an ethnic Macedonian identity within Yugoslavia. In 1944, the Germans attempted to establish an independent Macedonian puppet state. Later, the Yugoslav Partisans reasserted control and marked a tangible victory for pro-Yugoslav Macedonianism. Socialist Yugoslavia recognized Macedonia as a distinct nation in the federation and granted the republic considerable autonomous rights. Scholar Hugh Poulton suggests that "the attraction of the Yugoslav state was in that it allowed and supported the Macedonian identity and that without it Macedonia might be torn apart by 'the four wolves,'" referring to Bulgarian, Greek, Serbian, and Albanian claims on Macedonian territory and people (Poulton, "Macedonians and Albanians as Yugoslavs," 125).

is a way of saying that I have been shaped by different parts of this region that used to be one country. And I think all of them have played a role in different ways. That's why the post-Yugoslav. Also, I don't want to cut out any part of my identity to the benefit of expedience.

INTERVIEWER: You lived in the region through high school, and then you went to college abroad, right? [Stavrevska: No, I spent three of my four years in college here, in Macedonia, and one in the US.] I'm curious about that moment when you left the Balkans and went abroad. How did you feel leaving the region, and how did you introduce yourself in the US?

STAVREVSKA: I got this scholarship through the Open Society Foundation. That's how I learned about CEU [Central European University, where Stavrevska completed her MA and PhD degrees] as well, a program through which I think about forty people from southeastern Europe plus Mongolia—I don't know how Mongolia got in the mix—were selected and then their applications were sent to different universities in the US. Then the expenses were covered jointly by the foundation and the university that selected you. That also meant that, in my case, there were three of us from the region together: one person was from Croatia, who remains one of my closest friends to this day, one person was from Bulgaria, who I'm still close to as well, and me. We had each other as a network to go together.

I stayed with a host family my first week, and then after that I was in a student dorm. I always presented myself as being from Macedonia. And then I don't remember how I was explaining it to people, whether it was just "north of Greece." Sometimes that's what I used for where it is. Of course, there were a lot of people who were confused. I remember a couple of French guys trying to convince me that Macedonia was not in Europe; they meant the European Union. So there were all sorts of interesting conversations. Some people were more curious. More devout Christians would know that Macedonia was mentioned in the Bible. I think that's how I found out about it [the mention of Macedonia in the Bible] too.

For me, [the US] was exciting; it was something new and different. And it blew my mind how different it was, in terms of the educational system, the opportunities that were around, and the different understandings of people. Culturally, we had this predeparture orientation program on the basis of the experiences of many generations before us. It kind of prepared us for what to expect. Because I knew it was a year, I didn't have too strong of feelings in terms of leaving. I knew it wasn't a permanent thing. I saw it as an opportunity to do something different for a year or be somewhere else for a year.

INTERVIEWER: What about later on, when you studied and researched in other places in Europe and the US? Did you introduce yourself differently or did you find you used different strategies for explaining what Macedonia was, or where the Balkans were, or where you came from? Did your identity or the way that you expressed it outwardly change?

STAVREVSKA: No, I don't think it changed, but I think I might have started using different strategies. In the US, I lived first in Seattle, then in Indiana. I think it's also different if you speak to [different] people. When I was in Indiana, I worked at the Kroc Institute for International Peace Studies at the University of Notre Dame, where of course people knew of the Balkans, so I might say, "I'm from the Balkans," and then explain where in the Balkans. But with ordinary people, you use different strategies. I'd explain it as being north of Greece or being on the Balkan Peninsula.

INTERVIEWER: Tell me about the collective that you started with your colleagues.

STAVREVSKA: The YugoslavWomen+ Collective, which is six of us, formed in 2019. Some of us were friends before. We always joked that if we wrote our personal histories of Yugoslavia, it would be like speaking about six different Yugoslavias because we all come from different places and have had different experiences. Some were refugees during the war. Some were displaced. Some of us stayed in the same countries even if the countries changed names and systems of governance. So it's quite diverse in those terms. Also, our experiences have been different. Our families have had very different histories as well. But we all know each other through working in the same field.

Some of us recognized [one another] through the frustration we'd expressed at different conferences and being in the audience and hearing someone say, "Could you elaborate a little more on your bias?" You have a German person next to you, and no one has ever asked them about their bias in studying the Balkans. But of course, the Bosnian person studying Bosnia will still [be asked to] elaborate on their bias. We were brought together through this and other similar frustrations around knowledge production more broadly. It was in a bar during the biggest annual international studies conference, the International Studies Association Annual Convention. We said we need to write something about this. We have some things published, some under review, other things that we are writing, but it's mainly about changing the discourse at least a little bit. On the one hand, why is it that when one of us makes a claim, that it has to be attached to our identity, while the same kind of scrutiny is never ever extended to other people? And on the other hand, there is this assumption that the only thing we can know is the region, which is to say that the assumption is that our contributions—and I don't mean just the six of us, but scholars from the region—can only ever be particularistic, never theoretical and applicable to a broader range of experiences. It's like being between a rock and a hard place. It's not the only thing that's problematic, but it's one of them.

We have also spoken out about our experiences of being *naša*, or "ours," in the region, like what it means when you do research in the region. I did research in Bosnia, and there was a lot of that, of being *naša*: the our-ness of how I was perceived, the conversations I would have with people and what that means. I remember some of them really emphasizing their agency and [saying], "Okay, you're going to tell our story authentically." In and of itself, this comes with a different kind of weight.

So in some ways, the collective was formed out of love for where we come from. It was also formed, as I mentioned, out of frustration with knowledge production in general as well as knowledge production about the region in particular in international relations as a discipline.

INTERVIEWER: Has being a scholar, and especially being in international relations, shaped the way you think about your childhood in Yugoslavia? Have you, as an adult and as a scholar, reframed some of your own memories or feelings toward Yugoslavia?

STAVREVSKA: Yeah, I think so. This is specifically about the Albanian community in Macedonia. There were a lot of things that I did not know about the treatment of the Albanian community in Macedonia during Yugoslavia. That same treatment continued during the independence and then eventually led to the conflict—or rather, contributed to the armed conflict—in 2001. Being a scholar, part of my work included doing interviews with people who were teachers, Albanian teachers at the time, some of whom were in prison at the time. There's a lot of history around that as well that has not been included in the broader public discourse and certainly not in the history books that are written in Macedonian. When I was in school, I think, to the best of my knowledge, history lessons ended in 1991 with independence. And those lessons never covered how minorities have been treated, how Roma have been treated throughout Yugoslavia, actually, and how Albanians were treated during Yugoslavia, in all parts of Yugoslavia, including in Macedonia. Especially if this is a country I self-identify with, I'm meant to know these things.

And to this day, people still don't know. I remember one guy I was interviewing, and he was telling me that people walked from Kumanovo to Belgrade as a form of protest. I said, "Oh, I didn't know," and he said "Well, you should know, and your parents should know." And he had every right to say that. I feel that it's not about me being a scholar. It's more about being curious and learning about this aspect that made me not only aware of a part of history but also helped me reframe some of the understandings that I had. I mean, I knew Yugoslavia was not ideal and there was violence in different forms against certain parts of the population throughout its existence, but some of the understandings I had of how people in Macedonia were treated changed.

I try to have these conversations with my mom as well as members of the family who do not necessarily research or know this. Especially because Macedonia is still—and probably not just Macedonia—quite a divided society. If anything, I think [right] after the conflict was a better time to acknowledge some things than it is now. I think saying that the armed conflict in 2001 started for a reason and people were mistreated would make you really, really unpopular right now. It's much harder to say these things and to raise these issues now. [It's harder to] have these conversations now than it was in 2001 or 2003, when it was closer to the conflict, which is somewhat counterintuitive.

INTERVIEWER: What does Yugoslavia mean to you today?

STAVREVSKA: Well, it means several things. It means inspiration in terms of what it meant then, with the kind of radical idea it was at that time. As a feminist scholar, the type of liberation thinking that was at the heart of the Antifascist Feminist Front, for instance, blows my mind,[15] to say nothing of the rights that women had and the reproductive health rights as well. The educational opportunities that existed for everyone in the country. The understanding that the socioeconomic and political were so closely linked and that you could not speak about one without the other. This is based on my research, not on my experience, of course. The Non-Alignment Movement,

---

15. The Antifascist Feminist Front, or *Antifasistički Front Žena*, was founded to mobilize women to join the resistance movement. After World War II, it transformed into a pioneering women's group that advocated for political, economic, and social change in the first decade of the Cold War (Bonfiglioli, "Women's Political and Social Activism in the Early Cold War Era," 1–25). Women participated in mass in the Yugoslav Partisan resistance during World War II. See Batinić, *Women and Yugoslav Partisans*.

the fact that the world does not need to be locked into bipolarity. So I think as an IR [international relations] scholar, it is definitely an inspiration. I wouldn't have existed without Yugoslavia because [my parents] wouldn't have met.

But at the same time, I'm fully aware that it had its shortcomings. It had its shortcomings in centralization, in terms of oppression of people who even questioned the idea or questioned anything, in terms of people who were not recognized in the different republics and how they were treated. I am fully aware of that. One thing that has frustrated me for a long time is how, like Andrew Gilbert says about Bosnia, the past is in parenthesis.[16] There is sometimes this assumption that the war has wiped everything clean in a way, and everything that was before we need to forget. It really brings me a lot of joy that more and more scholars and activists—people who work on the commons, who work on feminism, and, of course, historians—draw inspiration from what was done before and how the local communities were arranged. Throwing out the baby with the bathwater is something that has always frustrated me about the analysis of Yugoslavia but also the political imagination that existed and exists since then. So now, in terms of the imagination of what is possible for everyone in the Balkans, it is only the EU. But thinking about what can be—if there is a different form of alliance, a different form of organization which learns from the past but picks up some of the good lessons as well—that is something that brings a little bit of hopefulness.

INTERVIEWER: Do you find yourself nostalgic about anything from Yugoslavia or even just the idea of Yugoslavia?

STAVREVSKA: I don't know if I would call it nostalgic. I wish it didn't end the way it ended. I wish it didn't bring all the violence it brought. But that's just imagining futures otherwise. I just do wish that some of the good things that were done then or learned then—well, actually, both those that were done and those that were learned—can be brought to imagining the future otherwise. No, I wouldn't say I'm nostalgic. It would be hard for me to be nostalgic for something I didn't really experience much firsthand.

INTERVIEWER: How do you relate to the Yugoslav diaspora? Do you seek it out? How do you relate to folks who are also from the region or had once been from Yugoslavia?

---

16. See Gilbert, "The Past in Parenthesis."

STAVREVSKA: I don't think it's a singular answer because in academia, in the field where I work, we recognize each other, and sometimes we share not just frustration and love but also a common language. I don't mean the actual language—sometimes it is the actual language, like the former official language of the country—but sometimes it's language and grammar more broadly. Like with an Albanian from the region, I might speak the same language in terms of understanding. We might have the same cultural registry in understanding things.

More broadly with the Macedonian diaspora, let alone the Yugoslav diaspora, I don't seek it out. If I meet them, sometimes we connect; sometimes we don't. Even in the diaspora, feelings of superiority of certain parts of the diaspora of the former country towards other parts of the diaspora still remain. Being Macedonian, sometimes you feel that quite strongly, and that is not something that I want to reproduce. In terms of food, I always do find [that] wherever I go I do make sure to find a Balkan food store [and] the restaurants as a way of finding comfort food and a taste of home. And I have brought Balkan food to all sorts of potlucks and barbeques with my friends who have nothing to do with the Balkans and who have now embraced ćevapčići and ajvar.[17] But as far as the diaspora is concerned, I think it is a bit of a complicated relationship. It depends on with whom and in what context. It is not something that I avoid. It's just [that] I don't necessarily think a relationship is worthwhile if we do not start from positions of mutual respect and equal footing.

INTERVIEWER: What do you call the languages you grew up speaking?

STAVREVSKA: Macedonian is the primary language, but then, because of the complex family that I have, we were all very exposed to what would now be called BCMS [Bosnian/Croatian/Montenegrin/Serbian], what was then called Serbo-Croatian. I speak both fluently as first languages, even though Macedonian is a bit more of my first language because I studied in Macedonian. But I remember sometimes my dad would say that I sounded like

---

17. Ćevapi, or ćevapčići in the diminutive, is a dish of rolled pieces of grilled minced meat (often a mixture of beef, lamb, or pork, depending on the region) commonly served in a flatbread called a *somun* with chopped onions, a milk cream called *kajmak*, and a drinkable yogurt. The dish is common across the Balkans and thought to predate the Ottoman period. The word ćevap comes from the Turkish word *kebap*. Ajvar is made from smoked and minced peppers, eggplant, and herbs. It is often sweet but can be seasoned to be piquant. It is consumed as a spread on breads or a condiment on meats or other dishes.

I was from Leskovac [now Serbia] when speaking Serbo-Croatian.[18] [This was] because of the cases; we don't have cases [in Macedonian], so I would hit and miss the cases [in Serbo-Croatian]. But in the family, it was always Macedonian that was spoken. But we were very, very exposed to Serbo-Croatian as well.

INTERVIEWER: I know you're visiting Macedonia right now. How do you feel when you're back in the region?

STAVREVSKA: I have always had a strong physical connection to the region, even while living away. Living in North America was a separate case, but when I was in Europe, I would be here frequently. I don't have a singular relationship to the region, though. In terms of my hometown, for instance, I'm proud of some of the positive changes I have seen. My hometown has had a lot of good changes happen to it in the last five years because it has an exceptional mayor.[19] I don't say this lightly. This is the first time I see the town actually developing nicely, in a positive direction. And I don't mean development as only economic, but human development too.

But at the same time, there are also a lot of negative developments. In Skopje especially, I see some divisions a little more. But Skopje is very hard to like in general, especially after Skopje 2014. It is capitalism-meets-antiquity-meets-kitsch.

I visit Sarajevo [now Bosnia and Herzegovina] frequently. I visit Belgrade [now Serbia] frequently. I visit Prishtina [now Kosovo] not as frequently as I want. But you see the changes that happen across the region, and you see capitalism flowing in, not in the most fortunate of ways. You see the urban changes. I have this kind of love-hate relationship. I will always like the bonds I have with people and how people are with each other. I'm not romanticizing it. It's the informality of how people are, which sometimes can be frustrating,

---

18. Leskovac is in southeastern Serbia, a part of the country that is largely impoverished. In other parts of the region, the dialect spoken in and around Leskovac is coded as peripheral, rural, and backward. Scholar Tanja Petrović suggests that some residents are aware of this stereotype and embrace the dialect as a way to critically engage with their identity (Petrović, "Place-Making through the Use of Dialect in a Facebook Chronicle of Leskovac (Southeast Serbia)").

19. At the time of the interview, the mayor of Kavadarci was Mitko Jancev (1981–), who had served in the role since 2017. Jancev was well-known for donating his mayoral salary back to the city and declining taxpayer-supported services like personal drivers. During his term, he spearheaded a wide range of social services and municipal improvement projects.

but I quite like that. So there are a lot of things I continue to like, that I've always liked, and maybe I started appreciating more, especially after being in London, where things are very different. But there are also a lot of things I notice a lot more than if I was here all the time. So yeah, it's complicated.

INTERVIEWER: As we've been talking, has anything come to mind that I haven't asked you about or that you haven't had a chance to mention in the previous questions?

STAVREVSKA: I was just reminded of how some parts of Yugoslavia that were not in the war directly, even those that did not have direct connections to the frontlines, were affected through relationships being broken. I think that was the case even for children who were not aware that there was war going on or what was going to happen. That's one thing. The other thing is that you really made me question which of my memories were mine and what is a heavy reinterpretation of what happened. So yeah, not sure. Still cannot untangle that, but you have all of it now.

INTERVIEWER: You lived more of your life without Yugoslavia being present then you lived during its existence. You've also lived many years abroad. All of that shapes our memories, and that's what I'm trying to get at. Because the folks I'm interviewing who were the oldest were in their late teens and early twenties [when Yugoslavia fell apart], that means that more than half of their lives have not been in Yugoslavia. I thought that was a critical juncture to start thinking about Yugoslavia.

STAVREVSKA: Yeah, you're right.
Oh! There is another thing that I remembered. I remember that during the war in Bosnia—and I think maybe this was through the news—my view was largely shaped around just the three ethnicities. No shades of gray or in between. No mention of the Roma population anywhere, as if they ever existed, or any other minorities. No mention of Bosnians, no mention of Bosniaks other than them being expelled and killed from what is now Republika Srpska. No mention of the Serbian population in what is now the Federation [of Bosnia and Herzegovina]. I think that is something that being there and actively seeking to understand these experiences as part of my research—these experiences at the margins, so to say—made me understand things about both Yugoslavia and the post-Yugoslav period with much more nuance than what I had before.

INTERVIEWER: I think it connects to your comment about memory too. Memory is not just changing or fading but also expanding when you're adding new understanding, new research, new things that we just didn't know about. You were mentioning earlier Tito's treatment of Albanians and other minorities in Yugoslavia, that, in a way, is the accordion opening up in your memory. Then you can say, "I remember this little thing that is actually indicative of something I know now as a bigger thing."

STAVREVSKA: Yeah, I remember I was doing other research—because I've been active in civil society in Macedonia a lot as well—with local communities, or *mesni zaednici*, here in Macedonia. People were talking about Yugoslavia as if it were yesterday. These people talked about how there were functional *mesni zaednici* and [said that] the *mesni zaednici* were the strongest link between the people in the villages. Well, not the strongest link, the *mesni zaednici* were not dependent on the town: they were their own. But they [the *mesni zaednici*] had actual resources, and they [the people] felt they had agency. And this is something interesting, and it would be really interesting for you in terms of nostalgia as well. People felt they had more agency back then in their fate, in their *sudbina*, than they have now in a pluralistic, democratic society. I write about this a little as well. It's something that I think a lot of people who have been promoting liberal democracy in this part of the world have not accounted for—the part that people might be nostalgic for an arguably centralized, single-party system where they felt they had more of a say. It was much more, I feel, decentralized at the local level, to the point where issues that mattered to the people in the village were likely decided on by the people in the village. And they not just had a say but funds, too, to do things.

INTERVIEWER: Oftentimes people mention this sense of community that existed because they were invested locally, because they were invested in that kind of community space. That is also the memory of Yugoslavia.

STAVREVSKA: Yeah, I mean the *komšiluk* thing, I started with that, and I might as well end with that. It used to be stronger also in terms of trust. Leaving your kids with your neighbor was not something that you would avoid doing because of lack of trust [in them]. But I think that also fits into this local community sense of people forming a network, a family of sorts, and understanding that doing things as a community makes everyone's life easier.

INTERVIEWER: Well, that is a fantastic bookend. Thank you so much for your thoughts and your memories.

STAVREVSKA: It's my pleasure.

7

INTERVIEW WITH

Bojan Števin

Bojan Števin was born in Zrenjanin (now Serbia) in 1981, where he stayed until his early thirties. Since then, he has lived and worked in Egypt, China, and Malaysia. When we spoke over a video call in late 2021, he was employed as an English teacher in Kuala Lumpur and hosted the podcast *Izokvireni* under the moniker Bojančina. During our conversation, Števin spoke about the social and economic opportunities the former Yugoslavia had provided his working-class family and imagined that it might have been an ideal society for him had it survived. In contrast, Števin spoke critically about the Serbian successor state, explaining that he had emigrated for his own well-being. He had struggled to build a sustainable life for himself in Serbia and feared for his safety as an openly queer man. However, Števin shared that his experiences abroad did not necessarily live up to how he had imagined the West as a child; they instead deepened his appreciation for Yugoslavia.

Števin's earliest memories of childhood in Yugoslavia were shaped by opportunities the state made availbale to his family. His parents built their own home in Zrenjanin, where they grew vegetables; his father had a steady job with the national oil company, and the family could afford to take vacations to the Adriatic Sea because his father's firm owned a subsidized holiday center in Montenegro. For Števin, like many other members of the youngest Yugoslav generation, childhood memories were generally carefree and comprised of unbound play with other neighborhood children. Yet he was keen to note that his happiness was mediated by the broader social world in which he was raised. He described Yugoslavia as a "humane place": "People were kinder there because they were taken care of, they were provided for, and they didn't work long hours. They had economic stability, and they didn't have to worry about what's going to be on the table the next day. They had more time to socialize because they didn't have to work from dawn until dusk." He stressed that late socialist Yugoslavia cultivated a sense of collective support and belonging. He also speculated that the Yugoslavia of his childhood might have been a "utopia" compared to the present day. "I would like to have that ability to start my work at eight a.m., finish at two p.m.," he explained. "I would like to not have to take any work home and just have from two p.m. until ten p.m. in the evening to hang out with my family, my friends, do my hobbies, do chores, run errands, and then still be able to afford a vacation and health care." Števin certainly criticized some aspects of Yugoslavia, such as limitations on freedom of speech, but his memories of everyday life were overwhelmingly positive.

Števin spoke in a markedly different tone when recalling his adolescence and early adulthood in Serbia during and after the Yugoslav wars. In the context of the widespread shortages and poverty that impacted most Serbian residents in the 1990s and 2000s, Števin explained that his life prospects had been grim. While he did have a job as a middle school teacher (at a time when Serbia's unemployment rate was 19.2 percent), Števin earned a low salary and saw few opportunities for advancement even as a college-educated adult. In 2010, the average monthly salary in Serbia was $610, about one-sixth the average in Germany at the same time. It was simply not enough. "On that salary, I couldn't even afford to live by myself and feed myself," Števin told me. "I could only afford food, so I still had to live with my parents." He remembered that he felt stuck in his job and started seriously exploring pathways to leave the country permanently in the early 2010s.

Another factor that made Serbia unlivable for Števin was its hostile social climate toward queer communities. The state introduced some laws to protect LGBT rights in the early 2000s, but these laws did not curtail discrimination. Števin speculated that he was among the few openly queer people in Zrenjanin, and he said that he often worried about how his identity might impact him, his family, and his employment. On a local level, he felt isolated. "Because I was the only out gay person in the town, I just felt like I was a bit of a scarecrow," he said. "No other gay people wanted to be around me out of fear of being outed by being seen with me. So dating was not happening. It just felt very lonely." On a macro level, he underlined that life as a queer person in Serbia in 2010 was simply dangerous. That year, ultranationalist groups attacked the Pride parade in Belgrade (the first parade, held in 2001, was similarly met with violence) and precipitated a homophobic riot. The state subsequently banned parades in 2011 and 2012 on the grounds that it could not protect public order. After criticism from the international community, Serbia's Constitutional Court declared that the bans were an unconstitutional restriction of freedom of assembly and freedom of expression, and the government reluctantly allowed Pride parades in subsequent years. Scholars have found similar instances of homophobia in other Yugoslav successor states around the same time.[1] In Serbia, in particular, social anthropologist Marek Mikuš suggests, homophobia was closely tied to ultranationalist resistance to European Union membership and the "perception of LGBT rights by their opponents as something foreign and 'elite.'"[2] This larger understanding of social dynamics did not change the fact that, for Števin, life in Serbia was unsafe and ultimately unfeasible.

In the decade after his emigration, Števin rearticulated his memories of both Yugoslavia and Serbia in relation to the realities of life in the West. He recalled that he associated socialist Yugoslavia with "characteristic communist colors" like dark browns and greens, whereas he associated Western culture with the vibrant pink hues of American movies. Watching MTV as a teenager, he had yearned to go abroad because he perceived elsewhere to be more fun. "There was more color over there; there was pink over there. I wanted to go there," he said. "There was glitter and stuff, you know? [There was] a lot of variety and diversity, like Black artists and Asian artists." After he emigrated, however, he gained a new perspective on his childhood and adolescence: "Talking to all these people who were Americans or Brits or Australians or French or Spanish or whatever—people from the West whom I imagined had had this amazing, fun adolescence—I realized mine was a lot more fun despite its scarcity. Although they had those concerts and they had those parties, their adolescence in Western countries was a lot more controlled than mine was in Serbia." He cited that he had far fewer social restrictions as a teenager. It had been socially and legally permissible for him to drink in cafes, go to clubs, and stay out late. Thinking back on his teen years, Števin concluded that they had been better than he had realized. He jokingly remarked that his one regret was not appreciating that time sooner. "I wish I'd had somebody back then to tell me what the reality was like in the West," he said. "It would have saved me from a lot of wanderlust. In Germany, they have *Fernweh*, like you're really dying to be somewhere far. Had I known what the reality was like, I wouldn't have had that strong feeling to have to leave. I would have probably enjoyed the present a lot more." While life abroad gave Števin a new perspective on his childhood and young adulthood in the region, it did not make life in present-day Serbia any more sustainable for him.

INTERVIEWER: Can you tell me a little bit about your hometown, where you were born, and what you remember about it?

---

1. See Moss, "Split Pride/Split Identities" and Swimelar, "LGBT Rights in Bosnia."
2. Mikuš, "'State Pride,'" 836.

ŠTEVIN: I was born in Zrenjanin, which in the beginning of the 1980s and around that time used to be one of the industrial centers of the former Yugoslavia.[3] It was a thriving city for skilled workers, and it was also famous for sports.[4]

I remember for the first five years, we were renting a little house, and during that time my parents were building their own. They finished it, and we moved when I was six. It was a little modest house with a nice big garden at the edge of town, but everything was easily accessible by car and even by bike. You could bike anywhere in twenty to thirty minutes. It was just flat and very agricultural. Everyone grew some kind of fruits or vegetables in their gardens. If they didn't, they probably had some relatives in the surrounding villages with a garden and probably some farm animals. I remember an abundance of food—high-quality food—because everything was organic, and you knew its source. Only the staples were store-bought. Everything else came from a person you knew.

INTERVIEWER: What was it like to be a child in Zrenjanin? What do you remember about your childhood?

ŠTEVIN: I remember spending a lot of time with my grandparents because they lived in the same town and not far away from us. It was walking distance. If my parents were at work, I would just go to my grandparents' house, or they would pick me up from school and take me to our house. They were kind of my babysitters.

I remember schools and kindergartens being very dark brown and dark green. They were very much those characteristic communist colors. I don't really think I experienced the color pink in my childhood or in my vicinity. When we saw pink, it was in American movies and on TV.

I remember having a lot of [neighborhood] friends. There were a lot of kids my age, and we played a lot outside. In my grandparents' neighborhood, too, there were a lot of kids, and I just remember us being outside in the street or in somebody else's yard hanging out. I remember drawing a lot with my friends and playing tag almost until my early teenage years. Somehow I remember mostly nice weather, us being outside. But even when it was winter, we were also always outside. Every day after school we would go sledding,

---

3. The agro-industrial combine Servo Mihalj, the largest producer of food in socialist Yugoslavia, was based in Zrenjanin. In the 1970s, Servo Mihalj operated forty-two factories that processed goods like oil, sugar, flour, and meat, employing twenty-four thousand people. One of its partner groups, the pharmaceutical company Jugoremedia, was Yugoslavia's first joint venture with a foreign company, German Hoechst AG.

4. Most notably, Zrenjanin was the hometown of the Proleter soccer team (Fudbalski klub Proleter Zrenjanin) from 1947 to 2005.

snowball fighting, building snow people, and going to each other's houses. That's what I remember. I don't know what it's like over there now.

Living here in Asia in a big city, kids these days go on playdates. We didn't have that. Whenever you wanted to play, you would just go outside and knock on other kids' doors, like, "Hey, are you free? Do you want to play? Come out and come to my house!" Or we would just take the phone and call the neighbor on the landline, like, "Hey, wanna come over? Let's watch something together! Let's draw together!" But these days, at least here, they have to ask their parents to call the parents of their friends to arrange playdates. There's none of that immediacy here. But I don't know what it's like now in my hometown in Serbia.

INTERVIEWER: Do you remember if you participated in any Yugoslav children's activities or youth activities?

ŠTEVIN: We didn't really have that. And I don't remember anybody from my hometown having anything like that. I just know that once we started first grade, we had to take the oath that we would be good Pioneers. We had to wear the school uniform just on that day. We didn't have school uniforms otherwise. I think for a couple of years during elementary school, we were still celebrating Tito's birthday. That was probably [an occasion] to learn some poem—I don't know which one—and draw a picture of Tito or a flag. I don't remember a lot of propaganda.

INTERVIEWER: Do you remember if you were aware of being around people who were different than you when you were a child?

ŠTEVIN: Yes. But I'm not sure if that has anything to do with the location. It was more my sexuality [that made me feel different]. Of course, I didn't recognize myself as gay back then. I was too young to be aware, and especially because there was no visibility of that community and population around me.[5] But I knew. I recognized it. Unlike other boys who liked to hang out with other boys, I just wanted to be friends with girls and do girly stuff. I would

---

5. Socialist Yugoslavia initially adopted the 1929 criminal code of the Kingdom of Yugoslavia (itself a holdover from Serbia's nineteenth-century codes), which made sexual intercourse between men punishable by up to four years of imprisonment. From 1959, Yugoslavia made male homosexuality punishable by up to a year of imprisonment, and the state imprisoned about five hundred individuals on that charge from the 1950s to the 1970s. In the wake of global sexual liberation movements, the Socialist Autonomous Province of Vojvodina, where Zrenjanin was located, decriminalized homosexuality in 1977 alongside the Yugoslav republics of Croatia, Slovenia, and Montenegro (other regions followed suit only after the Yugoslav wars). Several LGBT groups formed in Yugoslavia in the 1980s, but queerness remained largely marginalized from mainstream culture and society.

have these strange feelings in my tummy when I would see a boy that I liked. I never felt that about a girl. I heard adults talking about how you should feel when you meet a person of the other sex. I never felt that way [toward girls].

Also, in Zrenjanin and in that area of Yugoslavia [Vojvodina], there were a lot of minorities. There were four official languages. There was a big Hungarian population, a Romanian population, and other ethnicities, but this didn't seem to matter. I was just aware of them because some people in my family and my parents' friends were members of those minorities, so I knew of their existence through acceptance until the war started.

I was surrounded by different people. I was also the different one.

INTERVIEWER: Whether it's sexual differences or ethnic, cultural, or national differences, were you aware that people were treated differently or unequally in the context of Yugoslavia?

ŠTEVIN: Based on ethnicity, no. And I also didn't know how queer people were treated. I just didn't see any representation of them. Because I didn't see it, I felt like there was something wrong with me. And I don't know, I probably heard some awful jokes about [queer people], about that population, and so I didn't dare discuss any of that with people around me.

INTERVIEWER: Can you tell me who constituted your family growing up?

ŠTEVIN: Well, in my household it was just me and my parents. I'm an only child. We were very good friends with the landlords while we were living at the house we rented from them, so they kind of became my second family. And we're still friends with them, down to this day. My parents see them every day. They also had a son who was an only child who was six years older than me. Now I have a connection with him as if he is my older brother. He was the one who played records for me. Music was not easy to find. Nobody in my family or in my household listened to music or cared about music, and so he was my gateway to music. As I was growing up, he was the first one to take me to a bar and take me out and give me my first joint. He also protected me.

But then there were also my uncle and aunt—that's my mom's brother and his wife. She's Hungarian, so that's how I was aware Hungarians existed. I had grandparents whom I would see every day, also from my mother's side. We were not really in touch with my dad's side of the family. I would see some uncles and cousins occasionally, but there's a big [age] gap between all my cousins and me. They're either ten years younger or ten years older, so I never fit in. I knew them, and we'd maybe see each other at birthday celebrations and religious festivities, but I've never been close to them. My parents, like me—maybe I got that from them—tend to socialize more with their chosen families, like with their friends rather than blood relatives. They have stronger connections with friends than with family, just like I do.

INTERVIEWER: Were you aware of your family as mixed in any way?

ŠTEVIN: I don't really think I thought about it that much. Like I only knew that my aunt was Hungarian because when I was staying at her house, she would talk to her mom, and I would hear her speak Hungarian. And I probably knew that my mom's best friend was Croatian because they were talking about their families, and I overheard that word. And she had a slightly different accent. But it was not something that was presented to me [as significant] in any way.

INTERVIEWER: Do you remember how your family members engaged with Yugoslavia?

ŠTEVIN: I don't think they did. Just like they don't engage with any kind of politics to this day. They were just very simple people who were not necessarily obedient or brainwashed. They just lived simple lives. They lived in their little microworlds. They provided for the family, and that's how far their thinking went. There's no kind of social activism built into them to this day. And maybe that's the old communist or socialist programming that they carry, but they were never vocal about politics when it wasn't allowed, and they are not even vocal about them now [when it is].

Like, in our town, there's a big problem—we don't have drinking tap water, and we haven't had it for decades now.[6] And [my family] would never join protests or anything like that. Now the Chinese are building some kind of factory, a huge factory, to produce rubber and tires, and it's going to be a major pollutant, but [my family] just doesn't see much beyond their household.[7]

---

6. Zrenjanin's industrial history has left a legacy of pollution, such as high levels of arsenic in the water.

7. Zrenjanin is located in a free economic zone in Serbia. There are fifteen free zones in Serbia intended to bolster economic growth through foreign investment and export. Free zones offer exemptions from the Value Added Tax (VAT), custom duties on imported materials, and custom duties on exported goods. The Chinese company Linglong Tire started construction of a factory in Zrenjanin in 2019. Residents began protesting it on environmental grounds in 2020, citing concerns about pollution. In 2021, moreover, Serbian NGOs and the Balkan Investigative Reporting Network exposed a series of potential human rights violations at the Linglong Tire factory. Whistleblowers suggested that the Chinese company had brought in Vietnamese workers to build the factory, and that it confiscated their passports, withheld their pay, and housed them in inferior conditions. The Serbian state turned a blind eye not only to the potential case of human trafficking but also to the labor and living conditions that violated national law.

They were not that opinionated about religion in the same way. They're not religious, but I'm not sure if this is [because they're just not religious or] because they lived during communism. When communism stopped and religion was allowed again, all these former communists started converting and being more overtly Orthodox Christian. Those people were probably not people of faith. It was just a trend that started, and everybody was suddenly a practicing Orthodox Christian. But my parents didn't [do that]. It was not a part of their household, so they didn't care if there's God or if there's not. In a similar way, the president is not a part of their household, so they don't care who the president is as long as they can survive, they have money for food, and they can go to the doctor.

INTERVIEWER: Do you remember if any of your family members talked about Yugoslavia or mentioned Tito? Was there was a positive, or negative, or neutral association with the state at home?

ŠTEVIN: I don't think my mom ever expressed any kind of thoughts or beliefs about Yugoslavia. But I think my dad had a generally positive view of Yugoslavia. He had this romantic vision of Yugoslavia. But I know that my dad worked in the national oil company that was quite profitable, so he managed to earn a decent living. He had a job, and everything was set out for him. Whenever he talks about Yugoslavia, he talks about fairness. I think he has a biased view of Tito. He only sees Tito as a big investor in Yugoslavia. But he doesn't see the side where he got Yugoslavia in major debt because of the investments.

Also, my dad could afford vacations at the seaside every year because his company had resorts in Montenegro and all over the Adriatic coast. They could go on summer vacations for free—not for free but for very cheap because [the resorts] were company-owned. He has that image of a country that has your back. Maybe you don't get great pay, but at least you're provided with a more stress-free life. Like there was health care, there were places to go on vacation, and then there were also things organized for kids that were cheap and affordable. I guess he saw that everything was affordable, and then it didn't matter to him that he wasn't rich or that he didn't have freedom of speech. And maybe he just didn't need it because he had what he needed.

INTERVIEWER: Were you aware when the Yugoslav wars started in 1991?

ŠTEVIN: Yes, I remember the news. That was a time when some of my cousins who were ten years older than me were called to serve their regular military service. They weren't necessarily being sent to war, but they had to be stationed and go through the training. And that caused a lot of stress and anxiety in the family. They didn't know if they were just going to be taken for training and be kept safe or if they were actually going to be drafted and sent to war, sent to the battlefield. In the end, they were sent for training to Croatia and Slovenia, not [kept] in Serbia. I remember sending letters and postcards to all those cousins as a ten-year-old, using a lot of snail mail.

INTERVIEWER: Do you remember how your immediate environment changed when the wars started?

ŠTEVIN: Winters got very cold because of the lack of heating and electricity. And schools were getting a big intake of refugees all of a sudden. There was a big embargo on the whole of Yugoslavia, so you could see lines of people forming in front of the supermarkets waiting for the chance to buy milk and bread and lines forming in front of gas stations waiting for gas. There was a big scarcity of basic human goods.

INTERVIEWER: How long did you continue to live in Serbia?

ŠTEVIN: My first trip abroad [after the Yugoslav wars] was in 2000 when I went to Budapest for New Year's Eve. Then, the first time I left Serbia to work was in 2004. I went to the United States. That was for seasonal work, so I knew that was just temporary. And I did that twice in a row. I left Serbia in 2012 when I moved to China, and I haven't moved back since.

INTERVIEWER: How did you feel leaving Serbia as well as your family and hometown?

ŠTEVIN: I really had to leave in order to survive. I hit rock bottom. I found myself very stuck in Serbia because I was still living in my hometown. I became a teacher at a public school, teaching English in middle school. On that salary, I couldn't even afford to live by myself and feed myself. I could only afford food, so I still had to live with my parents.[8] I couldn't see any possibilities of progressing in any way in the job because it was a strict [path that] you just followed. There's a lot of laddering in which you progress in your career over there. If you were a teacher, then maybe you could become a principal. I didn't want to become an administrator. So it was like, "Uh-oh, I'll be doing this for the rest of my life."

---

8. According to the United Nations Economic Commission for Europe, the lowest gross average monthly wages in Serbia, adjusted for current currency exchanges, coincided with the international sanctions and trade embargo in response to the Kosovo War. Salaries had recovered somewhat by the late 2000s and early 2010s as Števin was struggling to make ends meet as a middle school teacher, but they were still disproportionately lower than in other European states. In 2010, for instance, the average monthly salary was $610 in Serbia and $3,663 in Germany.

And it was also kind of dangerous for me. Although I was enjoying working with kids, [my job] was at the same time always on shaky ground because of my sexuality. I was not in the closet anymore. And I was probably the only person who was not in the closet in that town. I never knew what kind of backlash I would eventually get from [my students'] parents and how the administration would react, how the parents would react, and how students would react. Also, [I didn't know] how that would reflect on my own parents. Would they be able to cope with that? It just felt like there was a lot of pressure.

Because I was the only out gay person in the town, I just felt like I was a bit of a scarecrow. No other gay people wanted to be around me out of fear of being outed by being seen with me.[9] So dating was not happening. It just felt very lonely. I felt like, "This is it—I'm barely thirty, and this is the rest of my life." So I really need to get out.

Even before that, I always wanted to live abroad. Even when I was a five-year-old, I knew that I wanted to get out. When I started working in public schools, I did start working on applying to jobs abroad everywhere in the world. I remember mostly applying in the Chinese market because there was high demand, but I never got a single response. It was mostly through the agencies, and they wanted certain passports and certain profiles. It's machinery, and I just didn't fit in their profile. They couldn't sell me to a school. But then I heard from a friend who went to China to work and teach English that it was

---

9. Serbia decriminalized homosexuality in 1994 and has been gradually introducing laws to protect LGBT rights since 2002. However, the social climate for queer communities remains hostile. In 2001, nationalist, neo-Nazi, and right-wing groups violently attacked the first Pride parade in Belgrade. The Serbian government canceled many subsequent events around the country, alleging that it could not provide protection for participants. The second Pride parade in Belgrade, in 2010, precipitated a homophobic riot; just as Števin was making plans to leave the region, the state banned parades in 2011 and 2012, citing concerns over public order. In addition to criticism from organizers and activists, foreign observers like the Norwegian Helsinki Committee declared that "the decision is in effect the Serbian state succumbing to pressure from violent and intolerant groups, preventing a peaceful celebration of human rights" (Norwegian Helsinki Committee, "Belgrade Pride 2011 Banned"). Serbia's Constitutional Court declared the bans an unconstitutional restriction of freedom of assembly and freedom of expression, and the government reluctantly allowed Pride parades. As scholar Safia Swimelar suggests, Serbia's weak support of LGBT rights is related to ultranationalist resistance to European Union membership that conflates queerness with Europeanness. "State and national identity has been constructed more in *opposition* to Europe and as more exclusionary and religious, with elites struggling to politically balance EU conditionality and a nationalist public," Swimelar writes. "The threat perception from the LGBT community was stronger and framed primarily as '*threat to the nation*'" (Swimelar, "LGBT Rights in the Balkans").

a completely different scenario once you're there and they can see you. There were a lot more doors open. So she just told me to go to China. And then, out of despair, I managed to get three years of unpaid leave from my school to have something as a safety net in case China didn't work. I bought a one-way ticket to Shanghai, and within two months I managed to find a job. I stayed. Then I kept moving to different countries. I never went back to Serbia.[10]

I felt bad about leaving my parents, especially being an only child and them being very typical Balkan parents. Especially my mom. She's very attached to me, and we have a very strong bond. But I knew I needed to leave to survive. She didn't need a depressed or dead son. She made it very easy for me despite being a typical, possessive Balkan mother. I'm sure she experienced it as a tragedy, me leaving permanently, but she never expressed it. She never asked me to come back. She knew that I was not happy, and although she misses me still, terribly, she doesn't miss seeing me miserable. That's why she gets over herself every time we speak. That's just not our topic of conversation, like, "Come back, you can always come back; we miss you, blah-blah-blah." There was never any kind of emotional blackmail, no matter how sad she was.

INTERVIEWER: When you're abroad, when you're living in Asia or traveling elsewhere, how do you introduce yourself? Where do you say you come from?

ŠTEVIN: I hate that question. [Laughs] How I answer where I'm from depends on my mood. [Laughs] Sometimes, I just ask [people] to guess to see how they're going to stereotype me based on my looks. Sometimes I say Yugoslavia. Most of the time, I actually say Yugoslavia, unless I really don't feel like going into that conversation about how Yugoslavia doesn't exist anymore. If I don't really feel like going into the conversation explaining my background, then I just say Serbia. I just feel like I identify myself as coming from Yugoslavia because Yugoslavia was the place which shaped me for twenty-something years. In what is today Serbia, I only lived for three or four years.

---

10. Although Serbia does not keep detailed data on emigration, it has experienced a notable brain drain of educated and professional citizens seeking better education, work, and life opportunities elsewhere. The 2011 Serbian national census, taken the year before Števin moved out of the country, recorded 313,411 Serbian citizens living and working abroad (out of a total population of 7,186,862). Scholars Ognjen Radonjić and Marjana Bobić speculate that this number is marred by underreporting. They cite demographic studies that estimate 367,000–422,000 people migrated out of the state between 2002 and 2011 (Radonjić and Bobić, "Brain Drain Losses," 6).

And I grew up in that Yugoslav system of values, which is not the same as the Serbian system of values. I grew up being taught and educated in Serbo-Croatian, not Serbian. I find Yugoslavia a lot more multidimensional than Serbia. Serbia to me is just a monoculture. And I never felt that I'm just a Serb. Serbia to me now is just [a state] that didn't want to collaborate with Croatians and Bosnians and Slovenians. I grew up having no problems with any of those people or any kind of people being around me and being part of my family. I grew up with that notion of brotherhood and unity that was a big part of propaganda in all of Yugoslavia. Serbia doesn't have that. Those are the big elements that I miss and why I don't identify with Serbia. I feel like my domain is much broader mentally than what Serbia stands for today.

INTERVIEWER: How do you identify nationally, ethnically, or culturally today?

ŠTEVIN: I think I'm definitely 100 percent Serb. But culturally I think I'm just cosmopolitan. I mean, I've lived and worked on four different continents. I can't really segregate what part of me belongs to what piece of geography. There are some things that I definitely have that are typically Serbian, but I also adopted some habits from the Chinese, and the Americans, and the Germans, and the Egyptians, and now the Malaysians. Like, I eat better with chopsticks than the Malaysian Chinese. I'm more Chinese in that way than Malaysian Chinese because Malaysian Chinese don't use chopsticks. They use forks and spoons. So every time I'm eating with the local Chinese in Malaysia, I'm the one who dominates the table [with their chopstick proficiency]. And I like drinking hot water like the Chinese do. I like being direct like Egyptians—staring in the eyes and not beating around the bush when leading conversations. But I also know how to be very political in work environments, and I learned that from Americans. Culturally I really think I'm a mishmash, a patchwork of stuff. There are also definitely aspects of all these cultures that I really dislike and don't identify with.

INTERVIEWER: What part of your identity do you think is shaped by your childhood experience in Yugoslavia?

ŠTEVIN: I think there's plenty, but I think the major ones would be simplicity and modesty. Like simplicity in any way but also what I mentioned about friendships. I feel that that environment shaped me in the way that I'm just used to friends being around and always being available for friends. Whereas when I started living in Western countries and experiencing Western cultures, [I found that] there's a calendar. Serbians don't really socialize like that. There's always time for friends. Maybe not on a daily basis, but you're going to find time. Even now during capitalism, when work life picked up, there's always time for friends. I don't know any Serbian [person] who has a calendar. [Laughs] It's like, "Oh, when are we going to hang out?" And they pull out a calendar from their pocket, like, "Oh, let me see, I have an hour in three weeks." No. Friendships don't work like that for me.

I also don't throw away anything. And I think that's very communist of me. I remember that my grandfather and my parents would save everything. Like, there's a shoelace, even a piece of a shoelace, and you don't throw it away because you might need it. And it's not the problem that it's too expensive. You can afford it, but you may not be able to find it in a store. I'm not hoarding because I have sentimental connections with stuff, but it's just like, "Oh, it might be reused." I might need it for something. Instead of having to go to a store to look for it, I can just open the closet and take it out and repurpose it.

Because we would always go on these vacations that were cheap but decent, I don't really know how to enjoy luxury vacations even though I can [now] afford them occasionally. I go [on these vacations now,] and I just find them wasteful. And I feel like I have a guilty conscience for spending that much money knowing that my friends and family back home would never be able to afford them. I'm like, "I should have just sent them that money. I don't even need this. Why do I need this expensive room on the beach when I'm just on the beach getting dirty in the sand?" I tried a couple of times to open my mind, but it really didn't work. Maybe I can enjoy it for a day or two, but not a long vacation.

And also, all my clothes are cheap. I won't buy brands. But I'm not sure if that's the influence of communism or if it's just my style, you know? I was a grunge kid.

INTERVIEWER: I think they're all influences.

ŠTEVIN: Luckily, we had MTV. MTV saved my life. [Chuckles] And MTV used to be good.

INTERVIEWER: What do you remember about MTV?

ŠTEVIN: Just videos and that grunge scene, an alternative scene. [The show] *120 Minutes*. The visual experimentation in short form because music videos were a new format; they blended [video] with music. [MTV showed] a scene that didn't exist in Serbia. Growing up, it was like, "I want to be there." Like I wanted to be on that scene. I wanted to go to that concert. Like, "There's more to life than what I have here in Yugoslavia/Serbia." There was more color over there, there was pink over there, I wanted to go there. [Laughs] There was glitter and stuff, you know? [There was] a lot of variety and diversity, like Black artists and Asian artists. When I was in Serbia, everyone was just white. That's why I'm thankful for MTV.

But I'm also thankful to Tito. Tito was a big movie buff, so we were not part of that Eastern bloc [practice] that blocked culture from the West and elsewhere.[11] We had access to all cultures. He built movie theaters in all towns. He wanted people to watch movies from all over the world. And I think that was also a big influence on me and how I became so cosmopolitan. I wanted to be in those movies. Although I can't really say I had a bad childhood, it was just monotone.

INTERVIEWER: Do you think Yugoslavia would have been a kinder place to live in if it didn't fall apart, for example, in terms of being more accepting of queerness or being more accepting of ethnic diversity? Do you think Yugoslavia would have been a more welcoming place for you to live in as an adult?

ŠTEVIN: I think it would have. I know that after coming out and joining the gay scene and meeting older queer people and talking to them, they would tell me that it was a lot easier in the 1970s and 1980s. It wasn't talked about, and there was no representation, but also it wasn't a big taboo. There was no backlash against [the queer community]. They were just left alone. They had their scene. It was underground, but they felt safer. And I think that gradually, with Western influence, had it stayed like that and been more open and more diverse without all this tension, I think it would be much easier for

---

11. The documentary *Cinema Komunisto* explores how Tito's love for film impacted the development of a vibrant film industry in socialist Yugoslavia. The state's central film studio, Avala Film, produced heroic war epics that romanticized Partisan fighters in World War II and extolled the glory of the Yugoslav state throughout the socialist years (*Cinema Komunisto*, Mila Turajlic, dir., 2010). However, scholars argue that Yugoslavia also readily welcomed cultural influences from the West. Scholar Dean Vuletic shows that Yugoslavia abandoned Soviet-style cultural policies after the Tito-Stalin split in 1948 and immediately opened up to significantly more Western culture than other socialist states (Vuletic, "Generation Number One," 862). By the 1950s and 1960s, Yugoslavia encouraged Westernization as a form of cultural diplomacy. As a result, residents had access to film, music, fashion, and foods from Western countries. Historian Radina Vučetić suggests that Westernization did not change Yugoslav ideology but that it did shape generations of Yugoslavs. "Yugoslavs chose jazz and rock'n'roll music, Hollywood movies, Coca-Cola and Levi's," she writes. "They were the most sought after icons of American popular culture, and satisfied their need to belong to the West, at least in a cultural sense" (Vučetić, "Džuboks (Jukebox)," 161).

people to be more accepting of diversity. But if you're afraid for your life, then everyone else is a threat. You build walls and barriers and just want to protect yourself. I guess you see everyone else as an enemy. But if you're well fed and can afford vacations, you probably don't care about what gay people do because you don't see them as a threat.

INTERVIEWER: Is there anything that you're nostalgic about when it comes to Yugoslavia?

ŠTEVIN: I didn't really experience Yugoslavia's vast territory because we didn't really travel much around Yugoslavia. I only knew the northern part of Serbia in Yugoslavia. But when I think of Yugoslavia and what it used to encompass, I miss the geography of it. I wish I could say that my country still has the Alps, and the beautiful sea, and Roman ruins, and the mountains of Bosnia for skiing, and the Colosseum, you know? But no, that's all taken away. All nature everywhere is beautiful, every country is beautiful, but I think that Yugoslavia had so much variety on such a tiny territory. It's very rare to find that anywhere else in the world. And not just when it comes to land formations, but also in terms of culture and religion and language.

I wish I could just have the freedom to live in one of the other [former] republics, but that's not possible. I mean, it's possible, but there are bureaucratic hurdles. I wish I could just pack my life and just go to a city in Croatia and start to build a life there. That would come with a lot of hurdles these days. [I also wish we had] the ability to just travel to these places. We don't need visas anymore, but [we still have to] exchange currency and deal with stuff. I think it was a nice little idea that failed.

INTERVIEWER: What does Yugoslavia mean to you now?

ŠTEVIN: Maybe that—a utopia. I really wish it hadn't failed. I wish it hadn't revolved around a dictator. I wish it had had a more politically stable system so it could survive past the death of a dictator. I'm not a fan of capitalism. I think Yugoslavia was a more humane place to live despite the lack of complete freedom of speech. I do think that people were kinder because they were taken care of, they were provided for, and they didn't work long hours. They had economic stability, and they didn't have to worry about what's going to be on the table the next day. They had more time to socialize because they didn't have to work from dawn until dusk. That created time open for possibilities for people to build connections, and connections mean stability. I think it was a lot more carefree.

But I don't know. I was not an adult. I didn't have to go through adult problems. But I would like to have that ability to start my work at eight a.m. and finish at two p.m. I would like to not have to take any work home and just have from two p.m. until ten p.m. in the evening to hang out with my family, my friends, do my hobbies, do chores, run errands, and then still be able to afford a vacation and health care. So in that way, it was a utopia. I mean, it definitely wasn't perfect, but I find that it was better than what we're living now.

INTERVIEWER: What is your relationship today to the Yugoslav, or Serbian, diaspora since you've been living abroad?

ŠTEVIN: I don't really have a relationship with them. Everywhere I lived, the diaspora was actually very small. I think the biggest was actually in Shanghai. I tried to make connections, but I realized that they were the people who left Serbia because of their financial needs. I left because of cultural needs. So every time we would meet and hang out, they would be very nostalgic, and they would just be playing Serbian songs and eating Serbian food. I found that they were not being culturally immersed in a local culture the way I was. I didn't go somewhere to miss where I came from. And I didn't really miss it. I missed the people, but I didn't miss the place. I didn't miss listening to Serbian music. I didn't miss eating Serbian food. I missed my friends, I missed my family, and I missed some aspects of my culture, but I didn't miss Serbian-ness. That's why I never connected [with the Serbian diaspora]. That happened to me everywhere else.

The Serbian community and diaspora in Egypt, and now in Malaysia, was much smaller. In Egypt, there was an embassy, but they didn't really organize anything. There was one occasion when they organized something and I went. Everybody was very nice, and I exchanged some numbers. Cairo is a huge mess, so it's very difficult for people to meet because of traffic jams and all that, so we never got to actually hang out. There were a couple of people who worked with me. There were three of us from Serbia working at that school. One of them was a TCK [third culture kid]. She never actually lived in Yugoslavia. It was only her parents who were Yugoslav. The other one of them left Serbia when she was a teen, before high school, and she moved to Australia. So they had very little connection to Serbia. Now, in Malaysia, I've only met one Serbian so far. I don't think there are any more. There was another one, but she left. We don't even have an embassy here.

I don't avoid Serbian people, but I avoid socializing with them if it involves nostalgia over Serbia. I can maybe be nostalgic over Yugoslavia, but not over

Serbia. And I guess also maybe it's because I'm antireligious. I don't care about our Christmas, our Easter, you know? If we're going to hang out, let's connect, let's mingle. But I'm not going to hang out with you just because it's Christmas and we have to celebrate. I have the impression that they're hanging out just because of that. They miss something from home, and they're trying to compensate. I feel like I cannot contribute to that feeling, so I may as well not sabotage them. I should just let them enjoy it, whatever they choose to do, and I'll do my own thing. I do miss the language though. I do miss the language.

INTERVIEWER: What do you call the language that you speak, and with whom do you speak it?

ŠTEVIN: I say Serbian, although I was educated in Serbo-Croatian. I cannot pull off the Croatian accent. I know Croatian grammar and vocabulary, but I cannot pull off the accent, so I can't really say that I speak Croatian. On my resume I want to come across as more open minded and inclusive, so my resume says Serbo-Croatian. If someone asks me in an everyday context, I just say Serbian.

I miss expressing my humor in Serbian occasionally. That's why I keep my journal in Serbian, and it's in Cyrillic. And I do talk to my family, but I feel like my Serbian is getting rusty in a way that it's just stuck in what it was ten years ago. I'm not acquiring any new slang or any new vocabulary, and my active vocabulary is diminishing. I still know a lot of words, but they're just not coming up. And I feel like the same is happening to me in English and German. I'm forgetting all the languages because I'm constantly thinking in three, and I just have a limited amount [of space] to not overburden my poor little aging brain. [Chuckles] I notice that when I go home, I understand the words that people are saying, but I don't understand the sentence because of the way they're speaking it. They've just become more playful, and the language evolved while I was away. And I'm not as quick at it anymore. I can't say I'm witty in Serbian anymore.

INTERVIEWER: How do you feel when you return to Serbia now or when you visit your family in Zrenjanin?

ŠTEVIN: Generally, it's sad because Zrenjanin is a very sad town. It used to be a very thriving industrial city. When Yugoslavia fell apart, everything got centralized in Serbia, and all industry moved to either Belgrade or Novi Sad. Zrenjanin just died economically and therefore died in all other ways. There's very little investment [from the state] and very few opportunities [for residents].¹² You can see it. You can feel it on the street. When I walk on the street, I feel like I'm walking in a little sepia film. It feels like this ugly yellow, brown, heavy thing.

I guess [I feel] happy/sad. If I went to visit in the winter, I would probably be sad. But since I mostly go home in the summer, I do have that nice and cozy feeling of being in my parent's garden, eating their food, eating their vegetables, and feeling like I'm being taken back to childhood. Like, "Ah, I'm out of the big city now." I can go to the garden and pluck an eggplant and go and fry it. I can go and pluck a plum or an apricot. They have so many fruits and vegetables. They taste richer and fuller than when I buy them anywhere else.

For some reason, Zrenjanin was also very clean this year. Normally, whenever I'd go to Serbia, I'd see a lot of garbage in Zrenjanin. It frustrated me. But for some reason, this year it was very clean. There was no garbage anywhere.

This summer also felt much nicer because Malaysia was very rough during the [COVID-19] lockdown, and it was very lonely. I just needed to experience some freedom of movement. When I landed in Serbia, I didn't have to scan in anywhere or be indoors all the time. I had more freedom to go to the movie theater, to enjoy life. It was not to the extent I was used to before the pandemic, but it was a closer version to it than what Malaysia had to offer to me. It was very liberating. And it was like, "I love being in Serbia." When I spent two months in Germany in 2017 and I went back home, I couldn't last more than a month. Then I took a job in Malaysia. It was like, "Get me out of here!" So there are times when I looked forward to Malaysia to escape from Serbia, but then this year was the other way around. I guess it depends on life's circumstances.

INTERVIEWER: As we've been talking, is there anything, any memory that I have not asked you about that you want to share?

---

12. NATO sanctions and bombing in the late 1990s, followed by the transition to a market economy in the 2000s, significantly impaired Serbia's industries. In the coming years, economic revitalization was more pronounced in some regions than others. In 2019, Belgrade held 41.7 percent of the total GDP, Vojvodina 26.5 percent, western regions 18.1 percent, and southern and eastern regions 13.7 percent. According to Serbia's Agency of Business Registers, twenty-one of the thirty-four largest revenue producers in 2021 were located in Belgrade. While several other businesses had headquarters in cities like Novi Sad and Senta, also located in Vojvodina, none were housed in Zrenjanin. Residents felt the regional economic disparity in their salaries as well. In 2019, the average salary in Belgrade was $1,177, while it was $831 in Vojvodina.

ŠTEVIN: I find that I had an amazing adolescence. I hated it at the time. I hated being an adolescent in Serbia, and I just wanted to get out. But then, working abroad and talking to all these people who were Americans or Brits or Australians or French or Spanish or whatever—people from the West who I imagined had had this amazing, fun adolescence—I realized mine was a lot more fun despite its scarcity. Although they had those concerts and they had those parties, their adolescence in Western countries was a lot more controlled than mine was in Serbia. I learned that there's no way that I would have been able to do any of what I did in Serbia during my adolescence in the West without being arrested on a weekly basis. It was just tolerated in Serbia, and in the West it wouldn't have been. Like, I started to go to bars legally when I was thirteen. I went clubbing when I was fourteen.[13] Although it was probably fun and there was definitely clubbing happening in the West, I probably wouldn't have been able to enter those clubs. It's kind of like the same situation reversed. They couldn't go to it [because of age restrictions], and I couldn't go to it [because I didn't live in the West].

I just didn't know at the time that people my age were not allowed to do the things that I was actually allowed to do in Serbia. In fact, I wasn't missing out on anything. Even if I had been there [in the West], I wouldn't have been able to do what I thought I should have been able to do. But I did a lot more fun stuff that people in the West couldn't do. I had a lot more freedom. I didn't have curfews. I could stay out until three or four o'clock at night. In high school, after classes, I would go to a bar to do homework with my friends over a glass of wine. There's no way I would have been able to do that in America.

INTERVIEWER: You were imagining the West as permissive or more exciting, yet in retrospect it turned out to be much different.

ŠTEVIN: Blame it on Hollywood! Later, when I went to New York City for the first time, I was like, "Oh, a dream coming true!" Like, "I am in the Big Apple." I didn't know what was happening to me. And then I realized that you couldn't actually dance in bars in New York City. Not legally possible—you have to go to a club. And I'm like, "What?" So even New York City wasn't as fun as I thought it would be. I mean, I loved my experience in New York City, but it was just like, "Why do you have to drink from a paper bag when you're in the street? Even if you're forty years old? What's the matter with you? You can't see porn magazines on a newsstand!?"

---

13. Like many other European countries, Serbia does not have a legal drinking age. There is a de jure alcohol purchase age, but it is loosely enforced.

So in that way Serbia was a lot more, I guess, liberal. I guess because it's in Europe. When it comes to that, Europe is a bit more liberal. Again, you didn't see that in Hollywood movies in the 1980s. In the Hollywood movies in the 1980s, everyone was dancing all the time. Everything was a party. Everything was a dance-off. You know? I didn't see a lot of dancing when I was in the States. I wish I'd had somebody back then to tell me what the reality was like in the West. It would have saved me from a lot of wanderlust. In Germany, they have *Fernweh*, like you're really dying to be somewhere far. Had I known what the reality was like, I wouldn't have had that strong feeling to have to leave. I would have probably enjoyed the present a lot more. So it wasn't such a bad place. It had its perks.

INTERVIEWER: Thank you for your time.

ŠTEVIN: You're welcome.

8

INTERVIEW WITH
Melinda Vuković

Melinda Vuković (name changed) was born in the late 1970s in a city now located in central Croatia. She attended school in Zagreb (now Croatia) and lived there until her midthirties. Soon after Croatia joined the European Union, Vuković moved to the Czech Republic with her family, where she was residing when we spoke over a video call in spring of 2022. In our conversation, Vuković characterized her childhood in Yugoslavia as generally happy, but she found the transition to independent Croatia jarring. She recalled how the growing presence of nationalism and Catholicism in everyday life worked to erase Yugoslavia from public consciousness. She also discussed why she felt increasingly alienated from Croatian society as an adult. Like many members of the youngest Yugoslav generation, Vuković found an inclusive community of former citizens far from home long after the state had collapsed.

At several instances, Vuković underlined that her memories of her Yugoslav childhood were overwhelmingly positive. She cited having had a general sense of comfort and belonging as a child. "I was really happy," she said. "I always had pocket money, so I could buy myself snacks all the time. There was nothing really missing. I had a family who could afford things like technology, so my dad bought some music equipment and speakers. I could listen to music and radio and watch music on TV. At that time, I didn't feel like I missed anything." Vuković also recalled numerous instances when she felt like part of a larger whole. For example, she remembered watching Eurovision and cheering on the Yugoslav contestants. Listening to the Yugoslav anthem in school made her feel like she was "a part of Yugoslavia." Like others interviewed in this volume, Vuković had detailed memories of her inauguration into Tito's Pioneers. She explained that it was "a really important event for every family with young children. I can't even think of what I could compare it to today because those events don't exist in school anymore, but it was something like a little wedding. It was a really happy moment. Everyone was proud. 'Oh, look at my little Pioneer,' they would say. We took a lot of pictures." Vuković only regretted that her family did not travel abroad when she was a child. She recognized that it was probably because they had most everything they needed in Yugoslavia, yet she wondered if her childhood would have been even more open to the world had she had the opportunity to visit other countries.

Vuković was a teenager when Croatia declared independence from Yugoslavia in 1991, and she lived through the starkness of its nationalization. The Croatian War of Independence impacted her family indirectly. She continued to attend school in Zagreb but had less money and fewer everyday comforts. Moreover, Vuković discussed how the war shifted the social climate. She suddenly became aware of nationalist rhetoric reframing her identity. She told me that her generation had been "raised at home as Yugoslavs, and we were brought up in schools like that too." After independence, she remembered that "all of a sudden, I started to hear words like 'Croatians, Croatians, Serbians, Serbians.' Before that, I never heard those words. In my mind, I now had to shift that this was Croatia and [that was] Serbia. It was no longer Yugoslavia. It was really difficult to understand as a child." As leaders sought to legitimize newly independent states, they differentiated constituents' linguistic, cultural, and historic identities, creating new national subjects on the one hand and erasing Yugoslavs on the other. "The elimination of the Yugoslav idea from peoples' day-to-day reality was achieved through various means," scholar Hana Srebotnjak writes. "Nationalism permeated the everyday reality of Yugoslav citizens and newly fabricated national concerns began to infiltrate the citizens' private sphere. The new nationalistic climate promoted identity declarations, previously considered irrelevant."[1] Vuković saw many people unquestioningly replace their Yugoslav identity with a Croatian one, but the reasons behind this change did not necessarily make sense to her as a young adult.

Vuković was just as surprised by the swift introduction of religious education into her school's curriculum. She had been neither brought up with religion nor educated in it. She shared a vivid memory of a new instructor who banned the music magazines she was accustomed to bringing to school. "This new person was a priest, and he was there to teach us Catholic religion," Vuković narrated. "[He said that] reading that magazine was not in accordance with Catholic religion. You can imagine my shock as a child. I had never heard about Catholic religion.... This subject was thrown into our faces overnight. No one explained this was now going

---

1. Srebotnjak, "Tracing the Decline of Yugoslav Identity," 73.

to be a new subject. Nothing! All of a sudden, you came to school, and you had another subject, which was hard-core Catholic religion, where you're not allowed to even read a magazine." After Croatia's independence, the state signed a series of concordats with the Holy See that allowed the Catholic Church to incorporate religious education into primary and secondary schools. While religious instruction was officially optional, most students attended classes because they feared stigmatization and had few alternatives. When her own children approached school age, Vuković found it hard to imagine sending them to school with religious education, and this influenced her decision to leave Croatia as an adult.

Vuković emigrated to the Czech Republic after Croatia joined the EU in 2013. She came to this decision after years of dissatisfaction with Croatian society. Vuković's reasons for leaving Croatia were in line with what the European Council on Foreign Relations found to be common motivations for emigration: corruption, primitivism, religious chauvinism, and nationalism. "Everything that was valuable before was gone, forbidden, removed," Vuković told me. "It wasn't a natural transition. It was very forced. I didn't develop this emotional connection to it. I couldn't. Even when I was a child, I dreamed about going abroad. As a grown up, I couldn't wait to leave. The minute we entered the European Union, I started applying. That was always a 'no' for me to stay there, but I never thought about that in Yugoslavia. Maybe because I was young, but I felt at home there as a child." As an adult, Vuković never felt at home in Croatia, and she had little interest in moving back or even visiting. After she settled in the Czech Republic, she found a diverse community of former Yugoslav citizens who had emigrated since the 1990s. "You would expect that they would have some restraints toward each other based on what happened, but they don't," she said. "There's that sense of unity I was telling you about here, abroad." That sense of unity—the one she felt in Yugoslavia but not Croatia—reassured her that the Czech Republic was her home.

INTERVIEWER: What are your earliest memories from your childhood?

VUKOVIĆ: I had a fun childhood. We had a big house in a city in central Croatia. We lived there with my mom, dad, my sibling, and grandparents from my father's side. I had a really fun childhood. [I remember] we played a lot with the neighbors' kids outside, on the street, and in our big garden. That's how I remember it from my childhood. When I think about my childhood in Yugoslavia, it was basically perfect. It has a special place in my heart. Later on, it was a different kind of life, but it stayed in my memory as a good place to be.

INTERVIEWER: Do you have recollections of the neighborhood where you lived?

VUKOVIĆ: Yes, it was a neighborhood where lots of houses were built. All the young families lived around there, and they had kids, one or two usually, in the same area. The usual way we communicated with each other was to go outside and play with each other. Sometimes [other kids] would come to our house, or we'd go to their houses, mostly for birthday parties. It was a very lively neighborhood with everyone very well connected in terms of friendship and everyday gatherings. It was fun. Today, I can't imagine living like that. It reminds me of village life because we mostly didn't [travel] anywhere else. We would just be there playing with other kids, and that was it.

INTERVIEWER: Who constituted your family when you were growing up?

VUKOVIĆ: [There was] my mom, dad, my younger sibling—three years younger than me—and then grandma and grandpa from my dad's side. We had a big house, so everyone had their own flat [or section of the house]. The house was not really like [an apartment] building [where individual apartments are usually private]; everyone knew what the others were doing. We had our own spaces, but technically there was no privacy in the house. As a kid, I didn't mind that. It was totally okay with me. I felt confident walking into any flat or going to visit any person in my house because I knew that I was always welcome. Today, at this age, I cannot imagine living like that. [I can't imagine] someone walking in at any time of day or evening without knocking. But back then, that was great for me. I felt secure. I was happy. I could go to my grandparents' [flat] on the lower floor. We lived in the same house together, and then we had neighbors around.

INTERVIEWER: Do you remember traveling to visit family anywhere else in Yugoslavia?

VUKOVIĆ: We had relatives in Macedonia, so we used to go there during the summer. That's it. Everything was inside of Yugoslavia. Maybe once we went to visit an aunt in Vienna, but we didn't do any international travel other than that.

INTERVIEWER: What do you remember about school?

VUKOVIĆ: I started school in Yugoslavia, and I think I was maybe in seventh or eighth grade when Yugoslavia dissolved. I went to school in Zagreb, in a neighborhood where a lot of the kids from the same street went to the same school, so we hung out at school as well. It was an interesting school. Everyone wore blue uniforms. There was lots of conformity. We had to look the same, and everyone had the same sandwiches, the same lunch bags, the same shoes. [Laughs] For me, at the time, it was interesting. I enjoyed it, but now I'm a mother of two teenagers, and I can't imagine them living like that. Times have definitely changed.

We didn't know anything better. For me, at that time, it was perfect. I was really happy. I always had pocket money, so I could buy myself snacks all the time. There was nothing really missing. I had a family who could afford things like technology, so my dad bought some music equipment and speakers. I could listen to music and radio and watch music on TV. At that time, I didn't feel like I missed anything. It was a happy childhood and a very good experience with primary school.

INTERVIEWER: Do you remember if you participated in any Yugoslav state activities?

VUKOVIĆ: The Pioneers. I remember that like it was yesterday. It was a big celebration in school, so parents had to buy us new clothes. We needed to dress up. Although we still had to wear our uniform underneath, we could wear new clothes. That was a massive gathering of parents, and there was a lot of music and food. It lasted all day long. It was a really important event for every family with young children. I can't even think of what I could compare it to today because those events don't exist in school anymore, but it was something like a little wedding. It was a really happy moment. Everyone was proud. "Oh, look at my little Pioneer," they would say. We took a lot of pictures. It was an important event for every family, I think.

INTERVIEWER: Was this the induction of the new generation of Pioneers?

VUKOVIĆ: Yes, that's the one. You would take the oath; after that, the celebration started. It seemed like a really important event. Everyone looked forward to it. I think it was in the second grade. I remember when I started school [that year], I would ask my parents, "When is the Pioneering happening? When is it? When is it?" I had to wait a few months for that event to happen. Everyone was super excited.

INTERVIEWER: Why do you think you looked forward to becoming a Pioneer? What made you excited about that?

VUKOVIĆ: I felt like a part of a community. I felt like once I was accepted into the Pioneers, I became a part of Yugoslavia as well. I became a Yugoslav. Before, I was just a kid watching and observing how everyone [else] was a Yugoslav. Then I felt like I was becoming a part of the community as well.

Probably that wasn't actually what was happening, but that's how I imagined it. So for me, it was really important to be accepted because that was part of the community that I lived in. I was also super excited about seeing my parents happy and proud. It was a moment that I really remember to this day, at this age. I wish we had something similar today.

INTERVIEWER: Do you remember if the idea of Yugoslavia was taught in any other ways at school?

VUKOVIĆ: I remember that there was always a picture of Tito on the wall and that there was always a flag on the side of the wall. Folded or spread, it didn't matter, but it was always somewhere. I can't really recall how often we listened to the Yugoslav anthem, but I know we did. It wasn't every day, so I think it was at some point during the week or the month. They played it in school, and we needed to stand up until the whole song finished. Even today, I remember that song. It's a beautiful song, and it made me happy to listen to it over and over again as a kid. That made me feel a part of Yugoslavia.

We were raised at home as Yugoslavs, and we were brought up in schools like that too. I never heard the words "Croatia," "Serbia," "Montenegro," "Macedonia." I never heard them. [It was] only during geography lessons when we would point at the map where those republics were. But everything else was only about Yugoslavia. We grew up thinking like Yugoslavs, not like [citizens of] specific republics.

INTERVIEWER: Were you aware of any kind of difference between you and the kids in school?

VUKOVIĆ: No, not at all. We never heard about anything else other than the village where their parents or their grandparents lived or the other towns where they would visit [family] during weekends or summer holidays. [It was] all in terms of [other] villages or towns or cities. We never heard about someone being, let's say, Slovene or Macedonian. That never existed. We were all basically one nationality. That was how I experienced it.

INTERVIEWER: Do you remember if anybody was treated differently based on their identity?

VUKOVIĆ: Maybe the Roma, but only because we kids teased them. I don't remember anything that came from teachers. It was us kids [who teased them] because [there was] usually one Roma student in school or in the classroom. The color of their skin was different, so kids always teased them. I think it's like that even today, unfortunately. But that's the only thing I recall.

The only person in our class who was sometimes treated differently was someone of a different race.

INTERVIEWER: Were you aware of your family being mixed in any way?

VUKOVIĆ: Yes, we all knew that my grandma was from Macedonia. [We also knew that] my grandpa and my dad were from the eastern part of Croatia and that my mom was from the northern part of Croatia. That was clear as day. I never understood why that was that important, but we all knew who was from where.

INTERVIEWER: Do you remember if religion played any role in your life when you were growing up?

VUKOVIĆ: Nope. Never. Not even a single word was mentioned. We did celebrate Easter and Christmas, but they were explained to us as celebrations or festive times of year. Church or anything related to church was never mentioned.

INTERVIEWER: You mentioned earlier that teachers spoke about Yugoslavia and, in a way, made you into Yugoslav citizens. How did your family speak about Yugoslavia?

VUKOVIĆ: Everyone was pretty quiet about that. I don't know if it was forbidden to talk about that or not. I remember that my dad and my grandpa were part of the communist party and that they had red cards.[2] That was pretty much it. Nobody really talked about it, but everyone would sit and cheer for Yugoslavia during Eurovision or other contests. You could feel this unity. There was never a conversation about it at all.

INTERVIEWER: Were you aware of the Yugoslav wars starting?

VUKOVIĆ: I don't remember how I heard war started, but I know at some point that was the only thing on TV. At the same time, we didn't really experience it like that. It looked to me as if it was a movie on TV or like it was

---

2. The League of Communists of Yugoslavia issued red identification cards to members. Membership grew steadily over the postwar decades in all the republics. In 1981, there were 2,154,627 members in Yugoslavia as a whole, about 9.6 percent of the total population (22,438,331). In Croatia, which had a population of 4,601,469 in 1981, 348,054 people—7.5 percent of citizens—were members of the League of Communists of Yugoslavia. Croatia was home to about 20.5 percent of Yugoslav citizens but only 16.1 percent of League of Communists of Yugoslavia members. Serbia, by contrast, had a proportionally high membership (Burg, "New Data on the League of Communists of Yugoslavia," 555).

happening a million miles away. Maybe they wanted to protect us, but our family members did not talk about it.

I still went out to play. I didn't have any connections to war other than knowing that it was happening somewhere in Croatia very close to our city. Probably as a child you just cannot understand the complexity of it. So for me, the war was something that I was aware of, but I didn't have any emotional connection to. I continued living my childhood like nothing was happening.

INTERVIEWER: Did anything change in your everyday life after the war in Croatia started?

VUKOVIĆ: No, I remember I attended English lessons just a little bit further from my house, and I still continued attending them. I really loved them. They were my connection to the world. The teacher would bring books and magazines from outside, from the West, and we would discuss them.

The only thing I remember is that sometimes there were these sirens, and we had to leave the house and go to the cellar of that building. Those were something like microinterruptions, which to me, as a child, were fun. It was like, "Hey, we're in the cellar, and there are candles, and oooh! It's so much fun!" But that was it. Those were the only interruptions I remember. Everything else was as normal as it was before. We were probably lucky because we were in Zagreb, and things were not happening in Zagreb.[3] Other than running to the cellar from time to time, I don't recall anything else that was missing or anything that I had to stop having because the war was going on.

INTERVIEWER: What kind of changes did you notice over the course of the war?

VUKOVIĆ: I noticed that the kids that I used to play with on our street were no longer on the street. I had to ring the doorbell and say, "Hey! Is this or that person here? Can they come out?" Before, they were always outside, or if I came outside and they heard me, they would come outside. Now, kids were indoors. You actually had to go to play inside or ask them to come outside to play in the garden. It was so probably because their parents were afraid.

---

3. Zagreb was far from the frontlines of the Croatian War of Independence, but it was not entirely spared. There were several air raids on government buildings, including the residence of the president at Banski Dvor in October 1991. After the Croatian army's offensive Operation Flash, the army of the parastate Republic of Serbian Krajina launched a serious retaliatory civilian attack on Zagreb in May of 1995 that killed seven and wounded more than two hundred people.

INTERVIEWER: Did you remember if the war impacted your family in any particular way?

VUKOVIĆ: No, it didn't. Although now that I think about it, I know my mom was very worried. I don't think she was well. But I didn't notice that as a child. I can imagine why a mother with two children would be totally scared, but I didn't notice it then. When I remember it now, I remember her face and her reaction to things. Back then I didn't notice.

INTERVIEWER: You lived through this very interesting moment of transition from living in unified Yugoslavia to living in independent Croatia. Were you aware of that political shift as it was happening?

VUKOVIĆ: Everyone was super excited when we became independent. Then there were some countries that accepted our independence. I can't remember which ones—Iceland and maybe one or two more. So that was a very exciting time. Everyone was celebrating. I was celebrating with them: "Yay! We're now Croatia." But I didn't understand really what that meant at that time. I knew at some point we were Croatians. All of the sudden, I started to hear words like "Croatians, Croatians, Serbians, Serbians." Before that, I never heard those words. In my mind, I now had to shift that this was Croatia and [that was] Serbia. It was no longer Yugoslavia. It was really difficult to understand as a child.

INTERVIEWER: What kind of signals did you receive from the media, from school, or from parents that began to change your understanding of your identity?

VUKOVIĆ: Well, in school it was overnight. Abruptly Tito's face was no longer on the wall. They changed it, and they put up Croatia's coat of arms. And a cross! There was a cross on the wall all of a sudden, and I had never seen that in my life. That was really obvious. The [Yugoslav] flag was gone, so all of a sudden the new [Croatian] flag was *everywhere*, literally. It was in school. It was on people's windows. The flag was really intense. It's similar to [how] Ukraine flags [appeared everywhere when Russia invaded Ukraine].[4] That's how it was in Zagreb in those days. Even if you didn't understand what was going on, you could see, "Okay, Croatia, Croatia, Croatia, flag, flag, flag." [It was] a bit traumatic for me. [Laughs] [It happened] all of a sudden. There was

---

4. Most Eastern European states viewed Russia's invasion of Ukraine in early 2022 as a callback to Soviet imperialism and rallied behind Ukraine. Popular forms of support, such as protests and displays of the Ukrainian flag, were common across Eastern Europe. See "Central and Southeastern Europe Show Support for Ukraine on Russian Invasion Anniversary."

no transition period. All of a sudden you woke up, and you were Croatian. You had to remember that, and luckily, you had reminders everywhere. [Laughs]

INTERVIEWER: Nationalism at its finest.

VUKOVIĆ: Yes. Thanks for asking me that question. When I think about it, it was so traumatic to make such a shift overnight. No one explained it or anything. All of sudden, [there was a] new flag and a new picture on the classroom wall.

INTERVIEWER: Do you remember how your family responded to this quick change?

VUKOVIĆ: My family was always very stoic when it came to those topics. You would never understand from their expressions or behaviors that there was a problem. So I didn't see anything. It could be because, except for my grandma, my family members were all Croatian, so maybe it suited them. I remember my grandpa was very proud. He was the oldest one in the family back then, and he was always talking about how proud he was. The rest of the family was not really [vocal]. Everyone went with the flow. There was a referendum [about] independence. I imagine everyone circled "Yes" because you were not allowed to circle "No." If you circled "No," [it implied that] you were not a part of us. That's how it was explained. They did their duty, but they never really openly talked about it, or I didn't hear anything really like that from them.

INTERVIEWER: How did you yourself relate to this quick erasure of Yugoslavia?

VUKOVIĆ: I just understood it was gone. Now we had a new flag and a new coat of arms. I didn't think about it at all. But you could tell later on that there were some massive changes that constantly reminded me that it wasn't like that [before]. Probably as I started to grow up and as I started to see what was happening, I started to think back and compare the two environments.

INTERVIEWER: What kind of changes did you notice? What were things that you noticed that were different in independent Croatia?

VUKOVIĆ: We used to have these youth magazines in Yugoslavia. One of them was called *Ok*.[5] We even bought some German ones like *Bravo*.[6] I used to read them as a child all the time. My father used to buy them for me. That's

---

5. *Ok* was a German teen magazine first published in 1964 that focused on culture, music, and entertainment.

6. *Bravo* was a German teen magazine first published in 1956. It featured articles about Western rock 'n' roll, fashion, and entertainment.

how I got introduced to Western music and movies. I always took these magazines to school, and I would read them with my friends. I would pick some [of the pictures] to put on my wall. Then, all of a sudden, I came to the *same* old school with the *same* old magazine, and a new person at the school ripped the magazine out of my hand and cut it into pieces.

This new person was a priest, and he was there to teach us Catholic religion.[7] [He said that] reading that magazine was not in accordance with Catholic religion. You can imagine my shock as a child. I had never heard about Catholic religion. I was like, "What are you talking about? Who are you? Why do I now have to sit in your class? And, above all, why you are ripping up my beloved magazine?" This subject was thrown into our faces overnight. No one explained that this was now going to be a new subject. Nothing! All of a sudden, you came to school, and you had another subject, which was hardcore Catholic religion, where you were not allowed to even read a magazine. That, for me, was a shock. I couldn't recover from it.

That was the first time I got introduced to Catholic religion, and [it was also] the last time. I never [wanted to] enter that class again. But there were no options. You couldn't choose not to go. I had to go, but I was there only physically, not mentally and emotionally. I just waited until it finished, and that was it. When I went to high school, I never wanted to hear about those lessons ever again.

INTERVIEWER: It's interesting that that was such a prominent experience and that it continues to be such a prominent memory. It sounds like it made a very large impact on you.

VUKOVIĆ: [It had a] massive impact. I was shocked, and I felt disrespected. If at least he could have asked me what I was reading or asked to see my magazine in a polite way. But abruptly ripping my magazine out of my hands? It was a *youth* magazine, a *music* magazine. It wasn't a grown-up magazine. So for me, that was a shock, and I remember I came home and was like, "What's that? We didn't have that before. Where did that come from all of a sudden?" I can easily tell you that things are still like that there in some areas of the city and the country. It's probably one of the main

---

7. After Croatia's independence, the state signed a series of concordats with the Holy See in 1997 and 1998 that allowed the Catholic Church to incorporate religious education into primary and secondary schools. The concordats mandated that the state pay the Catholic Church for teachers' salaries and grant the Church authority over selecting teachers. Some schools placed crucifixes in classrooms (Milekic, "Croats Uneasy over Church Role in Kindergartens").

reasons why we moved out because we didn't want our children to be under that influence.

INTERVIEWER: In that shift to Croatia, was there anything you started to actively miss from the time of Yugoslavia?

VUKOVIĆ: I remember that I noticed the difference in my pocket money. All of a sudden, it was gone. My family no longer had money.[8] I don't know, I can't connect that to what was happening, but I assume it was the switch from nationalization to privatization. My parents were a part of some companies, and they were privatized. So my pocket money was gone, and I could no longer afford anything I wanted during school breaks. I had to choose between a sandwich and a cake, but before I had been able to buy both. That was a huge difference for me. Probably the prices rose. I can't remember. We probably changed currency as well, so all of this had an influence.[9]

Then, some later years at the end of primary school, everyone all of a sudden started to speak about God. I guess if they had these classes then it was probably expected, but God and Croats, Serbs, and Bosnians became the main topics [of conversation]. I was wondering where that came from because I didn't really hear about those topics before. The words that were used [in conversation] with people definitely changed.

INTERVIEWER: You mentioned earlier that you sometimes traveled to Macedonia. Once Croatia became independent, did you notice that the new borders changed your mobility?

VUKOVIĆ: Yeah, that's a great question. After we became independent, I remember that we never went to Macedonia again. At the beginning, there was

---

8. According to the United Nations Economic Commission for Europe, the gross average monthly wage in Croatia at the end of the Croatian War of Independence in 1995 was $531, and it remained around that for the rest of the decade. The gross average monthly wage in Germany was $2,834 at that time.

9. Yugoslavia used the dinar during its entire existence. In the early 1990s, economic mismanagement led to severe hyperinflation and five reevaluations of the Yugoslav dinar. After declaring independence, Croatia used the Croatian dinar from 1991 until 1994. In 1995, it introduced the Croatian kuna, a currency with a name recalling the one used by the Ustaša-led Independent State of Croatia during World War II. Scholar David Bruce MacDonald points out that the currency also used symbols from the earlier Independent State of Croatia such as the medieval checkerboard coat of arms, signaling a revision of Croatia's history of fascist collaboration (MacDonald, *Balkan Holocausts?*, 103). Although Croatia joined the EU in 2013, it entered the eurozone and introduced the euro only in 2023, after it met economic requirements such as a stable exchange rate, controlled inflation, and sound public spending.

this fear because we had to drive through Serbia. I guess [my family] didn't want to do that with Croatian car plates. Then we were grown up, so we didn't want to [visit] with our grandparents anymore. After Croatia became independent, we didn't cross the border to the east anymore. And honestly, [we didn't cross] the west one either. It took many, many, many years [for us] to travel somewhere abroad.

INTERVIEWER: Do you remember how your feelings about Yugoslavia evolved over time?

VUKOVIĆ: I have to say that during the first few years of independence, that word "Yugoslavia" was hardly ever mentioned. I don't know if it was because people were afraid or if they knew they needed to create a habit of talking about Croatia. I can't really remember why that word disappeared, but it was gone. Like completely gone. I didn't hear anyone talk about it anywhere. And even [when referring to others, like] the Serbians, it was always "Serbians." It was never "ex-Yugoslavs" or something like that. The word "Yugoslavia" vanished completely. Because of that I think that I didn't spend much time thinking about it. In that environment, it became natural to feel Croatian, to be Croatian, and to say that you're Croatian. It never occurred to me to even talk about Yugoslavia. It was wiped out of our memory. Like this history never existed. That was sad to see.

INTERVIEWER: As a teenager growing up in newly independent Croatia, how did you identify?

VUKOVIĆ: In terms of citizenship, [I identified with] Croatia, definitely. There was nothing else you were allowed to say. I experienced it as normal because everyone was saying it. I didn't even dare to say anything else. It was Croatia, and that was it. There was this massive feeling of being proud. I felt like that was required and expected. But now that I think about it, that shift was a little bit too scandalous for children my age. That's not how it should be, especially with such topics like religion. But it felt like, "Oh, now we are independent, so now we can, you know, push it down your throat." And that actually created the completely opposite effect on me. There should have been some transition period, in my opinion.

INTERVIEWER: How do you identify today? If you had to explain who you are to someone who doesn't know you, how would you introduce yourself?

VUKOVIĆ: I would say, "I am Croatian, living in the Czech Republic." When you say Croatia, people have questions about Croatia, but I haven't been there for seven years. I still remember it, and I still have family there. But in my mind, I'm completely isolated from that nation, so I can't answer any questions [about it]. I always tell people that I'm Croatian but that I live in the Czech Republic, so they know that we should talk about the Czech Republic instead. That is also stated on my documents.

INTERVIEWER: Do you ever mention Yugoslavia when you introduce yourself?

VUKOVIĆ: No. I think I mentioned it a couple of times [at the university where I] studied when Yugoslavia came up. I would say, "Hey, you know, I was actually born in Yugoslavia." And then people would say, "Oh, really?" So then I would explain everything. But otherwise no, [it doesn't come up] in daily communication.

INTERVIEWER: To what extent do you think having grown up in Yugoslavia shapes who you are today?

VUKOVIĆ: I think it was mostly [through] upbringing and education. I can see the difference between myself and the younger generations and the people who were brought up in the West. When we went to school, we were never taught to provide any [of our own] opinions. We were just taught and then asked, "Did you do your homework—yes or no?" I never had an opportunity to express my opinions. I can see the difference with how we were brought up compared to the younger generations. I feel that they are more okay to say what's on their mind. For us, we always kept quiet. When I moved to the Czech Republic and started working for American companies, I [found myself in] a different environment where they wanted me to provide my opinion. It took me some time to unlearn my old habits from childhood. You have to change because the world doesn't sit still, right?

INTERVIEWER: Correct me if I'm wrong here, but another influence of your Yugoslav childhood seems to be your inclination to push back against religion and nationalism because you were not raised with them.

VUKOVIĆ: This is definitely what I didn't want [in my life]. I didn't want my children to be brought up with it either. Talking about religion and nationality was never an option for us as a family. It wasn't important. It was important who was a good person and who was a bad person, but someone's religion or nationality weren't really important. When Croatia became independent, this [religion and nationality] became very, very important in school and everywhere else. That was a shock for me. Especially when I became a mother, I couldn't imagine raising my children like that. It's so irrelevant. In Yugoslavia, it was irrelevant. We functioned very well without knowing who was from where and what religion [they practiced]. I would like to keep that from those times.

INTERVIEWER: As an adult now firmly living outside the Yugoslav region, is there anything that you feel nostalgic about related to Yugoslavia?

VUKOVIĆ: Back then, we had different music that was a little bit more urban than what is available [in Croatia] today. I mean, there are bands and musicians that are urban, but nonurban music prevailed in Croatia.[10] And even today, over there you have clashes between regions, which is nonsense to me. It's the same country, so I cannot imagine that. When I think about Yugoslavia, there were no clashes between regions or republics, or at least I don't recall any. Maybe I was too young. Maybe [they existed] on some political level. But that didn't exist in my everyday life.

I feel like back then, we had different values that were important. When Croatia switched to an independent country, our values switched as well. What we thought was important before was no longer important. Now it was nationality, religion, and race. Life values changed, and I preferred the ones we had in Yugoslavia.

INTERVIEWER: What does Yugoslavia mean to you today?

VUKOVIĆ: A kind of unity. In my mind as a child, it worked well. Now I can see that the challenges we had were probably not surmountable. I still think that

---

10. After Tito split with Stalin in 1948, Yugoslavia increasingly opened to Western cultural influences. See Vučetić, *Coca-Cola Socialism*. During the postwar years, Yugoslavs had access to foreign and domestic music. Yugoslav rock 'n' roll magazines like *Džuboks* regularly featured bands like the Beatles, Jimi Hendrix, and the Rolling Stones alongside articles on domestic performers (Vučetić, "Džuboks (Jukebox)," 161–62). During the Yugoslav wars, however, the nationalist regimes of most successor states sought to limit citizens' access to other cultures. Scholar Eric Gordy shows that Slobodan Milošević's regime in Serbia marginalized culture deemed urban, cosmopolitan, or antinationalist and in its place popularized culture deemed rural, peasant, and nationalist (Gordy, *The Culture of Power in Serbia*). Similar nationalization of popular culture occurred in Franjo Tudjman's Croatia. Scholar Catherine Baker suggests that "culture and entertainment were heavily politized during the Tudjman years through a range of explicit and implicit narratives, from songs which defined the nation in terms of its enemies, history, territory, religion and gender roles, to arguments among music professionals which contested the validity of pop genres depending on how well they implemented the ideological narratives of Croatia's geo-political identity" (Baker, "Popular Music and Political Change in Post-Tudjman Croatia," 1742).

the feeling of unity was fantastic. I never felt like that later, in the independent years. I think it was good for children back then. I felt like we had options back then, and in the new country these options were gone. Life values completely changed.

INTERVIEWER: It sounds like Yugoslavia means a sense of community or a sense of unified community to you, and that this is something you feel like you lost.

VUKOVIĆ: I think so. I think that it's still lost over there, even today. It's just not the same. I think people were more tolerant of each other back then. They were more relaxed and happier in general. Everyone was happy. I have pictures at home where we are together at the beach with friends. My parents were always social. That slowly disappeared later. I'm not sure whether it was connected to finance, the economy, or something else, but I think a lot of different factors changed that. Now that I think about it, it was a huge shift. Everything that was valuable before was gone, forbidden, removed. It wasn't a natural transition. It was very forced. I didn't develop this emotional connection to it. I couldn't. Even when I was a child, I dreamed about going abroad. As a grown up, I couldn't wait to leave. The minute we entered the European Union, I started applying.[11] That was always a "no" for me to stay there, but I never thought about that in Yugoslavia. Maybe because I was young, but I felt at home there as a child.

INTERVIEWER: Did Croatia ever feel like home?

VUKOVIĆ: No. I've been here [in the Czech Republic] for a while, and I haven't visited [Croatia] yet. I went just once for a day, but that was it. That feeling is gone. I feel at home here.

INTERVIEWER: How do you relate to other folks from Croatia or other folks from the former Yugoslavia? Do you find that sense of home with other folks who had a similar Yugoslav childhood?

---

11. Croatia applied to join the EU in 2003 and became the EU's twenty-eighth member state on July 1, 2013. EU membership allows Croatian citizens to travel, live, work, and retire in any other member state. According to the European Council on Foreign Relations, new member states often see an increase in emigration for better life, work, and education opportunities. The triggers for Croatian emigration include "corruption, primitivism, religious chauvinism, and nationalism" (European Council on Foreign Relations, "The Way Back," 7). Since Croatia joined the EU, its population has decreased by 10 percent due to emigration. In 2023, Croatia fulfilled the final requirements to join the eurozone, allowing it to introduce the euro, become a member of the Schengen Area, and do away with border control at mutual borders.

VUKOVIĆ: Yeah, this is incredible. The people that are here, they don't have those restraints or boundaries that they would have now in Croatia or Serbia. Everyone hangs out together. We go to the same concerts. If there is a Serbian rock band, we all go. I really enjoy that. You wouldn't see that over there—[people] are isolated, and they hang out in separate places. Over here, people don't mind. They get together no matter which former Yugoslav country they are from. All these people are forty and older. They moved here sometime before, during, or after the war. None of them were born here.[12] You would expect that they would have some restraints toward each other based on what happened, but they don't. There's that sense of unity I was telling you about here, abroad. Everyone is super friendly, and they don't care about each other's accents.

INTERVIEWER: When you're spending time with folks from the former Yugoslavia, what do you call the language that you speak?

VUKOVIĆ: I always think about what to say. I would say by default, "Hey, you speak Croatian." But people who are Serbian would say, "No, I speak Serbian," or others might say, "No, I speak Bosnian." So I figured I should stop using those words and just say, "Hey, you speak our language." Then they reply, "Yeah, we speak our language." And so it's interesting that everyone is happy when they can speak their own language.

INTERVIEWER: With whom do you get to speak "our" language?

VUKOVIĆ: I know some people who own a café bar in central Prague. They're very famous among the Yugoslav community in Prague, so a lot of people who came over from Bosnia, Serbia, Croatia, and Macedonia go there. I get to see them there. When they have events, like book or theater events with someone from an ex-Yugoslav republic, I also go there. There is always someone new there, and everyone is super excited to meet them. They always ask them, "Where are you from?" and then they exchange pictures. People like to talk about their homeland. They're happy to meet you, but they live here and enjoy life here in the Czech Republic.

INTERVIEWER: You mentioned that you don't have much of an interest in visiting Croatia. Do you think that you will ever live in the former Yugoslav region again?

---

12. Before the 1990s, there was almost no Yugoslav emigration to Eastern bloc countries like Czechoslovakia. By 2022, 3,272 residents of the Czech Republic were born in Croatia, 6,077 in Serbia, 2,725 in Macedonia, 2,403 in Bosnia, and 1,534 in Kosovo. Of the Czech Republic's total population of over 10 million, the community of former Yugoslavs constituted around 1 percent.

VUKOVIĆ: No, I don't so. I think that chapter is closed for sure. We'll see. When I'm retired, I might change my mind. At the moment, the chapter is closed. I need to visit, and I'm still delaying that because I need to switch my mindset to prepare for what's there. It's draining. When you come back, you're drained. That didn't happen when I came back from Slovenia this week. It's a different mentality [in Croatia]. I totally enjoy being away from it. It's a closed environment, and it's somewhere where I cannot develop emotionally and intellectually. I have no plans or desires to go back other than just to visit family.

INTERVIEWER: I know you have two children. To what degree are you teaching them about Yugoslavia or Croatia as part of their history and background?

VUKOVIĆ: The fact that they speak the language is probably the strongest factor. We speak to each other mostly in Croatian and only sometimes in English. They speak to their relatives and family in Croatia in Croatian. My older child sometimes reads books in Croatian to maintain the language because it's difficult to speak it here. Other than that, we sometimes watch Croatian football matches.

We are pretty open about why we are here and not there and the difference between living here and living there. Over there, nothing has changed, and probably nothing will change for many, many years. We sometimes compare them with other families' kids or friends' kids [in Croatia], and we ask them, "Do you see the difference? The difference is that we live here, and we wouldn't be able to provide you with what we have here if we were over there."

I don't mean that [only] financially. For example, my children speak three foreign languages by now, [and they learned them] free of charge here in the Czech Republic. If we were in Croatia, that wouldn't be possible. It would also cost a lot of money. I keep reminding them about what great opportunities we have abroad. My younger child speaks two foreign languages and is starting the third one in September. We also remind them about other opportunities. For example, we are big concertgoers as a family, and we tell them, "Look at all the cool bands and singers you get to hear abroad. If you were there, they would never visit Croatia." These microexamples make sense to them, and they see the difference. I would like them to see the difference so that they are more open toward the world. I think they should go somewhere in the world. That's why they speak three languages. I'd like for them to speak [Croatian] so they can talk to their relatives and friends, but other than that I don't think they should or will have any other connection to Croatia.

INTERVIEWER: As we've been talking, has there been anything that popped into your mind that I have not asked you about?

VUKOVIĆ: We all owned a weekend house back then, so every weekend we would spend time at the weekend house.[13] It was so much fun because there'd be other neighbors with kids. That really made my childhood even nicer, but now, when I think about it, what I missed was traveling. We didn't go abroad. We didn't get to see other cultures. We didn't have a chance to, or we didn't want to. I don't know. I've never asked my parents, "Why did we never travel abroad?" I know it wasn't easy to travel abroad, but then again it wasn't that hard. I think people could still normally travel, but my parents never did.

Today, I can't imagine that type of life for my children. They wouldn't be able to know the world, and that's what I think we were missing. We didn't know anything about anything. We were just in our own lives. It was just house, weekend house, school, and that was it. I was interested in music, and I could buy magazines and read a little bit about music and movies, but that was pretty much it. My children today know about the world in general and also about culture and politics. I am super proud of the way they think about the world and how they grew up being more diverse and inclusive than what we were back then.

INTERVIEWER: And on that note, I want to thank you for sharing your time and your memories. I really enjoyed our conversation.

VUKOVIĆ: Thank you for allowing me to remember what we had and what we didn't have. It was a really nice and pleasant conversation.

---

13. Weekend houses, popularly known as *vikendica* in Bosnian/Croatian/Montenegrin/Serbian, were privately owned second residences that ranged from spartan to luxurious. Some were used as holiday retreats on the seaside or in the mountains, while many others were used, as the name implies, as weekend getaways close to a family's primary residence. As Yugoslavia's economy improved, second homes became popular among political elites in the 1950s and white-collar workers in the late 1960s. By the 1980s, weekend homes had become accessible to a broader population of Yugoslavs. On the one hand, homeownership of second residences aligned with socialist ideas about workers' needs for rest and leisure, but on the other, it represented social inequality and personal gain. Scholar Karin Taylor points out that the number of registered weekend homes in Yugoslavia increased while there was an ongoing housing crisis in urban areas. Taylor argues that the state loosely regulated the social housing system and building of private homes and thus effectively "reproduced contradictions that actually advanced social inequality": "People who lived in social housing or owned their own property were the most likely to accumulate the necessary resources to build a *vikendica*.... In contrast, urban newcomers or people whose enterprise was unable to provide social housing for all employees exploited their resources in the struggle to purchase or build a city home in the first place. For these families, putting funds aside for a getaway was out of the question" (Taylor, "My Own *Vikendica*," 198–99).

SUGGESTED DISCUSSION QUESTIONS

General

1. How did interviewees remember their Yugoslav childhoods? What stood out in their memories?
2. Many interviewees mentioned their inauguration into the Pioneer youth organization. Why was this an important milestone?
3. How did interviewees engage with religion and religious rituals as children?
4. How did members of the youngest Yugoslav generation experience the collapse of the state? How did they experience war?
5. How did interviewees perceive differences among friends, classmates, and family members before the disintegration of Yugoslavia? How did their perception of difference change?
6. How did members of the youngest Yugoslav generation identify during the time of the unified state? How did their sense of identity change?
7. How did interviewees remember socialism?
8. What did Yugoslavia mean to interviewees at the time of the interviews, three decades since the collapse of the unified state?
9. How did the youngest Yugoslav cohort engage with the successor states at the time of the interviews, three decades since the collapse of Yugoslavia?
10. What value did interviewees find in Yugoslavia and its ideals?

Comparative

1. How did memories of growing up as the child of a mixed marriage compare for Gordan Pejić and Iva Radivojević?

2. How did memories of bilingualism compare for those who spoke Serbo-Croatian and another officially recognized language of Yugoslavia, such as Luka Lisjak Gabrijelčič (Slovene) and Elena Stavrevska (Macedonian)?
3. How did memories of bilingualism compare for those who spoke Serbo-Croatian and a minority language of Yugoslavia, such as Krisztina Rácz (Hungarian) and Artan Sadiku (Albanian)?
4. How did the childhood memories of Krisztina Rácz, Iva Radivojević, and Bojan Števin in Vojvodina, an autonomous province of Serbia and the most diverse region of Yugoslavia, compare?
5. How did the childhood memories of Elena Stavrevska and Artan Sadiku in the Republic of Macedonia compare?
6. How did the childhood memories of Luka Lisjak Gabrijelčič, who grew up in Slovenia, Yugoslavia's northmost and wealthiest republic, compare to those of Artan Sadiku or Elena Stavrevska, who grew up in Macedonia, Yugoslavia's southernmost and poorest republic?
7. How did memories of emigration from Yugoslavia due to war compare for Gordan Pejić, who fled as refugee from Bosnia, and Iva Radivojević, who emigrated from Serbia?
8. How did the adult-age decisions to leave successor states after the 1990s compare for Melinda Vuković (Croatia) and Bojan Števin (Serbia)?
9. How did the experiences of continuing to live in successor states compare for Luka Lisjak Gabrijelčič (Slovenia), Krisztina Rácz (Serbia), and Artan Sadiku (North Macedonia)?
10. How did the experience of living abroad compare for Melinda Vuković and Gordan Pejić (Czech Republic), Elena Stavrevska (United Kingdom), Bojan Števin (Malaysia), and Iva Radivojević (United States and Greece)?

BIBLIOGRAPHY

"About Us." Dubioza Kolektiv. Accessed on July 23, 2023. https://dubioza.org/about-us/.

Alexievich, Svetlana. *Secondhand Time: The Last of the Soviets*. Translated by Bela Shayevich. New York: Random House, 2017.

———. *Voices from Chernobyl: The Oral History of a Nuclear Disaster*. Translated by Keith Gessen. Funks Grove, IL: Dalkey Archive Press, 2005.

Anheier, Helmut, and Yudhishthar Raj Isar, eds. *Heritage, Memory & Identity*. Los Angeles: SAGE, 2011.

Archer, Rory, Igor Duda, and Paul Stubbs, eds. *Social Inequalities and Discontent in Yugoslav Socialism*. London: Routledge, 2016.

Ashbrook, John, and Spencer Bakich. "Storming to Partition: Croatia, the United States, and Krajina in the Yugoslav Wars." *Small Wars and Insurgencies* 21, no. 4 (December 2010): 537–60.

Babuna, Aydin. "The Albanians of Kosovo and Macedonia: Ethnic Identity Superseding Religion." *Nationalities Papers* 28, no. 1 (2000): 67–92.

Bacevic, Jana. "Education, Conflict, and Class Reproduction in Socialist Yugoslavia." In *Social Inequalities and Discontent in Yugoslav Socialism*, edited by Rory Archer, Igor Duda, and Paul Stubbs, 77–94. London: Routledge, 2016.

Bahar, Dany, Andreas Hauptmann, Cem Özgüzel, and Hillel Rapoport. "Migration and Post-conflict Reconstruction: The Effect of Returning Refugees in Export Performance in the Former Yugoslavia." *IZA Institute for Labor Economics* no. 12412 (June 2019): 1–39.

Baker, Catherine. "Cultural Space and Meaning in the Phenomenon of 'Crodance.'" *Ethnologie française* 43, no. 2 (April–June 2013): 313–24.

———. "Popular Music and Political Change in Post-Tudjman Croatia: 'It's All the Same, Only He's Not Here'?" *Europe-Asia Studies* 62, no. 10 (December 2010): 1741–59.

———. *Race and the Yugoslav Region: Postsocialist, Post-conflict, Postcolonial?* Manchester: Manchester University Press, 2018.
Bakić-Hayden, Milica. "Nesting Orientalism: The Case of Former Yugoslavia." *Slavic Review* 54, no. 4 (winter 1995): 917–31.
Ballinger, Pamela. *History in Exile: Memory and Identity at the Borders of the Balkans.* Princeton: Princeton University Press, 2003.
Banac, Ivo. *The National Question in Yugoslavia: Origins, History, Politics.* Ithaca: Cornell University Press, 1984.
Barany, Zoltan D. "Living on the Edge: The East European Roma in Postcommunist Politics and Societies." *Slavic Review* 52, no. 2 (summer 1994): 321–44.
Batinić, Jelena. *Women and Yugoslav Partisans: A History of World War II Resistance.* New York: Cambridge University Press, 2015.
Bieber, Florian. "The Serbian Opposition and Civil Society: Roots of the Delayed Transition in Serbia." *International Journal of Politics, Culture and Society* 17, no. 1 (fall 2003): 73–90.
Bloodworth, Aryn. "Educational (De)Segregation in North Macedonia: The Intersection of Policies, Schools, and Individuals." *European Educational Research Journal* 19, no. 4 (2020): 310–28.
Bonfiglioli, Chiara. "Women's Political and Social Activism in the Early Cold War Era: The Case of Yugoslavia." *Aspasia* 8 (2014): 1–25.
Borenstein, Eliot. "Our Borats, Our Selves: Yokels and Cosmopolitans in the Global Stage." *Slavic Review* 67, no. 1 (spring 2008): 1–7.
Bošković, Aleksandar. "Yugonostalgia and Yugoslav Cultural Memory: *Lexicon of Yu Mythology.*" *Slavic Review* 72, no. 1 (spring 2013): 54–78.
Botev, Nikolai. "Where East Meets West: Ethnic Intermarriage in the Former Yugoslavia, 1962–1989." *American Sociological Review* 59, no. 3 (June 1994): 461–80.
Boym, Svetlana. *The Future of Nostalgia.* New York: Basic Books, 2001.
Božić, Gordana. "Conversations with Bosnian Youth: From the Youth Relay Race to the Successor Generation Initiative." *Nationalities Papers* 35, no. 4 (September 2007): 743–72.
Bren, Paulina. *The Greengrocer and His TV: The Culture of Communism after the 1968 Prague Spring.* Ithaca: Cornell University Press, 2010.
Bren, Paulina, and Mary Neuburger, eds. *Communism Unwrapped: Consumption in Cold War Eastern Europe.* Oxford: Oxford University Press, 2012.
Brentin, Dario, and Dejan Zec, eds. *Sport in Socialist Yugoslavia.* London: Routledge, 2019.
Brunnbauer, Ulf. "'The People of Our Blood, Who Are Citizens of Foreign Countries': Yugoslav Diaspora Policies in the 20th Century." *Monde(s)* 2, no. 14 (2018): 97–121.
Bugarski, Ranko. "What's in a Name: The Case of Serbo-Croatian." *Revue des études slaves* 75, no. 1 (2004): 11–20.

Burg, Steven L. "New Data on the League of Communists of Yugoslavia." *Slavic Review* 46, no. 3/4 (autumn–winter 1987): 553–67.
Burić, Fedja. "Dwelling on the Ruins of Socialist Yugoslavia: Being Bosnian by Remembering Tito." In *Post-communist Nostalgia*, edited by Maria Todorova and Zsuzsa Gille, 227–43. New York: Berghahn Books, 2010.
———. "Sporadically Mixed: Lowering Socialist Expectations and Politicizing Marriage in the 1960s Yugoslavia." In *Intermarriage from Central Europe and Central Asia: Mixed Families in the Age of Extremes*, edited by Adrienne Edgar and Benjamin Frommer, 83–109. Lincoln: University of Nebraska Press, 2020.
Calic, Maria-Janine. *A History of Yugoslavia*. Budapest: Central European University Press, 2019.
Calori, Anna, and Kathrin Jurkat. "'I'm Both a Worker and a Shareholder': Workers' Narratives and Property Transformations in Postsocialist Bosnia-Herzegovina and Serbia." *Südosteuropa* 65, no. 4 (2017): 654–78.
Cave, Mark, and Stephen M. Sloan. *Listening on the Edge: Oral History in the Aftermath of Crisis*. Oxford: Oxford University Press, 2014.
"Central and Southeastern Europe Show Support for Ukraine on Russian Invasion Anniversary." *Balkan Insight*, February 24, 2023.
Cohen, Lenard J. *Broken Bonds: Yugoslavia's Disintegration and Balkan Politics in Transition*. Boulder: Westview Press, 1995.
Cohen, Lenard J., and Jasna Dragović-Soso, eds. *State Collapse in South-Eastern Europe: New Perspectives in Yugoslavia's Disintegration*. West Lafayette: Purdue University Press, 2007.
Cohen, Stephen F., and Katrina vanden Heuvel. *Voices of Glasnost: Interviews with Gorbachev's Reformers*. New York: W. W. Norton, 1989.
Čok, Lucija, and Susanna Pertot. "Bilingual Education in the Ethnically Mixed Areas along the Slovene-Italian Border." *Comparative Education* 46, no. 1 (February 2010): 63–78.
Cornips, Leonie, and Vincent A. de Rooij, eds. *The Sociolinguistics of Place and Belonging: Perspectives from the Margins*. Amsterdam: John Benjamins, 2018.
Crosby, Alan. "Mixed Marriages as Another Casualty of Bosnia's War." *Radio Free Europe/Radio Liberty*, July 8, 2017.
Dimova, Rozita. "'Modern' Masculinities: Ethnicity, Education, and Gender in Macedonia." *Nationalities Papers* 34, no. 3 (July 2006): 305–20.
Djokić, Dejan. *Elusive Compromise: A History of Interwar Yugoslavia*. New York: Columbia University Press, 2007.
———, ed. *Yugoslavism: Histories of a Failed Idea, 1918–1992*. Madison: University of Wisconsin Press, 2003.
Draghia, Dan. "Bordering Tito: The Romanian Borders under the Pressure of the Soviet-Yugoslav Conflict." *Romanian Political Science Review* 14, no. 2 (2014): 243–60.

Dragostinova, Theodora K. *The Cold War from the Margins: A Small Socialist State in the Global Cultural Scene*. Ithaca: Cornell University Press, 2021.

Dragović-Soso, Jasna. *'Saviors of the Nation': Serbia's Intellectual Opposition and the Revival of Nationalism*. London: Hurst, 2002.

Drakulić, Slavenka. "Letter from Vienna: Why I Haven't Returned to Belgrade." *Der Spiegel*, January 21, 2009.

Drnovšek Zorko, Špela. "See(m)ing Strange: Methodologies of Memory and Home." *Crossings: Journal of Migration & Culture* 7, no. 1 (2016): 81–95.

Duda, Igor. "Adriatic for All: Summer Holidays in Croatia." In *Remembering Utopia: The Culture of Everyday Life in Socialist Yugoslavia*, edited by Breda Luthar and Maruša Pušnik, 289–311. Washington, DC: New Academic, 2010.

Edgar, Adrienne. *Intermarriage and the Friendship of Peoples: Ethnic Mixing in Soviet Central Asia*. Ithaca: Cornell University Press, 2022.

Edgar, Adrienne, and Benjamin Frommer, eds. *Intermarriage from Central Europe and Central Asia: Mixed Families in the Age of Extremes*. Lincoln: University of Nebraska Press, 2020.

Engel, Barbara Alpern, and Anastasia Posadskaya-Vanderbek, eds. *A Revolution of Their Own: Voices of Women in Soviet History*. Translated by Sona Hoisington. New York: Routledge, 1998.

Erdei, Ildiko. "'The Happy Child' as an Icon of Socialist Transformation: Yugoslavia's Pioneer Organization." In *Ideologies and National Identities: The Case of Twentieth-Century Southeastern Europe*, edited by John R. Lampe and Mark Mazower, 145–79. Budapest: Central European University Press, 2004.

European Council on Foreign Relations. "The Way Back: Brain Drain and Prosperity in the Western Balkans" by Alida Vračić. ECFR/257. London: European Council on Foreign Relations, 2018. Accessed on January 29, 2025. https://ecfr.eu/publication/the_way_back_brain_drain_and_prosperity_in_the_western_balkans/.

Fenyvesi, Anna, ed. *Hungarian Language Contact outside of Hungary*. Philadelphia: John Benjamins, 2005.

Ferdinand, Siarl, and Flora Komlosi. "The Use of Hungarian and Serbian in the City of Szabadka/Subotica: An Empirical Study." *Hungarian Cultural Studies* 10 (2017): 1–13.

Fichter, Madigan. "Yugoslav Protest: Student Rebellion in Belgrade, Zagreb, and Sarajevo in 1968." *Slavic Review* 75, no. 1 (spring 2016): 99–121.

Fidelis, Malgorzata. *Women, Communism, and Industrialization in Postwar Poland*. Cambridge: Cambridge University Press, 2010.

Franičević, Vojmir, and Evan Kraft. "Croatia's Economy after Stabilization." *Europe-Asia Studies* 49, no. 4 (June 1997): 669–91.

Gerovitch, Slava. *Voices of the Soviet Space Program: Cosmonauts, Soldiers, and Engineers Who Took the USSR into Space*. London: Palgrave Macmillan, 2014.

Gheith, Jehanne M., and Katherine R. Jolluck. *Gulag Voices: Oral Histories of Soviet Incarceration and Exile*. London: Palgrave Macmillan, 2011.

Ghodsee, Kristen. *Muslim Lives in Eastern Europe: Gender, Ethnicity, and the Transformation of Islam in Postsocialist Bulgaria*. Princeton: Princeton University Press, 2010.

———. *The Red Riviera: Gender, Tourism, and Postsocialism on the Black Sea*. Durham, NC: Duke University Press, 2005.

Gilbert, Andrew. "The Past in Parenthesis: (Non)Post-socialism in Post-war Bosnia-Herzegovina." *Anthropology Today* 22, no. 4 (August 2006): 14–18.

Göncz, Lajos, and Ottó Vörös. "Hungarian in the Former Yugoslavia (Vojvodina and Prekmurje)." In *Hungarian Language Contact outside of Hungary*, edited by Anna Fenyvesi, 187–240. Philadelphia: John Benjamins, 2005.

Gordy, Eric D. *The Culture of Power in Serbia: Nationalism and the Destruction of Alternatives*. University Park: Pennsylvania State University, 1999.

Gorsuch, Anne E., and Diane P. Koenker, eds. *Turizm: The Russian and East European Tourist under Capitalism and Socialism*. Ithaca: Cornell University Press, 2006.

Gorup, Radmila, ed. *After Yugoslavia: The Cultural Spaces of a Vanished Land*. Stanford: Stanford University Press, 2013.

Grandits, Hannes, and Karin Taylor, eds. *Yugoslavia's Sunny Side: A History of Tourism in Socialism (1950s–1980s)*. Budapest: Central European University Press, 2010.

Grdešić, Marko. "Looking Back at Milošević's Antibureaucratic Revolution: What Do Ordinary Participants Now Think of Their Involvement?" *Nationalities Papers* 47, no. 4 (July 2019): 613–27.

———. "Thirty Years of Yugoslavia's 'Antibureaucratic Revolution': A Long-Run Appraisal and New Avenues of Research." *Nationalities Papers* 47, no. 4 (July 2019): 537–44.

Greble, Emily. *Sarajevo, 1941–1945: Muslims, Christians, and Jews in Hitler's Europe*. Ithaca: Cornell University Press, 2011.

Greenberg, Jessica. *After the Revolution: Youth, Democracy, and the Politics of Disappointment in Serbia*. Stanford: Stanford University Press, 2014.

———. "On the Road to Normal: Negotiating Agency and State Sovereignty in Postsocialist Serbia." *Anthropologist* 113, no. 1 (March 2011): 88–100.

Griffiths, Jennifer. "Enrico Toti: A New Man for Italy's Mutilated Victory." *Annali d'italianistica* 33 (2015): 341–54.

Guistino, Cathleen M., Cathrine J. Plum, and Alexander Vari, eds. *Socialist Escapes: Breaking Away from Ideology and Everyday Routine in Eastern Europe, 1945–1989*. New York: Berghahn, 2015.

Halilovich, Hariz. "Reclaiming Erased Lives: Archives, Records and Memories in Post-war Bosnia and the Bosnian Diaspora." *Arch Sci* 14 (2014): 231–47.

Hasić, Jasmin. "Diaspora as Digital Diplomatic Agents: 'BOSNET' and Wartime Foreign Affairs." *Migration Letters* 17, no. 1 (January 2020): 103–13.

Hawrylyshyn, Oli. "Ethnic Affinity and Migration Flows in Postwar Yugoslavia." *Economic Development and Cultural Change* 26, no. 1 (October 1977): 93–116.

Henkel, Reinhard. "Religions and Religious Institutions in the Post-Yugoslav States between Secularization of Resurgence." *AUC Geographica* 44, no. 1–2 (2009): 49–61.

Hetemi, Atdhe. *Student Movements of the Republic of Kosovo: 1968, 1981, and 1997.* London: Palgrave Macmillan, 2020.

Holmes, Leslie, and Philomena Murray, eds. *Citizenship and Identity in Europe.* Aldershot: Ashgate, 1999.

Horvat, Srećko, and Igor Štiks. *Welcome to the Desert of Post-socialism: Radical Politics after Yugoslavia.* London: Verso, 2015.

Ilic, Melanie, and Dalia Leinarte, eds. *The Soviet Past in the Post-socialist Present: Methodology and Ethics in Russian, Baltic, and Central European Oral History and Memory Studies.* London: Routledge, 2016.

Ivanova, Vanya. "Language Policy and National Equality in Socialist Yugoslavia (1945–1974)." In *Multilingual Europe, Multilingual Europeans*, edited by László Marácz and Mireille Rosello, 81–111. Leiden: Brill, 2012.

Jakovljević, Branislav. *Alienation Effects: Performance and Self-Management in Yugoslavia.* Ann Arbor: University of Michigan Press, 2016.

Jansen, Stef. "After the Red Passport: Towards an Anthropology of the Everyday Geopolitical Entrapment in EU's 'Immediate Outside.'" *Journal of the Royal Anthropological Institute* 15, no. 4 (December 2009): 815–32.

Jerman, Katja. "Border Town of Nova Gorica and Its Role in Forming a New Urban Center: Nova Gorica in Its First Years after the Foundation." *Studia Etnologiczne i Antropologiczne* 8 (2004): 103–18.

Jović, Dejan. "The Disintegration of Yugoslavia: A Critical Review of Explanatory Approaches." *European Journal of Social Theory* 4, no. 1 (2001): 101–20.

———. *Yugoslavia: A State That Withered Away.* West Lafayette: Purdue University Press, 2008.

Jurić Pahor, Marija. "Diaspora and Diasporisation: Slovene National Identity in the Contemporary Globalized World." *Journal of Ethnic Studies* 91, no. 91 (2023): 199–224.

Kenney, Padraic. *Rebuilding Poland: Workers and Communists, 1945–1950.* Ithaca: Cornell University Press, 1997.

Khanenko-Friesen, Natalia, and Gelinada Grinchenko, eds. *Reclaiming the Personal: Oral History in Post-socialist Europe.* Toronto: University of Toronto Press, 2015.

Kim, Gal. *The Partisan Counter-archive: Retracing the Ruptures of Art and Memory of the Yugoslav People's Liberation Struggle.* Berlin: De Gruyter, 2020.

Koinova, Maria. "Four Types of Diaspora Mobilization: Albanian Diaspora Activism for Kosovo Independence in the US and the UK." *Foreign Policy Analysis* 9, no. 4 (2013): 433–53.

Kojanic, Ognjen. "Nostalgia as a Practice of the Self in Post-socialist Serbia." *Canadian Slavic Papers* 57, no. 3–4 (2015): 195–212.

Koleva, Daniela. *Memory Archipelago of the Communist Past: Public Narratives and Personal Recollections*. London: Palgrave Macmillan, 2022.

Kolstø, Pål. "Identifying with the Old or the New State: Nation-Building vs. Yugo-nostalgia in the Yugoslav Successor States." *Nations and Nationalisms* 20, no. 4 (2014): 760–81.

Koneska, Cvete. "Vetoes, Ethnic Bidding, Decentralisation: Post-conflict Education in Macedonia." *Journal on Ethnopolitics and Minority Issues in Europe* 11, no. 4 (2012): 28–50.

Kriještorac, Mirsad. *First Nationalism Then Identity: On Bosnian Muslims and Their Bosniak Identity*. Ann Arbor: University of Michigan Press, 2022.

Lampe, John R. "The Two Yugoslavias as Economic Unions: Promises and Problems." In *Yugoslavism: Histories of a Failed Idea, 1918–1992*, edited by Dejan Djokić, 182–95. Madison: University of Wisconsin Press, 2003.

———. *Yugoslavia as History: Twice There Was a Country*. Cambridge: Cambridge University Press, 2000 (orig. 1996).

Lampe, John R., and Mark Mazower, eds. *Ideologies and National Identities: The Case of Twentieth-Century Southeastern Europe*. Budapest: Central European University Press, 2004.

Latham, Judith. "Roma of the Former Yugoslavia." *Nationalities Papers* 27, no. 2 (1999): 205–26.

Lavrence, Christine. "Making Up for Lost Time: Yugo-Nostalgia and the Limits of Serbian Memory." In *Global Memoryscapes: Contesting Remembrance in a Transnational Age*, edited by Kendall R. Phillips and G. Mitchell Reyes, 80–93. Tuscaloosa: University of Alabama, 2011.

Leinarte, Dalia. "Silence in Biographical Accounts and Life Stories: The Ethical Aspects of Interpretation." In *The Soviet Past in the Post-socialist Present: Methodology and Ethics in Russian, Baltic, and Central European Oral History and Memory Studies*, edited by Melanie Ilic and Dalia Leinarte, 12–18. London: Routledge, 2016.

Lemke, Jürgen. *Gay Voices from East Germany*. Translated by John Borneman. Bloomington: Indiana University Press, 1991.

Le Normand, Brigitte. *Citizens without Borders: Yugoslavia and Its Migrant Workers in Western Europe*. Toronto: University of Toronto Press, 2021.

———. *Designing Tito's Capital: Urban Planning, Modernism, and Socialism in Belgrade*. Pittsburgh: University of Pittsburgh Press, 2014.

Leydesdorff, Selma. *Surviving the Bosnian Genocide: The Women of Srebrenica Speak*. Translated by Kay Richardson. Bloomington: Indiana University Press, 2015.

Lindstrom, Nicole. "Yugonostalgia: Restorative and Reflective Nostalgia in Former Yugoslavia." *East Central Europe* 32, no. 1–2 (2005): 227–37.

Long, Michael. *Making History: Czech Voices of Dissent and Revolution*. Lanham, MD: Rowman & Littlefield, 2005.

Lóránd, Zsófia. *The Feminist Challenge to the Socialist State in Yugoslavia*. London: Palgrave Macmillan, 2018.

Luthar, Breda, and Maruša Pušnik, eds. *Remembering Utopia: The Culture of Everyday Life in Socialist Yugoslavia*. Washington, DC: New Academic, 2010.

MacDonald, David Bruce. *Balkan Holocausts?: Serbian and Croatian Victim Centered Propaganda in the War in Yugoslavia*. Manchester: Manchester University Press, 2002.

Majstrović, Vojin. "The Red Army in Yugoslavia, 1944–1945." *Slavic Review* 75, no. 2 (summer 2016): 396–421.

Maksimović, Maja. "Unattainable Past, Unsatisfying Present—Yugonostalgia: An Omen of a Better Future?" *Nationalities Papers* 45, no. 6 (2017): 1066–81.

Mariotti, Jasna, and Daniel Baldwin Hess. "Enlargement of Apartments in Socialist Housing Estates in Skopje under Transition: The Tension between Individual Preferences and Collective Action." *Journal of Housing and the Built Environment* 38 (2023): 39–59.

Martin, Upchurch, Anne Daguerre, and Daniel Ozarow. "Spectrum, Trajectory, and the Role of the State in Workers' Self-Management." *Labor History* 55, no. 1 (January 2014): 47–66.

Massino, Jill. *Ambiguous Transitions: Gender, the State, and Everyday Life in Socialist Romania*. New York: Berghahn Books, 2019.

Matthiesen, Anna. "Shifting Resources, Shifting Forms: Spontaneous Solidarity, Virtual Voluntarism and the Legacy of *Radne Akcije* in Postsocialist Serbia." *Südosteuropa* 68, no. 2 (2000): 252–73.

McConnell, Elysa. "International Disputes in the Italian-Yugoslavian Borderlands." *Les Cahiers Sirice* 1 no. 22 (2019): 117–34.

Mëhilli, Elidor. *From Stalin to Mao: Albania and the Socialist World*. Ithaca: Cornell University Press, 2017.

Messana, Paola. *Soviet Communal Living: An Oral History of the Kommunalka*. London: Palgrave Macmillan, 2011.

Micevska, Maja, Dimitar Eftimoski, and Tatjana Petrovska Mirčevska. "Macedonia's Transition Experience and Potential for Sustainable Economic Growth." *Economic and Business Review* 4, no. 3–4 (2002): 309–34.

Mihaljević, Josip. "Social Inequalities from Workers' Perspective in 1960s Socialist Yugoslavia." *Revue d'études comparatives Est-Ouest* 50, no. 1 (March 2019): 25–51.

Mikula, Maja. "Highways of Desire: Cross-border Shopping in Former Yugoslavia, 1960s–1980s." In *Yugoslavia's Sunny Side: A History of Tourism in Socialism (1950s–1980s)*, edited by Hannes Grandits and Karin Taylor, 211–37. Budapest: Central European University Press, 2010.

Mikuš, Marek. "'State Pride': Politics of LGBT Rights and Democratization in 'European Serbian.'" *East European Politics and Society* 25, no. 4 (November 2011): 834–51.

Milchevski, Ilija. "A Requiem for a Dream: The Name Issue and the Accession of Macedonia to the EU." *International Issues & Slovak Foreign Policy Affairs* 22, no. 4 (2013): 40–59.

Milekic, Sven. "Croats Uneasy over Church Role in Kindergartens." *Balkan Insight*, October 6, 2016.

———. "Franjo Tudjman: Strongman Obsessed with Forging Croatia's Independence." *Balkan Insight*, December 10, 2019.

———. "Rise of Yugo-Nostalgia 'Reflects Contemporary Problems.'" *Balkan Insight*, March 14, 2017.

Milich, Zorka. *A Stranger's Supper: An Oral History of Centenarian Women in Montenegro*. Woodbridge, CT: Twayne, 1996.

Minniti, Maria, and Lidija Polutnik. "Currency Conversion and the Role of Expectations: The Case of Slovenia." *Economic and Business Review* 9, no. 1 (2007): 5–21.

Molloy, Peter. *The Lost World of Communism: An Oral History of Daily Life behind the Iron Curtain*. London: BBC Books, 2009.

Molnar, Christopher. "Imagining Yugoslavs: Migration and the Cold War in Postwar West Germany." *Central European History* 47, no. 1 (March 2014): 138–69.

Moss, Kevin. "Split Pride/Split Identities." *QED: A Journal of GLBTQ Worldmaking* 2, no. 3 (summer 2016): 56–75.

Motadel, David. "The 'Muslim Question' in Hitler's Balkans." *Historical Journal* 56, no. 4 (December 2013): 1007–39.

Muhić, Maja. "Spiritual Assistance during Two Refugee Crises in the Republic of Macedonia." *Anthology of East Europe Review* 31, no. 1 (spring 2013): 75–92.

Neofotistos, Vasiliki P. "Postsocialism, Social Value, and Identity Politics among Albanians in Macedonia." *Slavic Review* 69, no. 4 (winter 2010): 882–902.

Neuburger, Mary C. *Balkan Smoke: Tobacco and the Making of Modern Bulgaria*. Ithaca: Cornell University Press, 2013.

Niebuhr, Robert. "Nonalignment as Yugoslavia's Answer to Bloc Politics." *Journal of Cold War Studies* 13, no. 1 (winter 2011): 146–79.

Nielsen, Christian Axboe. "The Symbiosis of War Crimes and Organized Crime in the Former Yugoslavia." *Südosteuropa Mitteilungen* 52, no. 3 (2012): 6–17.

Nikolić, Kosta, and Vladimir Petrović. "Organized Crime in Serbian Politics during the Yugoslav Wars." *Journal of Political Power* 15, no. 1 (2022): 101–22.

Ninković Slavnić, Danka. "Celebrating Yugoslavia: The Visual Representation of State Holidays." In *Remembering Utopia: The Culture of Everyday Life in Socialist Yugoslavia*, edited by Breda Luthar and Maruša Pušnik, 65–91. Washington, DC: New Academic, 2010.

Nježić, Zvonko, and Marijana Ačanski. "Da se ne zaboravi: Bombardovanje Novog Sada—ekološka crna tačka." *Hemijska industrija* 63, no. 2 (2009): 75–78.

Norwegian Helsinki Committee. "Belgrade Pride 2011 Banned." October 2, 2011.

Palmberger, Monika. *How Generations Remember: Conflicting Histories and Shared Memories in Post-war Bosnia and Herzegovina*. London: Palgrave Macmillan, 2016.

Patterson, Patrick Hyder. *Bought and Sold: Living and Losing the Good Life in Socialist Yugoslavia*. Ithaca: Cornell University Press, 2011.

Pavković, Aleksandar. *The Fragmentation of Yugoslavia: Nationalism and War*. London: Macmillan Press, 2000.

———. "Yugoslavism: A National Identity That Failed?" In *Citizenship and Identity in Europe*, edited by Leslie Holmes and Philomena Murray, 147–58. Aldershot: Ashgate, 1999.

Pavlaković, Vjeran. "Symbols and the Culture of Memory in Republika Srpska Krajina." *Nationalities Papers* 41, no. 6 (2013): 893–909.

Pavlowich, Stevan K. *The Impossible Survivor—Yugoslavia and Its Problems: 1918–1988*. Columbus: Ohio State University Press, 1988.

Pawson, Melissa. "Hot and Cold: Greece's Treatment of Ukrainians and Non-Ukrainians." *New Humanitarian*, August 16, 2022.

Perica, Vjekoslav. *Balkan Idols: Religion and Nationalism in Yugoslav States*. Oxford: Oxford University Press, 2002.

Petrila, Ann, and Hasan Hasanović. *Voices from Srebrenica: Survivor Narratives of the Bosnian Genocide*. Jefferson, NC: McFarland, 2020.

Petrović, Tanja. "Nostalgia for the JNA? Remembering the Army in the Former Yugoslavia." In *Post-communist Nostalgia*, edited by Maria Todorova and Zsuzsa Gille, 61–81. New York: Berghahn Books, 2010.

———. "Place-Making through the Use of Dialect in a Facebook Chronicle of Leskovac (Southeast Serbia)." In *The Sociolinguistics of Place and Belonging: Perspectives from the Margins*, edited by Leonie Cornips and Vincent A. de Rooij, 177–204. Amsterdam: John Benjamins, 2018.

———. "'When We Were Europe': Socialist Workers in Serbia and Their Nostalgic Narratives." In *Remembering Communism: Genres of Representation*, edited by Maria Todorova, 127–53. New York: Social Science Research Council, 2010.

Philipsen, Dirk. *We Were the People: Voices from East Germany's Revolutionary Autumn of 1989*. Durham, NC: Duke University Press, 1993.

Phillips, Kendall R., and G. Mitchell Reyes, eds. *Global Memoryscapes: Contesting Remembrance in a Transnational Age*. Tuscaloosa: University of Alabama, 2011.

Pichler, Robert. "In the Shadow of Kosovo: Divergent National Pathways and the Politics of Differentiation in the Socialist Republic of Macedonia." *Comparative Southeast Europe Studies* 69, no. 2–3 (2021): 289–311.

Pirjevec, Jože. *Tito and His Comrades.* Madison: University of Wisconsin Press, 2018 (orig. in Slovene, 2011).

Poulton, Hugh. "Macedonians and Albanians as Yugoslavs." In *Yugoslavism: Histories of a Failed Idea, 1918–1992*, edited by Dejan Djokić, 115–35. Madison: University of Wisconsin Press, 2003.

Praznik, Katja. *Art Work: Invisible Labour and the Legacy of Yugoslav Socialism.* Toronto: University of Toronto Press, 2021.

Prusin, Alexander. *Serbia under the Swastika: A World War II Occupation.* Urbana: University of Illinois Press, 2017.

Radonjić, Ognjen, and Marjana Bobić. "Brain Drain Losses—A Case Study of Serbia." *International Migration* 59, no. 1 (February 2021): 5–20.

Raleigh, Donald J., ed. and trans. *Russia's Sputnik Generation: Soviet Baby Boomers Talk about Their Lives.* Bloomington: Indiana University Press, 2006.

———. *Soviet Baby Boomers: An Oral History of Russia's Cold War Generation.* Oxford: Oxford University Press, 2012.

Ramet, Sabrina P. *The Three Yugoslavias: State-Building and Legitimization, 1918–2005.* Washington, DC: Woodrow Wilson Center Press, 2006.

Raykoff, Ivan, and Robert Dean Tobin, eds. *A Song for Europe: Popular Music and Politics in the Eurovision Song Contest.* Aldershot: Ashgate, 2007.

Rejmer, Margo. *Mud Sweeter Than Honey: Voices of Communist Albania.* Translated by Zosia Krasodomska-Jones and Antonia Llyod-Jones. New York: Restless Books, 2021.

Ritchie, Donald A. *Doing Oral History.* 3rd ed. Oxford: Oxford University Press, 2015.

Rogacheva, Maria A. *Soviet Scientists Remember: Oral Histories of the Cold War Generation.* Lanham, MD: Lexington Books, 2020.

Rugova, Barhd. "The Status of Albanian in Relation to Other Balkan Languages." *Slavia Meridionalis* 15 (2015): 139–48.

Rujevic, Nemanja. "A Home for Forgotten Balkan Refugees." *Deutsche Welle*, July 9, 2017.

Rusek, Benjamin, and Charles Ingrao. "The 'Mortar Massacres': A Controversy Revisited." *Nationalities Papers* 32, no. 4 (December 2004): 827–52.

Sadiku, Artan. "Public Art as Class Struggle in Post-socialist Yugoslavia." *Rosa Luxemburg Stiftung*, January 16, 2023.

Sahadeo, Jeff. *Voices from the Soviet Edge: Southern Migrants in Leningrad and Moscow.* Ithaca: Cornell University Press, 2019.

Scarboro, Cristofer. *The Late Socialist Good Life in Bulgaria: Meaning and Living in a Permanent Present Tense.* Lanham, MD: Lexington Books, 2011.

Scarboro, Cristofer, Diana Mincyté, and Zsuza Gille, eds. *The Socialist Good Life: Desire, Development, and Standards of Living in Eastern Europe.* Bloomington: Indiana University Press, 2020.

Shapiro, Susan G., and Ronald Shapiro. *The Curtain Rises: Oral Histories of the Fall of Communism in Eastern Europe.* Jefferson, NC: McFarland, 2004.

Smits, Jeroen. "Ethnic Marriage and Social Cohesion: What Can We Learn from Yugoslavia?" *Social Indicators Research* 96, no. 3 (2009): 417–32.

Spaskovska, Ljubica. *The Last Yugoslav Generation: The Rethinking of Youth Politics and Cultures in Late Socialism.* Manchester: Manchester University Press, 2017.

Srebotnjak, Hana. "Tracing the Decline of Yugoslav Identity: A Case for 'Invisible' Ethnic Cleansing." *Nationalities Affairs* 48 (2016): 65–84.

Stebej, Marko. "Size Isn't Everything: The Relationship between Slovenian and Serbo-Croatian in Slovenia." *International Journal of the Sociology of Language* 183 (2007): 13–30.

Stefoska, Irena, and Darko Stojanov. "Remembering and Forgetting SFR Yugoslavia: Historiography and History Textbooks in the Republic of Macedonia." *Südosteuropa* 64, no. 2 (2016): 206–25.

Štiks, Igor. *Nations and Citizen in Yugoslavia and Post-Yugoslav States: One Hundred Years of Citizenship.* London: Bloomsbury Academic Press, 2015.

Stubbs, Paul, ed. *Socialist Yugoslavia and the Non-Aligned Movement: Social, Cultural, Political, and Economic Imaginaries.* Montreal: McGill-Queen's University Press, 2023.

———. "Virtual Diaspora?: Imagining Croatia On-line." *Sociological Research Online* 4, no. 2 (July 1999): 1–13.

Surdu, Mihai. "Why the 'Real' Numbers on the Roma Are Fictitious." *Ethnicities* 19, no. 3 (June 2019): 486–502.

Swimelar, Safia. "LGBT Rights in Bosnia: The Challenge of Nationalism in the Context of Europeanization." *Nationalities Papers* 48, no. 4 (2020): 768–90.

———. "LGBT Rights in the Balkans: Accessing Two Decades of Change and Nationalist Challenges." *London School of Economics and Political Science Blog,* February 28, 2023.

Tanevski, Borjan. "The Problem between the Macedonian and Albanian Ethnic Groups in the Republic of Macedonia and Its Future." *New Balkan Politics* 9 (2005). Accessed on January 29, 2025. https://www.newbalkanpolitics.org.mk/item/The-problem-between-the-Macedonian-and-Albanian-ethnic-groups-in-the-Republic-of-Macedonia-and-its-future.

Taylor, Karin. *Let's Twist Again: Youth and Leisure in Socialist Bulgaria.* Vienna: LIT, 2006.

———. "My Own *Vikendica*: Holiday Cottages as Idyll and Investment." In *Yugoslavia's Sunny Side: A History of Tourism in Socialism (1950s–1980s),* edited by Hannes Grandits and Karin Taylor, 171–210. Budapest: Central European University, 2010.

Thomas, Marcel. *Local Lives, Parallel Histories: Villagers and Everyday Life in Divided Germany.* Oxford: Oxford University Press, 2020.

Todorov, Tzvetan. *Voices from the Gulag: Life and Death in Communist Bulgaria.* Translated by Robert Zaretsky. University Park: Pennsylvania State University Press, 1999.

Todorova, Maria. "Introduction: From Utopia to Propaganda and Back." In *Post-communist Nostalgia*, edited by Maria Todorova and Zsuzsa Gille, 1–13. New York: Berghahn Books, 2010.

———, ed. *Remembering Communism: Genres of Representation.* New York: Social Science Research Council, 2010.

Todorova, Maria, and Zsuzsa Gille, eds. *Post-communist Nostalgia.* New York: Berghahn Books, 2010.

Tokić, Mate Nikola. "Avengers of Bleiburg: Émigré Politics, Discourses of Victimhood, and Radical Separatism during the Cold War." *Politička misao* 55, no. 2 (2018): 71–88.

Tollefson, James W. "Language Policy and National Stability in Yugoslavia." *Canadian Slavonic Papers* 22, no. 4 (December 1980): 506–17.

Troch, Peter. "Of Private and Social in Socialist Cities: The Individualizing Turn in Housing in a Medium-Sized City in Socialist Yugoslavia." *Journal of Urban History* 47, no. 1 (January 2021): 50–67.

Tumbas, Jasmina. *"I Am Jugoslovenka!": Feminist Performance Politics during and after Yugoslav Socialism.* Manchester: Manchester University Press, 2022.

Ugrešić, Dubravka, *Culture of Lies.* Translated by Celia Hawkesworth. Philadelphia: University of Pennsylvania Press, 1997.

Vaněk, Miroslav, and Pavel Mücke. *Velvet Revolutions: An Oral History of Czech Society.* New York: Oxford University Press, 2016.

Vangeli, Anastas. "Nation-Building Ancient Macedonia Style: The Origins and the Effects of the So-Called Antiquization in Macedonia." *Nationalities Papers* 39, no. 1 (January 2011): 13–32.

Velikonja, Mitja. "Lost in Transition: Nostalgia for Socialism in Post-socialist Countries." *East European Politics & Societies* 23, no. 4 (fall 2009): 535–51.

———. "Slovenia's Yugoslav Century." In *Yugoslavism: Histories of a Failed Idea, 1918–1992*, edited by Dejan Djokić, 84–99. Madison: University of Wisconsin Press, 2003.

Videkanić, Bojana. *Nonaligned Modernism: Socialist Postcolonial Aesthetics in Yugoslavia, 1945–1985.* Montreal: McGill-Queen's University Press, 2020.

Vladisavljević, Nebojša. *Serbia's Anti-bureaucratic Revolution: Milošević, the Fall of Communism, and Nationalist Mobilization.* London: Palgrave Macmillan, 2008.

Volcic, Zala. "Post-socialist Recollections: Identity and Memory in Former Yugoslavia." In *Heritage, Memory & Identity*, edited by Helmut Anheier and Yudhishthar Raj Isar, 187–98. Los Angeles: SAGE, 2011.

Vučetić, Radina. *Coca-Cola Socialism: Americanization of Yugoslav Culture in the Sixties*. Budapest: Central European University Press, 2018.

———. "Džuboks (Jukebox)—The First Rock'n'roll Magazine in Socialist Yugoslavia." In *Remembering Utopia: The Culture of Everyday Life in Socialist Yugoslavia*, edited by Breda Luthar and Maruša Pušnik, 145–64. Washington, DC: New Academia, 2010.

Vucinich, Wayne S. *Memoirs of My Childhood in Yugoslavia*. Edited by Larry Wolff. Palo Alto: Society for the Promotion of Science and Scholarship, 2007.

Vuković, Drenka. "Migrations of the Labour Force from Yugoslavia." *SEER: Journal for Labour and Social Affairs in Eastern Europe* 8, no. 4 (2005): 139–50.

Vuletic, Dean. "European Sounds, Yugoslav Visions: Performing Yugoslavia at the Eurovision Song Contest." In *Remembering Utopia: The Culture of Everyday Life in Socialist Yugoslavia*, edited by Breda Luthar and Maruša Pušnik, 121–44. Washington, DC: New Academia, 2010.

———. "Generation Number One: Politics and Popular Music in Yugoslavia in the 1950s." *Nationalities Papers* 36, no. 5 (November 2008): 861–79.

———. *Postwar Europe and the Eurovision Song Contest*. London: Bloomsbury Academic Press, 2018.

———. "The Socialist Star: Yugoslavia, Cold War Politics and the Eurovision Song Contest." In *A Song for Europe: Popular Music and Politics in the Eurovision Song Contest*, edited by Ivan Raykoff and Robert Dean Tobin, 83–97. Aldershot: Ashgate, 2007.

Wehr, Demaris S. *Making It Through: Bosnian Survivors Share Stories of Trauma, Transcendence, and Truth*. Asheville, NC: Chiron, 2020.

Williams, John P., and Lester A. Zeager. "Macedonian Border Closings in the Kosovo Refugee Crisis: A Game-Theoretic Perspective." *Conflict Management and Peace Science* 21, no. 4 (2004): 233–54.

Winland, Daphne. "The Politics of Desire and Disdain: Croatian Identity between 'Home' and 'Homeland.'" *American Ethnologist* 29, no. 3 (August 2002): 693–718.

Yeomans, Rory. *Visions of Annihilations: The Ustasha Regime and the Cultural Politics of Fascism, 1941–1945*. Pittsburgh: University of Pittsburgh Press, 2013.

Zakić, Mirna. *Ethnic Germans and National Socialism in Yugoslavia in World War II*. Cambridge: Cambridge University Press, 2019.

Životić, Aleksandar. "Sanitetsko obezbedjenje odreda Jugoslovenske Narodne Armije na Sinaju 1956–1967." *Vojnoistorijski glasnik* no. 1–2 (2007): 130–38.

INDEX

Adriatic Sea, 39, 123n8, 145n17, 179, 186
Aegean Sea, 123n8, 127n10
Africa, 55, 55n12, 127n10
Afrika Korps, 55n12
Albania, 31, 32, 43, 63, 99, 100, 103, 103n20, 107, 107n26, 160, 160n6, 162, 168n13, 169n14
Albanian language, 90n3, 91, 92n5, 102, 105, 140n11, 164, 164n9; Albanian-language education, 23, 87, 90, 90n3, 90n4, 91, 96n11; Albanian-language universities, 90n4, 100, 100n17, 100n18, 106n24. *See also* Skopje University; State University of Tetova; University of Pristina
Albanian National Liberation Army, 20, 23, 32, 100n17
Albanians, 6, 24, 77, 90n2, 92n5, 93, 93n8, 96n11, 100, 105, 106, 128, 139, 175; discrimination against, 20, 23, 30, 31, 34, 88, 106, 154, 164, 172, 178; in Kosovo, 19, 20, 23, 30, 31, 88, 139n10, 164; in Macedonia, 20, 23, 32, 87, 90, 90n2, 96n11, 97n13, 98, 99n16, 106n24, 153
Alexander the Great, 168n13

Alps, 46, 138n8, 193
Anti-Bureaucratic Revolution, 19, 56–57, 56n14
anticommunism, 38, 145n17
antifascism, 16, 53, 89, 108, 131
Anti-Fascist Council for the National Liberation of Yugoslavia, 26
Antifascist Feminist Front, 173, 173n15
armed insurgency in Macedonia, 20, 23, 32, 100n17
Army of the Republic of Bosnia and Herzegovina, 33, 62n21, 140n12
Army of Republika Srpska, 61n19, 143, 150
Aromanians, 90n3
assimilation, 18, 39, 96n11
atheism, 23–24, 53, 158
Austria, 35, 45n2, 82, 138n8
Austria-Hungary, 17, 66n26, 68; nostalgia for, 66, 66n26
Autonomous Province of Kosovo. *See* Kosovo
Autonomous Province of Vojvodina. *See* Vojvodina

Bajram, 24, 93, 93n7, 96, 133
Balkans, 89, 93n8, 97n12, 104, 106n22, 112, 123n8, 126, 145n19, 170–71, 174, 175, 175n17
Balkan identity, 105, 124, 189
Bank of Slovenia, 59n17
Banja Luka, 143n15
Banski Dvor, 206n3
Battle of Kosovo, 139n10
Belgrade, 26, 67, 69, 76, 81, 85, 96, 106, 110, 113, 116, 117, 120, 126, 128, 132, 134, 136, 138, 142–43, 144, 147, 152, 160n5, 166n11, 173, 176, 180, 188n9, 195, 196n12
Bijelo Dugme, 44, 64, 64n24
Bosnia and Herzegovina, 2, 27, 33, 36, 47, 49, 51n9, 67, 93n9, 96, 98, 108, 124, 128, 130, 131, 135, 136, 138, 141n13, 149, 172, 174, 193; during Republic of Bosnia and Herzegovina, 24, 62n21; diversity in, 128, 133, 141; during World War II, 18, 145n19; intermarriage in, 96, 129n1
Bosnian genocide, 12, 20, 24
Bosnian identity, 134, 142, 144–45, 150
Bosnian language, 28–29, 34, 58n16, 71, 124, 132n4, 175, 215; accent and dialect of, 112, 129, 133, 148
Bosnians, 42, 41, 62, 116, 123, 126, 134, 149, 171, 177, 190, 210; Bosnian Muslims (Bosniaks), 24, 93n8, 97n13, 99n16, 128, 135n5, 177; Bosnian Serbs, 28, 36, 61n19, 139; in the diaspora, 151; refugees, 35, 61, 88, 97, 97n13, 99n16, 156, 167
Bosnian/Croatian/Montenegrin/Serbian (BCMS), 23, 28, 58n16, 71, 92, 132n4, 175. See also *ekavica, ijekavica, ikavica,* "our language," Serbo-Croatian; and names of individual languages

Bosnian War, 20, 24, 28, 33, 36, 36, 60, 61n19, 61n20, 62n21, 111, 140, 140n12, 141, 143, 143n15, 150, 152, 177
Bratislava, 143
Breadline Massacre, 61n19
Bregović, Goran, 44, 64, 64n24
Brioni Agreement, 25, 37
Broz, Jovanka, 26
Broz, Josip. *See* Josip Broz Tito
brotherhood and unity, 24, 92; ideal of, 83, 129; sentiment of, 113, 136, 139, 141, 190; state ideology, 16, 18, 35, 40, 124, 131
Brotherhood and Unity Highway, 18, 139, 139n9
Budapest, 66, 79, 80, 81, 143, 187
Bulgaria, 18, 107, 107n26, 120, 168, 168n13, 169n14, 170
Bulgarians, 90n3
bureaucratization, 107

Catholicism, 46n4, 52, 93n7, 199, 200, 201, 209, 209n7
Canada, 36, 128, 130, 145, 144, 148, 151, 152
capitalism, 15, 21, 39, 46, 68n28, 83, 107, 125, 167, 176, 191, 193
Ceausescu, Nicolae, 63–64, 63n23
Central European University, 66, 170
Četniks, 18, 24–25, 148
China, 21, 31, 179, 187, 188–89
childhood: during Yugoslavia, 14, 42, 43, 52–53, 55, 60, 69, 153, 182–83, 203, 206, 217; influences on, 1–2, 42–43, 44, 46, 66, 67–68, 71, 83, 101, 112, 146, 156, 179–80, 190, 212; memories of, 2, 3, 4, 5, 9, 10, 16, 72, 87–88, 89, 111, 113, 114, 128–29, 134, 155–59, 181, 192, 196, 199–200, 201
Christmas, 133, 135, 135n7, 163, 195, 20

INDEX 237

Christian Orthodoxy, 21, 93, 93n7, 135n6, 135n7, 158, 162, 170, 186
Christianity. *See* Christian Orthodoxy
circumcision, 97, 97n12
class difference, 6, 30, 52, 53–54, 95–96, 115, 154, 157, 159, 161n7, 165, 179
Cold War, 13, 19, 26, 29, 34, 38, 41, 63n23, 118n4, 173n15
communism, 53, 55, 103n20, 137, 151, 162–63, 181, 182, 185, 186, 191; rejection of, 46n4. *See also* socialism
conscription: during World War II, 54–55; during Yugoslav wars, 144, 187
Croatia, 46, 47, 48, 59, 60, 82, 97, 103, 108, 111, 112, 117, 118, 124, 126, 134, 137, 138, 144, 149, 151, 152, 193, 199, 201, 205, 216; economic disparities in Yugoslavia, 27; EU membership of, 201, 210n9, 214n11; independence of, 20, 25, 38, 57n15, 200–201, 207, 210–13; memory of Yugoslavia in, 93, 93n9, 106, 108, 200; nationalism in, 20, 140, 149, 200, 207; nationalist symbols in, 207, 210n9, 212–13; refugees from, 35; Serbs in, 22, 33. *See also* Independent State of Croatia
Croatian Defense Council, 33, 62n21, 140n12, 150, 206n3
Croatian identity, 9, 111, 112, 113, 123, 124, 128, 130, 131, 133, 138, 145, 208, 211–12
Croatian language, 28, 34, 58n16, 71, 124–25, 148, 215, 216; accent and dialect of, 113, 114, 124, 195, nationalization of, 124, 200
Croats, 6, 17, 42, 125, 126, 170, 185, 190; in Bosnia, 24, 29, 128; persecution of, 18
Croatian Parliament, 25
Croatian People's Peasant Party, 146n20
Croatian Spring, 14, 19, 38

Croatian War of Independence, 20, 25, 28, 33, 38, 60, 61n30, 62n21, 111, 141, 148, 150, 167n12, 200, 206–7, 206n3, 210n8
currency, 59, 187n8, 193, 210. *See also* dinar; tolar
Cyprus, 110–11, 120–22
Cyrillic, 28, 59, 77, 148, 195
Czechoslovakia, 11
Czech Republic, 128, 130, 144, 151, 199, 201, 211–12, 214, 215, 216; identity in, 145; xenophobia in, 130, 144, 144n16; Yugoslav emigration to, 215n12
Czechs, 114, 125

Dalmatia, 47, 55, 59
Danube River, 113
Day of the Republic, 26, 35, 147, 161, 163
Day of the Yugoslav National Army, 49n6
Day of Youth, 26
Dayton Peace Agreement, 24, 28, 36, 62n21, 143
democracy, 56, 167, 178
democratic elections, 19, 37, 38, 57
diaspora, 3, 65, 169, 175; Bosnian, 144, 151; Croatian, 130, 144, 148, 151, 214n11, 215, 215n12; Hungarian, 70, 74; in Canda, 148; in Czech Republic, 130, 151–52, 215–16, 215n12; in Egypt, 194; postwar émigré communities, 38–39, 130; Serbian, 144, 151, 194
dinar: Croatian, 210n9; Yugoslav, 28, 59n18, 210n9
Djinjić, Zoran, 119n6
Dubioza Kolektiv, 132, 132n4

Easter, 93, 93n7, 163, 195, 205
Eastern bloc, 13, 19, 63, 67, 83, 192, 215n12
East Europe: culture, 64n24; society, 13, 15; socialism and post-socialism, 11, 12, 13; states, 29, 163n8

East Germany, 67
Egypt, 34, 118n4, 179, 180, 194
Eid al-Fitr. *See* Bajram
ekavica, 28–29, 133. *See also* Serbo-Croatian
embargo, 98n14, 187, 187n8; Greek embargo on Macedonia, 33–34, 165; UN embargo of Yugoslavia, 28–29, 111, 161, 187
emigration, 3, 46n4, 9, 21, 39, 127n10, 151, 161m7, 201; brain drain, 110, 189n10, from Croatia, 214n11; from Serbia, 136, 181, 189n10. *See also* diaspora
English language, 80, 85, 92, 98, 121, 122, 132n4, 137, 179, 187, 188, 195, 206, 216
ethnic cleansing, 20, 24, 25, 34, 36, 143
ethnicity, 6, 37, 42, 75, 82, 88, 128–29, 131, 132–33, 162, 184; related to language, 28, 93n8. *See also names of individual groups*
Europe, 7, 10, 18, 29, 35, 36, 39, 41, 42, 43, 65n25, 69, 87, 104, 122, 127n10, 128, 152, 153, 156, 171, 176, 187n8, 197n13, 198; identity in, 7, 188n9
European Economic Community, 25, 27
European Union, 28, 30, 33, 108–9, 126n9, 170, 174, 181, 188n9, 199, 201, 210n9, 214, 214n11
Euroskepticism, 126n9
Eurovision Song Contest, 29, 160n4, 199, 205

fascism, 18; during World War II, 55n13
Federal Labor Act of 1958, 29
Foibe Massacres, 46n4
food, 16, 28, 79, 104, 133, 135, 135n6, 135n7, 138, 164, 180, 182, 182n3, 186, 187, 194, 196, 203; *ajvar*, 152, 152n22, 175; *ćevapčići*, 175, 175n17; coffee, 91, 139; *djevrek*, 159, 159n3; *kajmak*, 152, 152n22; pork, 92; *pršuta*, 152, 152n22; *rakija*, 147

Fourteenth Extraordinary Congress of the League of Communists of Yugoslavia, 20, 165n11

Gazimestan Speech, 139, 139n10
gender, 5, 11, 13, 14, 78, 129, 147, 158, 213n10
generations, 1–6, 9, 10, 14, 16, 42, 43, 53, 56, 56n13, 64, 69, 71, 72, 79, 80, 112, 125, 137–39, 147, 149, 155, 156, 179, 199, 200; identity of, 44, 66, 82, 83, 101, 105–6, 151, 170, 192n11, 212; of Pioneers, 26, 35, 47, 74, 203
genocide, 9, 13, 20; during World War II, 18. *See also* Bosnian genocide
Germany, 25, 35, 36, 64, 65m25, 82, 95, 101, 102, 140, 151, 180, 181, 187n8, 196, 198, 210n8
Gešovski, Sašo, 157, 157n2, 166
Gligorov, Kiro, 166, 166n10
Goli otok, 145, 145n17
Gorizia, 45n1, 45n2, 50
Greece, 45, 98–99, 103, 105, 107, 107n26, 110, 111, 112, 120, 124, 125, 126, 127n10, 169n14, 170, 171; Macedonian name dispute, 32–33, 98n14, 168n13. *See also* embargo
Greek language, 121, 124
Greeks, 122–23
guest workers, 41, 65n25, 110

Habsburg. *See* Austria-Hungary
Hanždar divizija (13th SS Waffen Mountain Division), 145, 145n19
health, 29, 123n8; health care, 37, 88, 89, 95, 107, 108, 127n10, 164, 180, 186, 194; reproductive health, 173
Hitler, Adolf, 18, 145n19
holidays, 16, 29, 60, 163, 167; at holiday centers, 29, 179; holiday travel, 47, 60, 75, 82, 88, 98, 99, 103, 105, 204; under

Holiday with Pay, 29; at weekend houses, 217, 217n13. *See* Bajram; Christmas; Day of the Republic; Easter; May Day; New Year's; *slava*
House of Flowers, 26
Hoxha, Enver, 30, 103n20, 160n6
Hungarian identity in Yugoslavia, 69, 70, 72, 74, 75, 77, 82; in Vojvodina, 39, 69, 70, 114, 125, 184
Hungarian language, 31, 39, 69, 72, 84; Hungarian-language education, 69–70, 72–74, 73n2; in Slovenia, 31, 58n16
Hungarians, 6, 84, 85, 184, 185; minority in Yugoslavia, 69, 70, 74, 77n3, 86; Yugonostalgia among, 85
Hungary, 18, 39, 45, 63, 67, 70, 74, 79, 80, 82, 83

Iceland, 25, 207
ideology: brotherhood and unity, 18; socialist, 40; Yugoslav, 192. *See also* socialism
identity. *See names of individual groups*
ikavica, 28–29. *See also* Serbo-Croatian
ijekavica, 28–29, 133, 148. *See also* Serbo-Croatian
Independent State of Croatia, 18, 149n21, 210n9
inequality: ethnic, 70, 153–54; social, 19, 37, 38, 217n13
International Criminal Tribunal for the former Yugoslavia, 33
International School of Prague, 143
International Workers' Day. *See* May Day
interwar Yugoslavia, 30, 38, 53, 66, 73n2, 146n20. *See also* Kingdom of Yugoslavia; Yugoslavia
Islam, 62, 92, 97n12, 99n16, 145n19. *See also under* Bosnians; Muslim
Israel, 118n4

Istria, 46, 46n4, 47, 59
Istrian Exodus, 46n4
Italy, 18, 35, 42, 43, 44–45, 45n1, 45n2, 46, 47n5, 50, 53, 60, 107n26, 151; Slovenian minority in, 45, 45n3, 56, 57; during World War I, 50n7; during World War II, 46n4, 54–55, 55n12, 169n14
Italian language, 31, 32, 58n16
Italians, 32
Italian Wars of Independence, 50

Jaganjac, Edo, 152
Jasenovac, 38, 149
JBTZ Trial, 54n11
Jews, 18, 38
Juka's Wolves, 140n12
Julian March, 46n4

Karadjordjević, Alexander I, 17, 146n20
Karadjordjević, Peter II, 17, 26
Karadjordjević, Paul, 17, 18
Karadžić, Radovan, 36
Kavadarci, 153, 154, 156–57, 157n2, 158, 161, 176n19
Kazakhs, 66
Kazakhstan, 67
Kingdom of the Serbs, Croats, and Slovenes. *See* Kingdom of Yugoslavia
Kingdom of Yugoslavia, 2, 17–18, 146n20, 183n5. *See also* Yugoslavia
Kishegyes. *See* Mali Idjoš
Klein, Richard, 26
Kosovo, 19, 30–31, 56n14, 67, 93, 99, 107, 107n25, 126, 137, 143, 150, 154, 161, 164, 165, 176; autonomous province, 19, 29; independence of, 21; inequality in, 30; language in, 91, 100n18, 106n24, 164n9; memory of Yugoslavia in, 89; Serbian repressive measures against Albanians in, 30, 33, 88, 90, 100n18, 139n10, 164

Kosovo Liberation Army (KLA), 20, 31
Kosovo War, 20, 23, 28, 31, 33, 34, 63, 88, 98, 99, 187n8; refugees from, 88, 99n16
Kragujevac, 99n15, 116
Kučan, Milan, 27, 37, 54n11
Kumrovec, 26
Kusturica, Emir, 64
Kuwait, 118

Lainović, Branislav, 111, 120, 120n7
Lajavi. *See* Branislav Lainović
Lastavica, 130, 151–52
language, 8, 45, 69, 71, 73, 82, 83–85, 90, 93n8, 110, 111–12, 113, 124, 126, 142, 144, 148–49, 150, 151, 175, 193, 195, 215, 216; diversity of, 7, 17, 43, 87n13, 111; language policy, 28, 31–32; official state language, 18, 28, 31, 39, 58n16, 90n3, 90n4, 164n9, 184. *See also* "our language" and names of individual languages
League of Communists of Yugoslavia, 32, 38, 54n11, 54–55n14, 166n11, 205n2
League of Socialist Youth, 35, 131
League of Young Communists. *See* League of Socialist Youth
leftist, 83, 84, 85, 87, 95
Lepa Brena, 141n13, 147
Leskovac, 176, 176n18
Levi's, 138, 192n11
LGBT identity, 6, 179, 180–81, 183–84, 183n5, 188, 188n9, 192–93
Lithuania, 25
Ljubljana, 31, 47n5, 54, 57, 64, 138n8
London Memorandum, 46n3, 47n5

Macedonia, 29, 49, 77, 87, 98, 102, 106n23, 106n24, 107, 138n8, 139, 139n9, 153–54, 156, 160, 164, 165, 167, 169, 169n14, 170–71, 178, 205, 210, 2015; army in, 98, 166; Christianity in, 24, 163; discrimination of Albanians in, 23, 172–73; economic disparity in, 27, 108–9; education in, 90n3, 90n4, 91, 100n17, 100n18, 161, 168, 172; independence of, 20, 23, 32, 88, 93, 103, 160, 166m10, 166n11, 168n13; Islam in, 93n7, 93n8; memory for Yugoslavia in, 38, 88, 89, 93, 93n9, 106; name dispute of, 32–33, 98n14, 168n13; post-socialist transition of, 95n10, 98n14, 101, 103n19, 108, 168n14; refugees in, 88, 97n13, 99n16; segregation in, 90n2, 96n11. *See also* armed insurgency in Macedonia
Macedonian identity, 87, 99, 104, 105, 155, 162, 169, 169n14, 175–76
Macedonian language, 18, 31, 90, 90n3, 91, 91n5, 93, 101, 102, 148, 159n3, 164, 164n9, 175
Macedonians, 6, 42, 51, 90, 90n3, 91, 93, 96n11, 116, 117, 124, 128, 157, 161, 161n7, 205; diaspora, 175. *See also* Albanians
Malaysia, 179, 190, 194, 196
Mali Iđoš, 69, 78, 80
Markale market massacres, 61n19
market economy, 2, 39, 59n18, 95, 95n10, 107, 196n12
Marxism, 93, 95, 104
May Day, 26, 151, 163
media, 12, 23, 27, 50n8, 60, 61, 61n19, 62, 63n23, 134, 140n11; magazines, 54; newspapers, 61, 103, 143, 149; radio, 140n11, 143; television, 54, 58, 61, 75, 78, 79, 122, 134, 137, 139–40, 140n11, 148, 149, 166, 167, 205
memory, 9–10, 15–16; generational, 2–3, 5; post-socialist, 3, 13; of World War II, 25
migration. *See* emigration
Mihailović, Dragoljub "Draža," 18, 24

military, 6, 18, 43, 50, 61, 80, 98, 103, 104, 117, 141, 143, 186–87. *See also* names of individual military units
Milošević, Slobodan, 19, 27, 33, 54, 57, 56–57n14, 62, 78, 100n18, 118, 126n9, 139, 139n10, 143, 146, 162, 166n11, 213n10
mixed marriage, 39, 96, 96n11, 129n1
Montenegrin identity, 92, 106n22, 128, 130, 134, 145
Montenegrin language, 28, 34, 58, 71, 92n5, 132n4, 175
Montenegrins, 24, 39, 90n3
Montenegro, 5, 6, 17, 20, 28, 49, 56, 107, 108, 137, 138, 141, 150, 167, 179, 186, 204; in interwar Yugoslavia, 146n20; as part of Serbia and Montenegro, 20, 27, 40; in socialist Yugoslavia, 183n5
Mostar, 12, 47
Mostar Bridge, 33, 47, 60, 166
Motol University Hospital, 152
multinationalism, 1, 3, 4, 7, 9, 21, 24, 42, 66n26, 70, 71, 124, 204
Munich, 65, 144
Muslims, 18, 24, 30, 62, 90, 93, 97, 105, 130, 133, 135, 135n5, 140, 141, 144, 145n19, 148, 152
Museum of Yugoslavia, 26
Mussolini, Benito, 55n12

Nasser, Gamal Abdel, 34
naš jezik. *See* "our language"
National Bank of Yugoslavia, 59n17
nationalism, 14, 16, 19, 68n28, 83, 88, 89, 106n23, 107, 114, 118, 130, 147, 149; Bosnian, 141n13; Croatian, 20, 36, 38, 157n2, 199, 200–201, 212–13; Hungarian, 70, 77; Macedonian, 100n17, 106n23, 168n13, 169; rejection of, 15, 46n4, 105, 132n4; Serbian, 16, 20, 24–25, 31, 33, 56n14, 139n10, 157n2, 180–81, 188n9; Slovenian, 47n5, 62
nationalized: culture, 213n10; diasporas, 3; identities, 155, 168n13; language, 71; media, 149; region, 7, 21; revisionist projects, 9
NATO bombing of Yugoslavia, 20, 31, 34, 63n22, 79, 80, 122–23, 123n8, 143, 196n12
Nehru, Jawaharal, 34
Neue Slowenische Kunst, 26
New Year's, 26, 163, 163n8, 187
New York, 111, 122–23, 197
Non-Aligned Movement, 19, 34, 173; nonaligned states, 13, 43
North Macedonia. *See* Macedonia
Norway, 35, 42, 151
nostalgia, 2, 13, 15–16, 15n43, 26, 41, 66, 67–68, 40–41, 67–68, 77, 88, 106–7, 125–26, 137, 165, 174, 178, 193, 194, 213. *See also* Yugonostalgia
Nova Gorica, 42, 43, 45n1, 53
Novi Sad, 56n14, 75, 80, 110, 113, 113n3, 116, 122, 123n8, 125, 195, 196n12

Ohrid Agreement, 23, 90n4, 100n17
Oluja. *See* Operation Storm
Open Society Foundation, 170
Operation Flash, 206n3
Operation Rösselsprung, 26
Operation Storm, 61, 61n21
Organization for Security and Cooperation in Europe, 104n21
organized crime, 111, 119n6, 120n7, 140n12
Osimo Agreement, 46n3
Otpor!, 33
Ottoman Empire, 17, 33, 139, 159n2, 175n17
"our language," 24, 71, 84–85, 149, 215

Pačić, Puniša, 146n20
Pale, 143, 143n15
Palestine, 121
Pančevo, 153, 155
Pan-Slavic, 40
paramilitary, 20, 31, 36, 120n7, 140, 140n12, 167n12, 169n14
Paris Peace Treaty of 1947, 45n1, 46n3
Partisans, 34; during World War II, 18, 38, 56n4, 169, 169n14, 173n15; memory of, 54, 55n13, 192n11; participation in, 42, 46n3, 53, 135, 136
Pavelić, Ante, 18, 38, 149
peacekeepers, 88, 99; peacekeeping missions during Cold War, 118n4; peacekeeping missions during Yugoslav wars, 32, 24, 98
People's Liberation Army of Yugoslavia, 49n6
People's Radical Party, 146n20
People's Socialist Republic of Albania, 103n20, 160n6. *See also* Albania
Philip II of Macedon, 168n13
Pioneers, 35, 75; inauguration into, 26, 48, 199–200, 203; memory of, 42, 47, 71, 160, 183; pledge of, 35, 48, 74, 131; uniform of, 91, 115, 129, 131
Poland, 40, 63, 67
popular culture, 16, 71, 82, 84, 99n15, 192n11, 213n10; magazines, 102, 197, 200–201, 206, 208–9, 208n5, 208n6, 213n10, 217; music, 14, 15, 29, 64n24, 101, 105–6, 132n4, 136, 141n13, 147, 149, 160, 160n4, 160n5, 162, 184, 191, 194, 199, 203, 213, 213n10, 217; movies, 57, 57n15, 63, 64, 64n24, 84, 98, 119, 119n5, 126, 149, 181, 182, 192, 192n11, 198, 209, 217; radio, 140, 199, 203; television, 15, 29, 63, 84, 102, 115, 199, 203, 181, 182, 191–92

postcommunist transition, 5, 10, 12, 13, 15, 33, 59n18, 67, 87, 88, 95n10, 96n14, 101, 102, 103n19, 165, 167, 196n12, 199, 201, 207–8, 211, 214
post-socialist transition. *See* postcommunist transition
post-socialism: in Eastern Europe, 10–11, 13; memory of, 2, 5, 16; in Yugoslavia, 12, 92n5
post-Yugoslav, 2, 7, 14, 25, 64, 71, 108, 177
post-Yugoslav identity, 4, 7, 44, 64, 66, 153, 155, 169–70
poverty, 79, 80, 88, 168n13, 180
Prague, 128, 130, 142, 143–44, 148, 149–52, 215
Prazina, Josuf "Juka," 140, 140n12
Pristina, 67
privilege, 5, 6, 45n2, 102, 138, 147; nostalgia for lost privileges, 71, 82
privatization, 25, 98n14, 103n19, 210
passport, 185n7, 188; Canadian, 144; Croatian, 112, 124, Serbian, 143; used with special permits, 45, 45n2; Yugoslav, 41, 95, 138, 138n8

queer identity. *See* LBGT identity

racism, 51, 62
Radić, Stjepan, 146n20
Radio Free Europe/Radio Liberty, 140n11, 143
Radio Sarajevo, 140
Rally of Truth. *See* Anti-Bureaucratic Revolution
Ramadan. See *Bajram*
Red Army, 145, 145n18
refugees, 6, 121, 127, 127n10, 142n14; after World War II, 38; from Yugoslav wars, 35–36, 61, 61n19, 88, 97, 97n13, 99, 99n16, 110, 127, 142, 143, 144, 151, 156, 167, 171, 187

INDEX 243

Relay of Youth, 26
religious identity, 1, 7, 15n43, 17, 18, 42, 52–53, 96, 98, 118, 129, 133, 139, 147, 184, 188n9, 193, 212–13, 213n10, 214n11. *See also* atheism; Catholicism; Christian Orthodoxy; holidays; Islam
Republic of Bosnia and Herzegovina. *See* Bosnia
Republic of Herzeg-Bosnia, 24, 36
Republic of Serbian Krajina, 20, 25, 28, 36, 61n19, 143n15, 150, 157n2, 206n3
Republika Srpska, 20, 24, 167, 177
Riblja Čorba, 147
Roma, 18, 24, 36–37, 39, 64, 74, 90n2, 90n3, 114, 128, 153, 154, 157–58, 159, 172, 177, 204
Romania, 63, 63n23, 67
Romanians, 39, 184
Russia, 21, 31, 66, 67, 95, 120, 126, 126n9, 136; invasion of Ukraine, 10, 207, 207n4
Russian language, 118
Rusyn, 39

sanctions, 27–28, 33, 111, 119n6, 126n9, 187n8, 196n12
Sarajevo, 61, 61n19, 67, 94, 96, 128, 129n1, 131–34, 135n5, 136, 141, 142, 143n15, 144, 148, 151, 152, 175
self-management, 37, 39–40, 137, 178
Šempeter pri Gorici, 42
Senta, 69, 72, 196n12
Serbia, 40, 49, 57, 67, 69, 72, 73, 76, 86, 99, 103, 106, 106n22, 108, 110, 112, 113, 116, 120, 122, 126, 128, 129, 133, 135, 136, 137, 138, 138n8, 139n9, 141, 142, 143, 149, 150, 153, 155, 161, 161n7, 168n13, 176, 176n18, 179, 183, 183n5, 190–91, 192, 193, 195–96, 197–98, 197n13, 200, 204, 205n2, 207, 211; autonomous regions in socialist republic, 19, 30–31, 33, 99, 164n9; crime in, 110–11, 119, 119n6, 120n7; diaspora of, 130, 148, 151–53, 189n10, 194–95, 215, 215n12; nationalism in, 15, 20, 27, 33, 36, 126n9, 130, 139n10, 149, 149n21, 157n2; nostalgia for Yugoslavia in, 83, 89, 93, 93n9; refugees in, 35, 142; rights of Albanians in, 20, 30, 31, 88n3, 100n18; Roma in, 36–37; during World War II, 18, 24–25, 35, 64n24, 80, 168n14, 180, 195n12; before Yugoslavia, 17; after Yugoslav wars, 2, 12, 180–81, 185n7, 187–89, 187n8, 188n9; during Yugoslav wars, 20–21, 24, 25, 31, 61n19, 61n20, 150, 167, 196n12, 187, 213n10
Serbia and Montenegro, 20, 27, 28, 40
Serbian Autonomous Oblast of Eastern Slavonia, Baranja, and Western Syrmia, 24
Serbian Autonomous Oblast of Krajina, 25
Serbian Autonomous Oblast of Western Slavonia, 25
Serbian identity, 75, 81–82, 84, 111, 112, 113, 124, 128, 130, 142, 144–45, 147–48, 189–91
Serbian language, 28–29, 34, 51n9, 71, 72, 73, 74, 77, 84–85, 100n17, 124–25, 132n4, 148, 175, 195, 215; dialect and accent of, 111, 114, 123, 133
Serbian Orthodox Church. *See* Christian Orthodox
Serbian Progressive Party, 126n9
Serbo-Croatian, 18, 28–29, 31, 34, 39, 54m11, 58, 58n16, 65–66, 70–71, 73n2, 124, 148, 164n9, 175–76, 190, 195–96. *See also* Bosnian/Croatian/Montenegrin/Serbian; *ekavica, ijekavica; ikavica;* "our language"

Serbs, 6, 17, 30, 39, 40, 70, 71, 84, 114, 116, 117, 122, 123, 125, 133, 134, 139, 140, 141, 146, 191, 200, 207, 210, 211; in Bosnia, 20, 24, 28–29, 36, 62, 93n8, 128, 139, 177; in Croatia, 20, 25, 62n21, 167n12; in Kosovo, 20, 30; in Macedonia, 32, 90n3; in Slovenia, 42, 51; persecution of, 18, 38

Servo Mihalj, 182n3

sexuality, 11, 102. *See also* LGBT identity

shopping, 41, 45n1, 79, 138, 138n8, in department stores, 156, in shops, 50, 53, 59, 60, 103n19, 126, 175, 191; shopkeepers, 56, 152; in supermarkets, 91, 187

shortages, 16, 19, 28, 180

Siege of Sarajevo, 24

Skopje, 87, 93, 103n19, 104, 105, 107, 154, 161, 165, 168, 168n13, 176

Skopje University, 100, 100n17

slava, 135, 135n6, 136

Slovak language, 39

Slovaks, 39, 40

Slovene Communist Party, 27

Slovene identity, 42, 51, 51n9, 64, 66, 204

Slovene language, 18, 31–32, 45n1, 56, 58n16; dialect and accent of, 52

Slovenia, 31, 42, 44, 46–47, 48, 52, 53, 53n10, 54, 54n11, 66, 73, 97, 107, 139n9, 140, 166n11, 183n5, 187, 216; economic disparity in, 27, 47n5; after independence, 59–61, 59n18, 62; independence of, 20, 25, 37, 50, 50n8, 55, 56–57n14, 58–59, 59n17; war in, 20, 37, 57–58; during World War II, 18, 45n1, 46n4; during Yugoslav wars, 54, 61–62

Slovenians, 6, 17, 45n1, 47n5, 54n11, 128, 138n8, 190; minority in Italy, 45, 46n3, 56

Slovenian Territorial Defense, 37

socialism, 10; collapse of, 11, 19, 24, 95n10; criticism of, 37, 72, 106–7; in Eastern Europe, 10–11, 13, 67, 103n20; education under, 40, 154; forgetting of, 38; growing up in, 1; housing under, 29–30, 95n10, 103n19; ideals of, 3, 21, 40, 42, 89, 138n10, 154; identity under, 35, 53, 106n23, 130, 169n14; ideology of, 40, 48, 125; inequality under, 90n2; language policy under, 31–32; legacies of, 4, 71, 185; market, 39; memory of, 1, 9, 181; migration during, 47; minorities in, 36–37, 73; nostalgia for, 15–16, 71, 83, 93n9; prosperity in, 2, 6; religion in, 93n7, 135n5, 135n6, 163n8; social benefits of, 29, 88, 153; symbols of, 93n9, 99n15; transition from, 46, 56, 59n18, 87, 88; travel during, 45; urban planning under, 42, 44–45; worker's self-management under, 30; work under, 180, 217n13; in Yugoslavia, 1, 12, 14, 19, 32, 38, 39, 67, 83, 161n7, 183, 192n11, 213n10. *See also* communism

Socialist Republic of Serbia, 33, 164. *See also* Serbia

Socialist Federal Republic of Yugoslavia, 2, 18, 24, 35, 40, 41. *See also* Yugoslavia

Sofia, 120

solidarity, 83, 88; ideal of, 3, 16, 19, 40, 87, 89, 105, 106, 108

Solidarnost, 87, 105

South Slavic and Albanian Language Broadcast Service, 140n11

South-Slavic language, 85, 104n11, 148

South Slavic state, 107n26

Soviet Union, 18, 19, 39, 160n6. *See also* Russia

Spain, 122

Split, 77, 157, 157n2

Srebrenica, 24, 67
Stalinism, 107
Stalinists, 19, 145n17
State University of Tetova, 100, 100n17, 100n18
student demonstrations, 19, 33, 37–38, 107, 107n25, 136
Suez Canal Crisis, 118n4
Switzerland, 35, 101
Syria, 121, 127n10
Szeged, 80

teachers, 47, 51, 58, 62, 69, 70, 73, 74, 77, 79, 91, 92, 93, 94, 96, 97, 100, 100n17, 115, 122, 131, 133, 137, 140, 157, 172, 179, 180, 187, 187n8, 204, 205, 206, 209n7
Ten Day War, 20, 37, 57–58
Tetovo, 87, 88, 90n2, 94, 96–97, 98, 100, 103–4, 106n24
textbooks, 38, 58, 93, 100, 141, 142, 172
Thessaloniki, 33, 138n8
Third Reich, 145n19
Third World, 27, 50n8
Tito, Josip Broz, 5n11, 13, 26, 24, 35, 38, 131, 136, 146, 178, 192, 192n11; criticisms of, 64; death of, 14, 19, 26, 47; during World War II, 18, 26, 131; pictures and celebrations of, 26, 59, 62, 93, 118, 183, 204, 207; split from Stalin, 19, 30, 32, 35, 63n23, 145n17, 160n6, 161n7, 192n11, 213n10; support for, 55, 186; Titoism, 27, 32
Tito's Pioneers. See Pioneers
tolar, 59, 59n17, 59n18
Toti, Enrico, 50n7
travel, 13, 19, 28, 29, 41, 43, 45n2, 46–47, 60, 61–62, 64n24, 76, 77, 82, 83, 87, 89, 95, 103, 103n20, 107, 110, 116–17, 120, 124, 128, 134, 136, 137, 138, 138n8, 149, 160n6, 167, 189, 193, 200, 202, 210–11, 214n11, 217. See also holidays

Trieste, 41, 45n3, 56, 138, 138n8
Tudjman, Franjo, 38, 119, 149, 213n10
Tunisia, 55n12
Turks, 90n2
Turkey, 35, 45n2, 127n10
Turkish language, 90n3, 164n9; Turkish words used in Yugoslavia, 159n2, 175n17
Tuzla, 67, 134
TV Sarajevo, 137, 139, 140n11

Ugrešić, Dubravka, 9
Ukraine, 10, 64, 112, 126n9, 127, 127n10, 207, 207n4
unemployment, 19, 27, 35, 37, 47n5, 60, 94, 98n14, 101, 165, 168n13, 180
United Nations, 27, 28, 34, 118, 118n4
United Nations Economic Commission for Europe, 187n8, 210n8, 187n8, 210n8
United Nations Emergency Force, 118n4, 98
United Nations Higher Commissioner for Refugees, 35
United Nations Human Rights Council, 142n14
United Nations Protective Force, 32
United Nations Security Council, 28
United States, 13, 33, 41, 61n20, 82, 104, 122, 123, 124, 125, 170–71
University of Belgrade, 116
University of Kosovka Mitrovica. See University of Priština
University of Priština, 100n18
University of Pristina, 30, 100n17, 100n18, 106n24
University of Skopje, 100, 100n17
Ustaša, 18, 25, 38–39, 148, 149, 149n21, 210n9

Vance, Cyrus, 61n20
Vance-Owen Peace Plan, 61n20

Vancouver, 148
Vienna, 144, 202
Vojvodina, 39, 56, 56n14, 69, 76, 196n12; autonomous province, 19, 29, 30, 33, 113n3, 183n5; diversity in, 39, 111, 184; education in, 73, 73n2; Hungarians in, 70–71, 77; identity in, 70, 75, 76, 77, 77n3, 81
Vojvodina Hungarian Alliance, 86
voting, 20, 25, 32, 37, 55, 57, 83; suppression of, 23
Vučić, Aleksandar, 126n9
Vukovar, 167, 167n12

war crimes, 24, 33–34
weekend house, 217, 217n13
World War I, 2, 17, 39, 50, 50n7, 53, 66n26
World War II, 2, 18–19, 24, 25, 29, 38, 40, 46n3, 46n4, 55n13, 56, 73n2, 92n5, 130, 131, 145n18, 145n19, 150n6, 161, 161n7, 166n10, 172n15, 210n9; memory of, 43, 50, 54, 149n21, 192n11; Partisans in, 34, 28

xenophobia, 36, 47n5, 130, 132n4
Xoxe, Koçi, 160n6

Yogurt Revolution. *See* Anti-Bureaucratic Revolution
Youth Work Actions, 18, 40, 138, 139n9
Yugonostalgia, 4, 5, 15–16, 56, 67–68, 69, 70–71, 82–83, 85, 93n9, 105, 130. *See also* nostalgia
Yugoslav anthem, 40, 147, 199, 204
Yugoslavia: autonomous regions of, 27, 30, 48, 56n14, bombing of, 31, 34, 123n8; border of, 43, 45, 45n1, 45n2, 36n4, 64n23, 138n8, 160n6; childhood in, 42, 52, 71, 116, 129, 146–47, 153, 179, 190, 199, 201, 214; currency of, 28, 58n18, 210n9; debt in, 26–27,

186; diasporas of, 3–4, 65–66, 123, 128, 130, 145, 148, 151–2, 175, 201, 215; dissolution of, 1, 7, 24, 25, 32, 37, 44, 54n11, 56, 56n15, 79, 88, 89, 97, 105, 108, 141, 166n11, 168, 168n13, 195, 200, 207; diversity in, 7, 43, 184; education in, 69–70, 73, 73n2, 90n3, 91, 94, 100n18, 154–55, 164; economy in, 27, 39, 59n18; economic disparity in, 30, 47n5, 98n14; erasure of, 58, 93, 199, 200, 207–8, 211; ethnicity in, 133; fertility in, 53; holidays in, 26, 26, 35, 161; housing in, 29–30, 89, 95n10, 105, 217n13; ideals of, 16, 24, 30, 37, 39, 40, 71, 83, 87, 89, 105, 108, 124, 125, 128, 129, 131, 146, 190, 193, 213; inequality in, 35–36, 71, 87, 90n2, 153–54; interwar, 17–18, 23, 30, 146n20, 183n5; language in, 28, 34, 39, 71, 85, 92n5, 111, 124, 148; language policy in, 31–32; legacy of, 15, 71; memory of, 1, 3, 5, 7, 9–10, 16, 38, 67–68, 87, 131; migration from, 3, 65n25, 110–11, 116, 140n11, 215n12; migration in, 47, 52, 161n7; mixed marriages in, 96n11, 111, 129, 129n1; multinationalism in, 1, 7, 24, 70, 71, 72; nationalism in, 20, 38, 47n5, 88, 89, 106n23, 107, 139, 139n10, 141n13, 149n21; nostalgia for, 70, 77, 88, 125, 138–38, 165, 186, 193, 194; opposition of, 58; politics in, 42; popular culture in, 29, 44, 64, 82, 84, 192n11, 208, 213n10; racism and discrimination in, 52, 62, 172; refugees from, 35–36, 38, 127; religion in, 93n7, 135, 158; republics of, 27, 29, 32, 33, 42, 44, 47, 48, 56n14, 60, 76, 83, 106n23, 134, 205; Roma in, 36–37, 157; sanctions in, 27–28, 187; socialism in, 1, 3, 10, 12–14, 18–20, 25, 29, 32, 34, 37, 39, 67, 71, 72, 83, 118n4, 125, 145n17, 178,

180–81, 182, 182n3, 183n5; support or patriotism in, 55, 56, 62–63, 66, 95, 136; unemployment in, 60; during World War I, 17; during World War II, 18, 26, 34, 38, 38, 42, 43, 46n3, 49n6, 56n13, 64n24, 145n13, 145n19, 169, 169n14, 173n15; during Yugoslav wars, 1, 2, 10, 12, 14, 20–21, 25, 27, 31, 33, 36, 47n5, 62, 71, 78, 88, 97, 99, 110, 111, 118, 139, 156–57, 157n2, 166, 167n12, 180, 186, 205

Yugoslav identity, 7, 18, 24, 42, 44, 85, 106, 110, 111–12, 124, 130, 144–45, 150, 200, 203–4. *See also* post-Yugoslav identity

Yugoslav National Army, 12, 20, 25, 27, 31, 32, 33, 34, 36, 37, 40–41, 43, 49n6, 50, 50n8, 57n15, 61n20, 77, 98, 116, 118n4, 131, 136, 139n9, 140, 157, 157n2, 167n12

Yugoslav passport. *See* passport

Yugoslavs, 1–4, 5n11, 34, 35, 122, 131, 147, 152, 194; in Bosnia, 24, 128; in Czech Republic, 216n12; in Macedonia, 106n23; in Slovenia, 51; in Vojvodina, 39

Yugoslav wars, 1–2, 10, 12, 12n34, 64, 110, 112, 129, 129n1, 130, 157, 157n2; aftermath of, 26, 28, 71, 99, 111, 180, 187; displacement from, 3, 35–36, 65n25, 110; international response to, 27; memories of, 10, 62, 78, 97, 139; nationalism during, 25, 47n5, 88, 149n21, 156, 166, 186, 205, 213n10. *See also individual wars*

YugoslavWomen+ Collective, 171–72

Zabranjeno Pušenje, 147
Zagreb, 29, 113, 116, 138n8, 139, 144, 147, 160n4, 199, 200, 202, 206, 206n3, 207
Zastava Automobiles, 98, 99n15
Zrenjanin, 69, 70, 72, 73, 74, 76, 78, 79, 80, 179, 180, 182, 182n3, 182n4, 183n5, 184, 185n6, 185n7, 195–96, 196n12

JOVANA BABOVIĆ is Associate Professor of History at State University of New York at Geneseo. She is author of *Metropolitan Belgrade: Class and Culture in Interwar Yugoslavia* and *Sleater-Kinney's Dig Me Out*.

For Indiana University Press
Sabrina Black, Editorial Assistant
Tony Brewer, Artist and Book Designer
Anna Garnai, Production Coordinator
Sophia Hebert, Assistant Acquisitions Editor
Katie Huggins, Production Manager
Alyssa Lucas, Marketing and Publicity Manager
David Miller, Lead Project Manager/Editor
Bethany Mowry, Acquisitions Editor
Dan Pyle, Online Publishing Manager
Pamela Rude, Senior Artist and Book Designer

www.ingramcontent.com/pod-product-compliance
Lightning Source LLC
Chambersburg PA
CBHW021351300426
44114CB00012B/1171